GENERATION
FREEDOM

GENERATION FREEDOM

*The Middle East Uprisings and
the Remaking of the Modern World*

Bruce Feiler

HARPER ● PERENNIAL

NEW YORK ● LONDON ● TORONTO ● SYDNEY ● NEW DELHI ● AUCKLAND

HarperCollins books may be purchased for educational, business, or sales
promotional use. For information please write: Special Markets Department,
HarperCollins Publishers, 10 East 53rd Street, New York, NY 10022.

FIRST EDITION

Printed on acid-free paper

Library of Congress Cataloging-in-Publication Data

ISBN 978-0-06-210498-4

11   12   13   14   15   DIX/RRD   10   9   8   7   6   5   4   3   2

For John Healey,
whose hands gave me the
power to walk again

CONTENTS

Prologue   xi

I   Freedom Comes Home   1

II   The Birthplace of Freedom   25

III   The Voice of Freedom   47

IV   Freedom to Believe   77

V   Generation Freedom   105

Acknowledgments   145

GENERATION
FREEDOM

PROLOGUE

FREEDOM FROM FEAR

The Twin Towers and the Two Doors

I heard the singing as soon as I crossed the Brooklyn Bridge. It came from the hole in the skyline where the Twin Towers had once stood. It was nearing 1 a.m. on Monday, May 2, 2011, a little more than an hour after President Barack Obama announced that American service personnel had just hunted down, trapped, and killed the world's most wanted man, Osama bin Laden. As soon as the president finished speaking, I told my wife I wanted to go to Ground Zero. She looked at me like I was crazy. It was after midnight. I told her I thought the still-open wound in lower Manhattan would be dark and tranquil at that hour, and maybe it would provide some insight into this near-perfect bookend to what had happened there a decade earlier.

Instead I found several thousand people—many who were only in grade school on September 11, 2001—gathered for an impromptu rally. They waved American flags, tossed toilet paper on the lampposts, and sprayed champagne on the crowd. The only thing missing was a sailor kissing a nurse. And just as I arrived, the crowd was finishing a rendition of "The Star-Spangled Banner"—*O'er the land of the free and the home of the brave?*—before breaking into chants of "USA! USA!" I felt like I was at a homecoming rally.

I waded into the crowd. About half of the people there

were raucous college students. One was dressed as Captain America. Another shimmied up a traffic light pole and recited the Declaration of Independence by reading it from his Black-Berry. Another sounded an Australian didgeridoo. "I just wanted something that made a lot of noise," explained Dinos San Pedro, a jazz student.

Others had come for more solemn reasons and were offended by all the fist-pumping. "I'm happy bin Laden is dead," said Constance Lauria, a flight attendant for United Airlines, whose Flight 175 flew into the South Tower. "But people are not remembering the victims here. This is a hollow victory. It's not going to bring back all those souls."

As she looked around, it occurred to me that the number of people who had gathered for this rally was near in size to the number who had been killed on September 11.

I also noticed something else about the crowd. It reminded me of one I had seen in Liberation Square in Egypt a few weeks earlier. I had gone to report on the historic youth uprisings sweeping the region and what they meant for the future of peace, coexistence, and relations with the West. There, like here, young people dangled from light poles, painted their cheeks with flags, and held up iPhones to snap photos they posted on Twitter. "When I heard that young people over there started a revolution," said Averie Timm, a writing student from Pratt Institute, "I was so happy. People say our generation uses Facebook as a drug. For us to take technology and change the world, that made me proud."

At first glance, the uprisings across the Middle East and the killing of Osama bin Laden appear to have little in common. One was a populist movement to topple brutal dictators and demand greater freedom for innocent people. The other was a masterful plot by an elite military force to take out a brutal murderer who despised freedom and slaughtered innocent people.

But having spent months exploring the roots causes and future impact of the Arab Spring, I believe the two events—coming at the same moment—will always be intertwined. The coming of age of a new generation of Muslim youth and the dramatic death of Osama bin Laden will be the Twin Towers of 2011. And for the one billion people around the world who are Muslims under the age of thirty, these two towers represent opposing life choices.

One path—the jihadist—offers a better life through religious conformity, violence, and self-annihilation. The other offers a better life through activism, voting booths, and job opportunities. Both of these paths have had people on them. But at this moment, one appeared headed toward the bottom of the sea and the other toward the Nobel Peace Prize. This year would be remembered as the moment those two paths crossed.

Hours later, after the crowd began to disband, I spotted a young man narrating a letter to his family in Arabic into his cell phone's video camera. His name was Nadir Bashir. He was twenty-eight-years-old, from Sudan, and he worked at the

General Assembly of the United Nations. Dark-skinned and animated, he was eager to show me his ID card to prove he had such a prestigious job.

"Young people in the Arabic world were the first victims of the terrorists," he said. "Osama bin Laden and other leaders of terrorist organizations brainwashed these people and made them focus on something other than spreading freedom in their own countries. The men who flew those planes on September 11 were nineteen young people from the Muslim world.

"But this year," he continued, "those young people woke up from a long dream and focused like young people everywhere not on attacking others but on building their own countries. They made revolutions from Tunisia, to Egypt, to Yemen, to elsewhere."

"Why was that other path so appealing?" I asked.

"I will tell you honestly," he said. "Young people in the Muslim world were thinking that the path the terrorists offered them was the easy path to happiness. If you choose that direction, you will go to heaven very quickly. This is Door No. 1. But if you choose the long way, you will have to go to college, study hard, suffer for a while, and then after seven or eight years still not find a job. This is Door No. 2."

"So which will be more popular going forward?"

"Today, Door No. 1 has been closed by the United States. Some people might slip through, but that door has lost much of its appeal. And Door No. 2, because young people across the Arabic world are creating such exciting opportunities for change, has just opened a little wider."

To me, this was the heart of the question I had been exploring for months. Are the changes transforming the Middle East potent enough to undo a generation of stagnation, resignation, and blame—a morass so powerful they helped make Door No. 1 so appealing in the first place? Are the calls for freedom coming from Tunis, Cairo, Tripoli, Damascus, and other capitals—along with the extraordinary display of interreligious, intergender, intergenerational cooperation they ignited—unifying enough to make the changes necessary to allow Door No. 2 to become a viable option again?

The youth uprisings in the Middle East set the stage for this choice. The death of bin Laden brought it into sharper relief. One population. Two doors. Which will they choose? And what will their choice mean for us?

The answers to these questions lie in the hands of one group of people: Generation Freedom. Now that bin Laden's passing allows us to close our own door on 9/11, maybe we're finally ready to open a second door ourselves and find out who this generation is. Our future clearly depends on it.

I

FREEDOM COMES HOME

Can What Was Born in the Middle East
Save the Middle East?

They started gathering just before noon. They walked across bridges, drove in from the Nile Delta, taxied in from the neighborhoods surrounding the pyramids. They brought their children, their mothers, their cell phones, their cameras. They packed water, sandwiches, oranges, and chocolate. A few brought scarves dipped in vinegar in case the police fired tear gas again; others wore padded jackets to absorb any blows from the hired thugs wielding wooden batons. They hoped, but they feared, too.

The night before, the largest crowds in more than seventeen days had gathered in Liberation Square in Cairo to witness the end of three decades of Hosni Mubarak's erratic, repressive rule and the spread of the Arab Spring to the cradle of the ancient world. Yet while encouraging leaks had emanated from the presidential palace all day and the military had issued "Communiqué #1," the traditional sign of a new regime, when the grim-faced president with the pancake makeup took to the giant screens in Tahrir Square he issued a rambling, heart-hardened speech that made it clear he was not abdicating his gilded perch. A stunned disbelief descended on the crowd. Many gasped in horror or wept. And soon the masses began shouting in unison, "Leave! Leave! Leave!" They removed their shoes and waved them in the air, a popular sign of contempt in the Arab world. (Remember when George W. Bush had a shoe thrown at him in Baghdad?) A few hundred even marched in anger toward the presidential palace in Heliopolis.

The protesters had little choice but to call for greater numbers of demonstrators the next day. If today was the "Great Disappointment," tomorrow would be "Farewell Friday." Some diehard activists camped overnight in the white-tented village in the heart of Tahrir Square that had become known as Freedom City. Others returned home for a shower or change of clothes. Still others, members of the much-maligned "Sofa Party" who had watched the uprisings from the seats of their pants, decided now was the time to leave their pillows behind.

All day Friday, the third Sabbath of the revolt, defiant residents streamed toward Tahrir. By dusk they had reached their largest numbers yet, more than 1.2 million people. The crowd, with their many brightly colored sweaters, pullovers, and scarves, buzzed about the crowded plaza, ebbing and flowing like a bucket of marbles dumped in a mixing bowl.

Just as the sun dipped behind the sands, the early evening call to prayer cried out across the city, and suddenly what seemed like half of Egypt stopped and formed into straight lines in the direction of Mecca. They unfolded pieces of newspaper on the ground and began the ritual of bending, rising, kneeling, touching their foreheads to the ground, then standing, chanting, and doing it again. Even soldiers climbed on the tops of tanks to join the prayers, with some inviting marchers to join them on the bulwarks of repression. The serpentine lines and weaving trails looked like the fingerprint of a changing world. It's as if they created a new koan for the sages to consider: What's the sound of a million people praying?

But not everyone paused to pray that night. Some of the protesters were secular, some were undercover loyalists looking to stir up trouble, some were Christians. To make sure no thugs attacked the worshipers and no rowdy protesters disturbed them, huge throngs of Christians locked their arms and formed a massive human chain around the Muslims to create a sacred space for them to pray. Earlier, during a Christian mass in the same spot, Muslims had done the same thing for Christians. And on occasions when a melee threatened Cairo's historic downtown synagogue, Muslims and Christians together had locked arms and formed a human shield in front of the house of worship. Three faiths. Three spontaneous armies of defense. A visual manifestation of an evolving Middle East.

Then, about three and a half minutes into the sunset prayers, a new and unexpected image flickered onto the giant television screens of Tahrir. It was Vice President Omar Suleiman, standing at a podium with an unidentified man hovering just over his left shoulder like a mother making sure her son properly apologized for throwing toilet paper in the neighbor's pool. (Later this unnamed military official—he was eventually identified as Major Sherif Hussein of the army—became the hero of a viral Internet campaign called "The Man Behind Omar Suleiman," in which his frowning face was photoshopped behind Saddam Hussein; Adolf Hitler; Darth Vader; Leonardo DiCaprio and Kate Winslet in *Titanic*; Martin Luther King, Jr., delivering his "I Have a Dream" speech; Franklin Roosevelt, Winston

Churchill, and Joseph Stalin at Yalta; Justin Bieber; Jesus; the Sphinx; and nearly every other icon in the history of celebrity.)

Suleiman read a terse, two-sentence statement. "In the name of God the merciful, the compassionate: Citizens, during these very difficult circumstances Egypt is going through, President Hosni Mubarak has decided to step down from the office of president of the republic and has charged the high council of the armed forces to administer the affairs of the country. May God help everybody." Those who were not praying unleashed an ebullient cheer across Tahrir. But even more striking, those who were praying did not stop. History could wait; God could not. For a remarkable three and a half more minutes, even as their prayers were being answered around them, they continued to maintain their silent vigil in the direction of God's holy ground.

Finally, with the last chant complete, hundreds of thousands of extremely patient worshipers leapt in the air, unfurled Egyptian flags, and unleashed a collective, guttural cheer that could be heard from the Nile to the Yangtze. "We are free!" they cried. "We are free!"

In the miracle of that moment, the world naturally focused on the toppling of a long-hated dictator. In less time than it takes to start a blog, a new population of revolutionaries, wielding little but cell phone snapshots, status updates, and hashtags, had felled one of the most sophisticated and entrenched police states in the world. But while everyone was understandably fixated on the ousted president, I couldn't help wondering if we hadn't missed the real news. Maybe the bigger story wasn't the president up on the screen but the young people linking their arms on the ground. Maybe this young generation of freedom-loving Muslims was creating a new triple helix of shared identity that could forge an updated DNA for the Abrahamic faiths. Maybe, after decades in which the dominant voice of the Muslim world was orthodoxy, extremism, and terror, we were finally hearing the call of shared destiny and trust. *What's the sound of a million people praying?* The remaking of the future of faith.

Two weeks later I was standing in Tahrir Square. I came with a host of questions: Who is this new generation? What are they creating? And what do they mean to the world?

I hadn't planned to be here. My first visit to Egypt was fifteen years earlier, on a summer tour of the Middle East. On a visit to St. Catherine's Monastery in the Sinai Peninsula, I sat beside a giant shrub that monks claim is the actual "burning bush" in which Moses heard the voice of God. Alongside it was a fire extinguisher. *Is this in case the burning bush catches on fire?* I thought. The next morning I climbed Jebel Musa, or Mount Moses, which tradition says is the mountain where Moses received the Ten Commandments.

That trip convinced me to undertake a three-year project retracing the Five Books of Moses through the desert. I climbed Mount Ararat looking for Noah's Ark, crossed the Red Sea where Moses led the Israelites to freedom, and trekked to the top of Mount Nebo in Jordan where Moses died overlooking the Promised Land. *Walking the Bible* was published in 2001. Six months later came the September 11 attacks. As the world teetered on the brink of religious war, I went back to the region to learn more about Abraham, the shared ancestor of Jews, Christians, and Muslims. In subsequent years, I was airlifted into Baghdad during Operation Iraqi Freedom and took my wife on a second honeymoon in Iran. Altogether, over more than a decade, I managed to hike, swim, camp, spelunk, bargain, baksheesh, and kebab my way through every holy site, camel depot, war zone, and hot spot from Casablanca to the Caspian Sea.

And then I stopped. After I got back home from one of my more arduous trips, my wife announced, "You've had your time as a war correspondent." The following week I packed up my body armor. I slowly put my camel years behind me.

But the past has a way of not letting you go, especially when it involves the desert. As 2011 dawned, I watched with awe as wave after wave of hope-starved young people across two continents—from Tunisia to Libya, to Bahrain, to Yemen, to Syria—took to the streets to reclaim their lives. They marched in the face of dictators. They withstood the rain of bullets. They prayed in the face of tanks. And as the volatile mix of rallies, recriminations, worship, crackdowns, topplings, repression, and still more cries for reform continued to spread, people outside the Middle East began to wonder how much change the revolutionaries were bringing.

Time and again, commentators told us these uprisings represented something new. They were driven by young people—a bulging generation burdened with no jobs, rising prices, few prospects for marriage, and limited opportunities to define or fulfill their dreams. These young people, we were told, were fueled by decades of repression, government torture, and corruption. They were fed by an underground dot-com samizdat of YouTube videos, Facebook pages, Flickr photos, and Twitter feeds. #Jan25 was this generation's "Give me liberty or give me death!" It was, in the iconic words of Wael Ghonim, "Revolution 2.0."

But was it, really? Sure, all these newfangled elements were present in this movement. But as someone steeped in the ancient world, I also heard a different cry coming from the protesters. I heard the prayers of a suffering people calling out to a higher authority to help overthrow an oppressor. I heard the promise of an earthly paradise where the children of the prophets finally claim their God-given liberty. I heard the echo of the oldest stories ever told.

And then, in the crowds in Cairo, I began to see the signs. "Since you are a pharaoh, we are writing you in the hieroglyphics," said one. "Mubarak, if you're a Pharaoh, we are all Moses," said another. And in the final hours before the dictator's fall: a banner depicting King Tutankhamen's mask with Hosni Mubarak's face on the left and the face of a mummy on the right. In between was a line from the Qur'an in Arabic, "So today we will save you in body that you may be to those who succeed you a sign." The verse comes from Sura 10, the climax of Moses's showdown with the Egyptian leader. Pharaoh dies, and God preserves his body as a reminder to other tyrants that they, too, shall not prevail.

Could it be that this new revolution had roots in the earliest revolution of them all? At its core, was Revolution 2.0 really not that different from Revolution 1.0?

I decided to do what I had done a decade earlier after September 11. I would go back to the lands where civilization was born. I would turn away from the tweets and text messages and go back to the original texts that still define these countries and much of the world. I would go deep inside the oldest questions ever posed and try to figure out: Is freedom a universal right, as God suggests in the Garden of Eden? Do the forces of freedom—like Moses—really stand a chance against the forces of oppression—the pharaoh? Can the sons of Abraham—divided by faith, trapped in a cycle of violence—really live side by side in harmony?

The connection between the attacks of 2001 and the uprisings of 2011 was more than just a coincidence. Their short-term objectives were the same—the toppling of sclerotic regimes across the Middle East. The terrorists who attacked the United States on September 11, after all, were hoping to compel Americans to withdraw their support for the kings and potentates across the Muslim world. Even the perpetrators were the same: The suicide bombers of 9/11, like the leaders of the uprisings of 2011, were largely drawn from well-educated, well-to-do, Westernized families.

But the messages were different. The earlier one was backward-looking; the new one forward-looking. The earlier one was designed to create restrictive, even theocratic states;

the new one was designed to create open, even civil states. The earlier one was built on fear and terror; the new one on hope and opportunity.

Yet they had one more vital aspect in common: Both events were founded on the same underlying narrative. It's the story of humanity's relationship with the divine, and how different people interpret their God-given freedom. Osama bin Laden and the legions of Al Qaeda extremists he helped train interpret the Abrahamic tradition as justifying the use of violence to create exclusive, Islamic societies. Ahmed Maher, Wael Ghonim, and the legions of moderates, secularists, and even temperate Islamists they helped unleash interpret the same tradition as sanctioning more inclusive regimes where believers, rival believers, and nonbelievers alike can live together in a functioning society.

In effect, the two events are twin responses to the same problem: how to improve life in the Middle East. The uprisings of 2011 are the antidote to the attacks of 9/11. They are the rival narrative to the prevailing argument of the ayatollahs, the Al Qaeda operatives, the Wahhabi madrassas, the Hezbollah bombers, and the Hamas rockets: that violent extremism and religious orthodoxy are the only answers to Middle Eastern decay. In the new coalition of change, some of the voices are clearly religious; others are secular. Many in the middle are struggling to find a balance.

But in their messy, uneven, pluralist totality, the new generation of Muslim youth represent the cry of moderate Islam the West has been yearning to find for so long. How these competing constituencies in the new Middle East balance their differences—and how we in the West support them—may go a long way toward determining the prospects for interreligious harmony in the decades to come.

To understand how we respond to that call, I deeply believe we must understand how the children of Abraham view the central stories of their own identity. For nearly three thousand years, three stories have linked the peoples of the Ancient Near East: the birth of human dignity in the Garden of Eden; the shared humanity of the children of Abraham; Moses's insistence on human freedom. A common theme among these stories is that humans have God-given rights to freedom, dignity, and justice for all, ideas that have helped animate moments of transformation from the Roman Empire, to the Reformation, to the American Revolution, to the civil rights movement, to the fall of the Berlin Wall.

But for decades, many in the West believed the Muslim world was immune from these same yearnings for freedom. This view, I daresay, had become the consensus. Samuel Huntington, in his influential book *The Clash of Civilizations* (1996), argued that humans are irreparably divided along religious and cultural lines, and that foremost among those is a fiery chasm that separates Jews and Christians from Muslims. The reason, Huntington argued: Muslims do not share the core desires of the West; they have learned from their religion to be hostile to pluralism, individualism, and a free society. And Huntington was not alone. The West seemed to agree that the children of Islam were tribal, medieval, backwards, and content to be ruled by mind-numbing dictators propped up by the oil-loving United States.

The uprisings of 2011 killed that idea for good. The world now knows that freedom lives in the sands where it was born. But what everyone wonders is "Can freedom prevail?" Can the ideas of openness, tolerance, self-determination, and opportunity compete against the countercurrents of repression, militarism, fear, and religious orthodoxy? Can this new generation really change the world? As I set out for the region during this season of change, I hoped to answer this question: Can freedom, an idea that started in the Middle East, finally come home and save the Middle East?

———

Once in Cairo, I was directed not to Tahrir Square but to the headquarters of the Syndicate of Journalists, a crumbling, concrete jail of a building—eight stories tall, in that drab, khaki color favored by British colonizing armies and early desktop computers. Since the Bread Riots of 1977, the front steps of the Syndicate of Journalists has been the unlikely beating heart of freedom in the Arab world. Because the land is owned by the syndicate, the police have no authority to arrest people who gather here. The small, savvy band of protesters around Cairo knew that if they ever got into trouble they could take refuge here.

And the police knew it, too, which is why they had a saying: Protesters could assemble around 150 people on the Syndicate stairs, but if they managed to make it to the street, they would instantly become 2,000; if they could round the corner onto

Champollion Street, they would gather enough momentum to become 8,000; and by the time they got to Tahrir Square, they would reach 150,000, at which point they would win. The riot police had a simple philosophy: Don't let the revolutionaries get to Tahrir Square.

That's why the events of January 25, 2011 were so monumental.

"Before January twenty-fifth, many people were not as comfortable, or brave, or interested in participating in the demonstrations," said Noor Ayman Nour, a twenty-one-year-old law student and bass guitarist, the son of prominent dissidents, and one of the hunks of Tahrir Square. With his trendy glasses, Brylcreem curls, and teen-idol smile, Ayman Nour quickly became one of the public faces of the revolution. He volunteered to take me on the path to Tahrir Square to show me how the greatest night of his life almost became the last night of his life.

"We called those people the 'Sofa Party,'" he continued. "They sat on the sofa and watched. But they were converted on this day. Before January twenty-fifth, people felt that if they demonstrated for the end of the regime they would be alone. But January twenty-fifth gave you this sense of community and comfort, knowing that if you walked the streets you would not be alone. There are other people who love this country as well."

We stepped off the stairs and into the street. A candy stand sold Chiclets, Ho Hos, Snickers, and Borios, a knockoff of Oreos. As we rounded the corner, I noticed the English street sign for Champollion, the famed Egyptologist who decoded the Rosetta Stone, was spelled Shampillon. "After the revolution, we're going to have a minister of spelling," Ayman Nour said.

Like many of the youthful leaders of the revolution, Ayman Nour had grown up in relative privilege. But he was thrust into politics at an early age when his father, a popular parliamentarian who ran for president against Hosni Mubarak in 2005 (he garnered a heavily undercounted 8 percent of the vote), was thrown into jail. Ayman Nour was thirteen years old.

"For the four years that my father was in prison, every day I woke up to the thought, 'Prepare yourself. You might get a phone call that your father has died.' I went through my teenage years with this numbness. On family occasions, lots of my friends would go on picnics. We would go see my dad in prison."

Ayman Nour soon gravitated to a community of activists who were inspired in part by his father's incarceration. These several dozen young people held underground strategy sessions where they scoured the Internet for details of nonviolent protests like the Otpor movement in Serbia, which helped topple Slobodan Milošević. The "Youth for Change" group eventually stumbled on the writings of Gene Sharp, a shy academic from Boston who culled lessons from Gandhi and Martin Luther King, among others, into a ninety-three-page manifesto, *From Dictatorship to Democracy*. The book contains tips on how to organize a student sit-in, plant flowers in symbolic places, or survive a hunger strike.

Ahmed Maher, a thirty-year-old engineer who cofounded

the group, tried to bring its nascent efforts to a boil in the spring of 2008 to support workers who were striking on April 6. A boyhood lover of video games, Maher started a Facebook group page to call on activists to wear black and stay home on the day of the strike. Seventy thousand people joined in three days. The "April 6 Movement," as it was called, even created a logo—a vaguely menacing white fist in a red disk—modeled on one used in Serbia. Though only a few hundred gathered for the event outside Alexandria, the protesters battled police and toppled a billboard of President Mubarak. Two protesters were killed. Within weeks, Maher was arrested, stripped naked, and tortured; his cofounder was detained and had to swear off protests to gain her release. The movement sputtered.

"But it was still the first successful online revolt ever," Maher later told me; "the first civil disobedience that made the Egyptian regime shake."

Against the wishes of his wife, who was then caring for their nine-month-old daughter, Maher called for a demonstration on January 25, 2009. He chose that date because it was Police Day, a national holiday and the perfect occasion to snatch a symbolic victory from the most hated part of the regime. Again the protest failed to catch fire. He tried again on January 25, 2010. Still no luck. Each time, the Sofa Party prevailed.

But then, unexpectedly, there was a grisly breakthrough. On June 6, 2010, a twenty-eight-year-old man named Khaled Said was at an Internet café in the port city of Alexandria when police attempted to arrest him on trumped-up charges of theft and weapons possession. When officers banged his head against a marble table, the café owner asked them to step outside. It was a critical misstep, because it gave the authorities a reason to remove him from view. The police dragged Said's body across the street, pummeled him repeatedly, and forced him to swallow a bag of hashish. He died on the spot.

The story disgusted and ignited the opposition. Maher started a Facebook group called "My name is Khaled Said." By year's end it had 250,000 members. Meanwhile, an anonymous administrator started another Facebook group called "We are all Khaled Said." It had 300,000 members. Both sites were filled with video clips and newspaper accounts of police brutality, as well as a simple message: "This is your country." Eventually Maher got an email from the anonymous administrator of the other site saying the two should cooperate.

On January 18, 2011, Maher was in Qatar at an Al Jazeera conference on digital media when he began speaking with his friend Wael Ghonim, the head of marketing of Google Middle East and North Africa. The two had met a year earlier. Bespectacled and respectable, Ghonim was another unlikely revolutionary—just a hacker trying to crack a firewall, only one erected with real firepower. Over lunch, Maher briefed Ghonim on his plans to call for a "day of revolution" on January 25, 2011. Ghonim approved, and Maher said he had to reach out to the administrator of "We are all Khaled Said" to coordinate.

"I sat down at my computer, which was right next to Wael's," Maher told me, "and I started to chat with the admin of the other site. I had no idea at the time that I was chatting with Wael Ghonim."

January 25 was once more becoming the focal point of the revolutionary movement.

———

Champollion Street is narrow, dark, and lined with car repair shops. Ayman Nour pointed out a fast-food shop that sells *kushari*, the brawny Egyptian national dish comprised of rice, lentils, chickpeas, and macaroni, topped with salsa and fried onions. "Now that's revolutionary food," he said. "Have one of those at noon, you won't be hungry until midnight."

On the night of January 24, 2011, the city held its breath. Ayman Nour's mother, Gamila Ismail, once a glamorous television host who was booted off Egyptian state television when her husband was imprisoned, was skeptical this date would be any different. "Last year we were expecting eighteen thousand," the now-divorced activist said at an event. "We got only a dozen."

Her son, meanwhile, was taking no chances. "That night I went shopping and saw people I didn't know buying knee and elbow pads," he said. "I just smiled at them, knowing we were on the same team." He also picked up spray paint to blacken the windows of police cars and lemons to sniff for relief from tear gas. The next morning he donned what he calls his "revolution jacket." "It's durable," he said, "and has lots of zippers. It's great for hiding things." Using more techniques he learned online, he took two cell phones, knowing that the police would confiscate one but stop looking after that. He patted the pocket over his heart. "They never look up here," he said.

Egyptians like to sleep late, so the protests began late in the morning on Police Day. By midday, small groups began taking to the streets, first dozens, then hundreds, then thousands. As the police had long feared, the crowds quickly begat more crowds. By late afternoon, tens of thousands of demonstrators were spread out across the city. "And it was not just the typical people!" said Ayman Nour. "You saw all these segments of society that never hit the streets before, calling for their rights. This is why January twenty-fifth was the best day of my entire life, even more than when Mubarak stepped down. A huge group of people, walking through the streets of Cairo, calling for something I've been calling for since I was thirteen. That day was definitely the rebirth of hope in Egypt."

"So what happened to make the change?"

"Tunisia," he said. On December 17, 2010, a young fruit vendor in rural Tunisia set himself on fire in response to years of harassment at the hands of government officials. The incident sparked weeks of demonstrations in the tiny North African country, culminating twenty-eight days later in the resignation of the president. "When President Ben Ali stepped down on January 15," Ayman Nour said, "the Egyptian people said, 'Wow! If a country that tiny can do it, so can we.'"

But if Egyptian protesters were surprised by the numbers who showed up on January 25, the police were even more so. Overstretched and underprepared, they did what authorities often do in such situations: They unfurled the full weaponry of repression. Rows of helmeted riot police paraded into the city center, security vehicles rolled in behind them, volleys of tear gas were launched. All through the evening the police tried to beat, berate, intimidate, and humiliate the protesters into submission.

By midnight, Cairo's streets were awash in debris, dense with smoke, tense with uncertainty. But they were still full of people. The government shut off the Internet to isolate the Twitter-happy crowds. A few blocks from Tahrir, several hundred protesters stormed an abandoned police truck, tipped it over, and set it ablaze. That's when plainclothes officers grabbed Noor Ayman Nour, battered his head and shoulders, and shoved him into a green paddy wagon. There were forty-four people piled one atop of another in a vehicle the size of an ambulance. One was praying; a number were crying.

One of the people inside was Jack Shenker, a young journalist from England. "I spotted a high-ranking uniformed officer, and shouted at him that I was a British journalist," he later said. "He responded by walking over and punching me twice. 'Fuck you and fuck Britain.' "

The van sped through the chaotic streets, careening around corners, lurching with the bruised and bloodied bodies of an astonishing cross section of the population: an old man who was taking part in his first demonstration, a young man whose eye was bleeding from a rubber bullet, a lawyer. "As I was being dragged into the vehicle," the lawyer said, "a police general said to me, 'Do you think you can change the world? You can't! Do you think you are a hero? You are not.' "

But one man inside was very calm. This was not his first demonstration. This was not his first encounter with brutality. His father had been imprisoned when he was thirteen. His mother's career had been ruined. His teenage years had been spent in a state of perpetual numbness. He had been waiting all his life for this moment. He had been waiting for any sign that the numbness might end. And he knew exactly what to do.

As that green paddy wagon lurched through the streets of Cairo, Noor Ayman Nour tugged the brass zipper above his heart, slid his hand into his pocket, and felt the cool metallic comfort of his backup cell phone. Then the twenty-one-year-old with the baby cheeks did what any boy in his situation might do.

He called his mother.

———

Talaat Harb Square is actually a circle. In the middle is a statue of the founder of the Bank of Egypt, and surrounding it is a cosmopolitan mix of bookstores, cafés, and political offices, including the one that once housed Ayman Nour's father. A row of four books in the window of one shop caught my eye. Their covers showed Condoleezza Rice, Madeleine Albright, Michelle Obama, and Khaled Mashal, the head of Hamas. *What a perfect representation of the choice Egypt faces*, I thought.

Inside the paddy wagon, Ayman Nour and the forty-three other captives were increasingly desperate. The detainees had no idea where they were going or what to expect. Several people fainted; one man collapsed to the floor, gasping for breath. The others ripped open his shirt and tried to steady him, but he was slipping into diabetic shock. The protesters screamed for the drivers. "Help, a man is dying!" They got no response.

At one point, the vehicle actually lunged to a stop, the door opened, and an armed police officer appeared. He called for Noor Ayman Nour to get out. As the son of a prominent dissident, Ayman Nour was considered a dangerous person to detain. But he refused to abandon his fellow passengers. "No," he said firmly. "I'm staying." When the officer pressed him, Ayman Nour repeated his insistence that he would not leave unless everyone was freed along with him. The other inmates burst into applause. Jack Shenker climbed over the others and urged the young activist not to pass up the opportunity. "Don't be a hero," he said.

"Either I leave with everyone else, or I stay with everyone else," Ayman Nour said. "It would be cowardice to do anything else. That's just the way I was raised."

The police gave up, and the wagon continued its grim passage. Once the other captives realized they had an experienced hand in their midst, they asked Ayman Nour where he thought they were being taken. "I have no idea," he said. "I'm in the dark with you." But once they reached the outskirts of town, which he could tell by the quieter surroundings, he had an inkling.

"At that point, I actually began singing," Ayman Nour said. "People just gave me the look of 'What are you doing?' I told them, 'It's one of two things. Either they are going to let us out in the middle of the desert to go home, so we're celebrating in advance. Or they're taking us to the Central Security Forces headquarters, and we're never going to celebrate, smile, or laugh again, so we might as well smile and laugh now.'"

Ayman Nour, though, had a plan. In those first moments

in the paddy wagon, he had furtively telephoned his mother and described to her the vehicle they were in, and where they had been seized. With a decade of political activism behind her, Gamila Ismail knew just what to do. She telephoned her ex-husband and notified her other son, and the three hopped in three separate cars and began chasing down the security vehicle that contained her son.

At one point Ismail thought she had identified the right vehicle, and was following it through the streets. Ayman Nour asked everyone in the wagon to quiet down and whispered to his mother to honk her horn so they could tell whether she indeed had the right vehicle. She did.

But Gamila Ismail knew something her son and his fellow captives did not. They were seconds away from Central Security Forces headquarters by now. "Lots of my friends drove through that entrance and were never seen again," Ayman Nour said. So as the wagon approached the gate, Ismail sped her car in front of the paddy wagon, swerved sideways, and blocked the entrance. As soon as she leapt from the vehicle, Ayman Nour's brother and father swarmed toward the back door of the paddy wagon and began attacking it with crowbars.

"The truck began to rock alarmingly from side to side," recalled Jack Shenker, "while someone began banging the metal exterior, sending out huge metallic clangs. We could make out that a struggle was taking place over the opening of the door."

When at last the door opened, a police officer had managed to push aside Ayman Nour's father and brother and pulled his gun, but the captives surged forward, sending him flying. One by one the protesters fled their sweaty cell. "I insisted on being the last person out," said Ayman Nour, "because I knew there were a lot of sick and injured people. Obviously my coming out last of forty-four people was very nerve-racking for my parents. They were thinking, *We just spent hours chasing the wrong truck and our son wasn't inside!*"

Once he did step into freedom, there was no celebration. His three family members quickly grabbed him and threw him inside one of their cars, along with the man who had taken the rubber bullet in his eye. They sped back to Cairo, took the victim to the hospital, and placed Ayman Nour in hiding at the home of a family friend. For the next two days he remained a fugitive. But when word began to spread that Friday, January 28, had been identified as another rally, this one a "Day of Rage," he knew he had to join.

"Did you think the protests would succeed at that point?" By this time we had reached the end of Talaat Harb Street and were arriving at the entrance to Tahrir Square. Cairo's largest, greatest public space was filled with palm trees and bordered by block-like government buildings. Sweeping vistas opened up before us. As a pedestrian, you mostly felt relief from the smog, the congestion, and the choking claustrophobia of all the accumulated crud. For the first time all day I noticed the sky. It was gray, but uplifting nonetheless.

"It felt like an unprecedented moment," he said. "We didn't know whether or not it would turn into a revolution. But we knew that after the twenty-fifth of January, nothing in Egypt would ever be the same."

II

THE BIRTHPLACE
OF FREEDOM

The Garden of Eden and the Roots of Revolution

The first time I set foot in the desert, I braced myself for the silence. I was in my mid-thirties, well-traveled, yet completely inexperienced in the arid landscape of the Middle East and North Africa. The desert would surely feel isolated, I thought, an island of serenity. But once I stepped into the Sinai Peninsula, I was amazed by the din—the wind whining through the mountains, the sand tinkling against your face, the rocks crunching beneath your feet. The desert was definitely empty, but it's the least quiet place I've ever been.

The Nile is the exact opposite. As I set off one afternoon on my latest trip to Cairo in a high-masted felucca from a bustling riverbank not far from Tahrir Square, I steeled myself for a clanky, cacophonous ride. Rush hour was honking around us; the floating casinos, bowling barges, and party boats topped with neon mermaids and dolphins were just getting revved up; the pulsing pace of Africa's largest city (15 million people and counting) was squeezing its watery aorta like a heart attack waiting to happen.

But the river was almost mute. Ten degrees cooler and a hundred decibels quieter than the city around it, the river had a cleansing breeze, a light chop, and the effortless ability to make tension melt away. In antiquity, Egypt was called the "gift of the Nile." That gift is still giving five thousand years later.

"The Nile used to be a much stronger reference point for Egyptians," said Mahmoud Sabit, the colorful, chain-smoking historian of modern Egypt whose mysterious, crumbling Grey Gardens–style mansion sits in the narrow stretch of land between Tahrir and the Nile. Wiry and intense, with white hair and deep-set lines across his face, he appears older than his fifty-two years. We were sailing toward the Qasr al-Nil ("Palace of the Nile") Bridge, the chief passageway from downtown Cairo to Gezirah Island, the cultural heart of the city. "Even twenty years ago it was much more of an economic highway for barges, water taxis, and feluccas. It was like Main Street. All this traffic going to the Delta, Upper Egypt, the Mediterranean, carrying bricks, or chickens, or cows."

"Does it still have a romantic place in people's hearts?"

"It's more of a psychological thing in the sense that Egyptians never let themselves get far away from the sight of the Nile. If you notice, ninety percent of Egyptians live within a few miles of the river. But I think the real attachment is atavistic. The Nile makes everything important."

Which is why it came as no surprise that on Friday, January 28, 2011, the pivotal day in the entire revolution, the central battle between protesters and police took place over who controlled Qasr al-Nil Bridge, and with it access to the city.

———

We pushed off the bank. Omar, our pilot, slowly lifted the sail, then sat down and offered us a beer. Of all the Muslim countries I have visited, Egypt is among the easiest in which to find alcohol, a testament to its undercurrent of liberalism. I asked

Omar how his life had changed since the start of the revolution. "I feel much safer now," he said. "I used to look over my shoulder all the time. The police used to take me away without warning, just so I would give them more money, or a free ride on the river. Now they just pass by without asking. I can sleep safely on my boat at night."

At first glance, it might seem like a stretch to say that the Egyptian Revolution—and the entire swath of uprisings that rattled the Middle East and North Africa beginning in 2010—had their roots in religion. After all, most of the high-profile organizers were young, not overtly spiritual, and their language appeared to be more secular than faith-based. But look beneath the surface, and it's easy to draw a straight line between the passionate cries for freedom across the modern Middle East and the earliest calls for freedom in the Ancient Near East. In fact, you can't understand the current yearnings without understanding their earliest written expression, and that was in the scriptures of the Abrahamic faiths. Long before the Enlightenment, the Reformation, or even classical Rome and Greece, freedom had its earliest and most influential expression in the Hebrew Bible.

Let me explain. Today, the religions that grew out of the Bible are holy to half the humans alive. That number includes 2 billion Christians, 1.5 billion Muslims, and 14 million Jews. Those faiths have dominated Western life for more than twenty centuries, and it's easy to think of scripture as inherently conservative, the tool of autocrats, slave masters, male chauvinists, and anyone who benefits from traditional ways of organizing society. And it's true that the Hebrew Bible, the New Testament, and the Qur'an can be read to serve those purposes.

But long before they were co-opted by the powerful, these texts were embraced by the powerless. If anything, it's easier to read them as revolutionary texts. As Jonathan Sacks, the chief rabbi of Britain, wrote, "The Bible was, and probably always will be, a radical political document, testifying to the right of prophets to criticize kings, the inalienable dignity of the human person regardless of wealth and status, and most importantly for the history of freedom: a clear sense of the moral limits of power."

Since Jews came first among the Abrahamic faiths, they were the first to use scripture to promote a radical agenda of human freedom. They didn't have to look far. In the opening chapter of Genesis, God announces, "Let us make man in our image, after our likeness." The significance of this formulation is hard to overstate: Humans are earthly manifestations of God. If you enslave, oppress, or in any way devalue another person, you are, by extension, doing the same thing to God.

This idea became a central theme of the Hebrew Bible. Because humans are made in God's image, we are fundamentally free. We may live in our own times, but we also have timeless values and are entitled to eternal rights. Throughout the narrative, God's children are constantly aspiring to achieve this ideal state of freedom.

The Bible even creates a handy vision of what that ideal world might look like. It's called the Garden of Eden. The Bible locates Eden at the confluence of four rivers. Two of those are known—the Tigris and Euphrates. The other two—the Pishon and Gihon—are unknown, though for centuries many believed they were the Ganges and the Nile. From the beginning, Eden was more than a physical place, it was also a symbolic place. It was an ideal world where "every man shall sit under his grapevine or fig tree, and no one will make him afraid." This notion that humans can achieve a better society was revolutionary in human history. The Bible doesn't just articulate this notion; it invented it. Before the Bible, most religions viewed gods as standing apart from history. Afterwards, the children of Abraham saw God as being everywhere and as intervening in daily life.

And one of the ways he most frequently intervened was by toppling powerful men—from Adam to Noah to Pharaoh to Goliath to David. The Bible consistently conveys the idea that absolute power and arrogant leaders are dangerous weapons. Even more important, it tells readers they have the right—even the obligation—to stand up to those leaders.

And they listened. Early Christians looked to scripture in their fight against Imperial Rome. Faced with torture, abuse, even being fed to lions, Christians clung to the idea that all humans were created in God's image. "I would ask you," wrote Clement of Alexandria in the second century, "does it not seem to you monstrous that human beings who are God's own handiwork should be subjected to another master?" Because of them, the tradition of reading scripture to argue for human liberty would always be present in the Western world. "From such beginnings," concluded historian Elaine Pagels, "Christians forged the basis for what would become, centuries later, the Western ideas of freedom."

But what about Muslims? What's their relationship with freedom?

Back on the Nile, Omar was tacking to the west. He and Mahmoud Sabit were trading tales about how the revolution was already transforming Egyptian life. Omar said there was less honking in Cairo now that people were less tense. Also, groups of local citizens were banding together to run neighborhood watch programs at night. One group was even tackling one of the city's most visible problems, traffic. They were affixing stickers to the windshields of illegally parked cars, saying, "Egypt is changing and you're still double-parked!"

Dr. Sabit told a story about how on the night of January 25, riot police on their way home from Tahrir Square looted the lingerie store he runs near his house. "The poor men," he said. "They had spent all night defending the regime and their only reward was a few bustiers and brassieres. I have a surveillance video with one of them holding a G-string on a bayonet."

I had asked him to help me understand the connection between the Qur'an and freedom, and we spent a few minutes discussing the origins of Islam's sacred text. The stories of the Hebrew Bible were written down in the mid-first millennium B.C.E. The New Testament followed around five hundred years after that, and the Qur'an another five centuries later. The timing is significant because it means Muhammad transcribed the divine words in the Qur'an at a time when the stories of the Bible were well-known in Arabia, along with a rich variety of extra-biblical legends.

The Garden of Eden was among these stories, and it appears frequently in the Muslim holy book. Unlike the Bible, the Qur'an is not linear, so the story of Creation is not confined to a few chapters at the outset. Even more important, the story differs from its counterpart in Genesis in subtle yet meaningful ways. For starters, Eden is not exactly an earthly place but rather a heavenly place, a celestial paradise where God creates man and woman. In addition, Eve comes across much better in the Islamic version. Adam is the one who initiates eating the fruit against God's orders, and God forgives both Adam and Eve for their transgression, instead of ostracizing them from Eden. Also, the Qur'anic version has no notion of original sin and no overtone of female subservience.

After God absolves Adam and Eve, he dispatches the first couple to earth as his representatives. In the hadith, the all-important commentaries gathered in the centuries after Muhammad, Adam is described as coming to rest in India, with Eve in Arabia. The two remain separate for hundreds of years, then finally find each other in Mecca, where they mate. After their union, Adam fasts for forty days, abstains from sex with Eve for one hundred years, then sets about building a sanctuary in Mecca that will be an earthly substitute for the

Garden of Eden. One idea behind the hajj, the annual pilgrimage to Mecca, is that all humans can return to Eden on a regular basis. Much more than Judaism and Christianity, Islam has a living, breathing manifestation of Eden built into its annual calendar.

The story has yet another ongoing potency in Islam through the power of the garden. Deserts dominate the Middle East, so it makes sense that gardens would be coveted places in Islamic culture. The word *paradise* even comes from the Persian word for walled orchard. A similar reverence extends to the color green. Muhammad wore a green cloak and turban; inhabitants of paradise wear it, too; and it's the color of many bindings of the Qur'an. In the Middle Ages, crusaders avoided putting green on their coats of arms so they wouldn't be confused with Muslims, who often had green on their battlefield markings. And green is the most popular color in the flags of predominantly Muslim nations. It appears on the flags of Iran, Iraq, Afghanistan, Pakistan, Saudi Arabia, Kuwait, the United Arab Emirates, Jordan, Lebanon, Syria, Turkmenistan, Uzbekistan, Azerbaijan, Bangladesh, Libya, Algeria, Morocco, the Maldives, Mauritania, Sudan, and Palestine. It was no accident that the first of the so-called "Twitter revolutions," the student-led protests that grew out of the disputed election in Iran in 2009, which many see as the spark of the entire youth movement in 2011, was called the Green Revolution.

Given this ubiquity of garden imagery, I was curious if modern Muslims drew the same lessons of fundamental human dignity from the Garden of Eden story as do Jews and Christians. I asked Dr. Sabit.

"The word *freedom* that we're now hearing on the streets of Cairo, Tripoli, and Damascus doesn't have a precise equivalent in Arabic," he said. "And I would have to say that freedom as a concept isn't central to the Qur'an. What does have precedence—and what many Muslims mean when they cry 'freedom'—is liberty, justice, not being a slave."

The most basic human right in the Qur'an, he continued, is to be regarded as the pure, sanctified creation of God. As is the case in Genesis, God breathes life into humans and grants Adam and his descendants a special place in his creation. "We have bestowed blessings on Adam's children," says God in Sura 17 of the Qur'an. "We gave them greater advantages and exalted them above our other creatures." Building on this basic human dignity, the Qur'an stresses that no one can deny these God-given freedoms to another person. Particular scorn is heaped on anyone who captures another human being and turns him into a slave. A hadith identifies three categories of people whom God shall oppose on Judgment Day; one is "he who enslaves a free man, then sells him and devours the money."

From this core concept of individual liberty, the Qur'an constructs a more comprehensive notion of political liberty. The key principle is that only God can limit human freedom. As Sura 12 puts it, "Judgment is Allah's alone." Since humans are forbidden from usurping God's will, if a ruling authority gives orders that violate human dignity, individuals are not required to follow them. The hadith go even further, providing the basis for citizens legitimately standing up against lawlessness and despotism. In one such commentary, the prophet declares, "The best form of jihad is to tell a word of truth to an oppressive ruler." And if fear causes a person to refuse to speak out against such a tyrant? "You should have feared me and put me above the fear of others," says God. Take that, Sofa Party.

Given this underlying foundation of freedom in the holiest teachings of Islam, I asked Dr. Sabit whether he thought the current revolution was consciously tapping into these ideas. "For some people, yes," he said. "But for most, probably not consciously."

"So for those other people, where does their notion of freedom come from?"

"You have to understand," he said, leaning forward, "we've all been oppressed. We've been living in a society that for all intents and purposes has been lawless. It was like a big zoo around here. We were the animals, and they were the keepers. There have been no fundamental rights: the right to an education, the right to health care, the right to work toward a decent life. These have all been denied to most of the population in this country."

"But the idea that people deserve those rights, where is that grounded? Does it come from the West, from nature, from the Internet? There's a widespread notion outside the Middle East that Islam and freedom are incompatible, that Muslims wouldn't know how to handle freedom if you got it."

He sat back. "We're not Burkina Faso," he said. "We've had

this debate for centuries. We've had periods of great liberalism and freedom. We've had a progressive political system. We don't have to look to the West for examples of these ideas. We can look to our own history."

He cited two examples in which the Muslim world has interacted with the West to create an Islamic brand of a free, open society. The first was in the eighth century. Following the death of Muhammad in 632, Islam quickly spread across the Middle East and North Africa. In 750, after a century of expansion and internecine warfare, the descendants of Muhammad's youngest uncle, Abbas ibn Abd al-Muttalib, led a revolution against the more restrictive, pro-Arab regime known as the Umayyads, and ushered in a multiethnic, pluralist, deeply learned dynasty. The Abbasids moved the capital from Damascus to Baghdad, set up vast bureaus for translating Plato, Aristotle, and other philosophers into Arabic, and held ornate salons where Jews and Christians were invited to debate Muslim theologians on the finer points of religious doctrine. To be sure, this religious tolerance was partly practical—the newly minted Muslim conquerors could not control the religious practices of everyone in their entire empire. And authorities sometimes turned violent toward other People of the Book at a moment's notice. But an extended period of freewheeling religious coexistence prevailed.

During this period, a powerful subgroup of the Abbasids introduced an idea called the Mu'tazila Doctrine, which argued that God's wishes are accessible to rational thought and inquiry. The core of liberal Islam, the Mu'tazilites said reason was a central element of Islamic faith and used this principle to argue against political tyranny. Face-to-face with authoritarian figures, the much weaker Mu'tazilites did what both Christian and Jewish leaders had done in similar moments in their history: They reached back to privileges granted to Adam and argued that all humans have a right to freedom. And since God is not capable of doing wrong, they argued, human evil must be the result of people using their own free will improperly. In these situations, other humans are authorized to correct those misdeeds. The ruling Abbasids embraced the Mu'tazilites' revolutionary ideologies when it was in the interests of their upstart regime. But within a few generations, once the Abbasids consolidated their own power, the Mu'tazilites were dispatched, their leaders burned at the stake.

"But not before they left behind an enduring antecedent of how a moderate, learned, pluralist civilization could thrive in the Islamic world," said Dr. Sabit. "The revolutionary leaders of today can take comfort in the fact that they were not the first to mix Western ideas with Islamic traditions to create an open society."

For the next thousand years, Islam largely stifled outside ideas. But the dream of a free society was reborn in the nineteenth century during another fruitful interaction between Islam and Western thought—this time inspired by the French Revolution. Egypt and other Arab states heard the infectious ideas of "*liberté, égalité, et fraternité*" and knew they held the promise that progress could improve their lives. Through technology, learning, and science, any state could unleash the full potential of its citizens. Muhammad Ali, the first governor of modern Egypt, who swept into power in the wake of Napoleon's invasion of 1798, dispatched young men to France to study the Enlightenment, translate writers like Voltaire and Montesquieu into Arabic, and articulate a vision for a new Islamic state. The most important of these emissaries, Rifa'a al-Tahtawi, rejected some of the libertine excesses he witnessed in Paris, but insisted that Egypt could build a society where democracy coexisted with Islam; religion and science could be partners. His vision climaxed in 1878 with Egypt's first homegrown constitution, which was updated in 1921.

"For thirty years until the first military takeover in 1952," Dr. Sabit said, "we had a parliamentary life, we had constituencies, we had governments that cared for the population, brought about health care, programs, and projects. When we're talking about freedom, we had a recent history that we can compare it to. Freedom is not something we're trying for the first time. We've had practice."

"So when you look at the current revolution, you're reaction is . . ."

"We're back on track, as we should be. And just like the best moments of progress from our past, this one was homegrown."

This is why for the first time in his life, on January 28, 2011, Mahmoud Sabit put down his history books and set out to help make history himself.

———

You actually can't sail very far on a felucca in Cairo these days. When Dr. Sabit was young, the bridges would open twice a day so the high-masted vessels could pass through with their wares. These days the automobile has overtaken the boat as the primary means of commerce, so the bridges no longer open. The roads have no need to bow down to the river.

As our short sail neared its end, we arrived at the concrete pylons underneath Qasr al-Nil Bridge. At either end of the bridge there are two bronze lions. (They reminded me of a similar stone lion I saw in Iraq that's still standing in the ruins of ancient Babylon.) Completed in 1933, the mile-and-a-quarter bridge is flat, which creates a grand entrance from the island of Gezirah in the west into the grand heart of Cairo to the east. Just as it arrives downtown, the bridge pours pedestrians and cars alike directly into the center of Tahrir Square. Or at least it does when the road is not blocked by twenty thousand riot police.

In the days after January 25, Cairo was tense. Noor Ayman Nour was in hiding. The seasoned protesters such as Ahmed Maher and his colleagues in the April 6 Movement decided to lie low, regroup, and amass for what they hoped would be a much bigger "Day of Rage" on Friday, January 28. Unlike in the Judeo-Christian world, where the Sabbath day might be considered a poor day to call for massive demonstrations, Fridays proved pivotal in the Muslim uprisings because a) it's a holiday from work, b) no Islamic government would dare intervene to stop people from gathering for noonday prayers, the holiest of the week, and c) you already have a sizable group of people in public on which to build, and those people are usually charged up from what are often highly politicized sermons. Glance at a timeline of the critical days of the revolutionary movements in Tunisia, Libya, Bahrain, Yemen, Syria, and elsewhere: Most are Fridays.

As a mark of how revolutionary fervor was spreading far beyond the young at this point, Dr. Sabit had four demonstrations to choose from. "But I wanted my wife to go," he said, "so we went to the fluffy one. We met at a coffee shop on Gezirah Island after prayers." The night before, they did some research on the Internet about what to bring: diving goggles, washcloths, and hooded sweatshirts.

"Ours was very much the latte demonstration," he said. "Or at least was supposed to be. We met around 1 p.m. and had our coffee at Beano's, which is our equivalent of Starbucks, and waited for our friends to appear. When we stepped outside, we caught the attention of two officers from state security, who very much thought we were highly amusing. We smiled, and started walking."

When I asked what exactly they were doing when they walked, he said, "We were demonstrating. We were heading toward the bridge, chanting 'Down, down, with the regime!' and 'Bread, freedom, and human rights!' even though unlike a lot of the protesters, we didn't really need the bread." He chuckled. "By the time we got to the Qasr al-Nil Bridge, enough people had joined us from their flats and surrounding streets that we were five hundred, at which point the security police didn't think it was so amusing anymore."

The regime had already deployed teams of riot police to cordon off the east side of the bridge and with it the entrance to Tahrir Square. "We had a choice to try to break through the line, which we thought was a bit premature, or go back and get more people. The police started shelling us with tear gas. People were vomiting and crying, but others started pulling over their cars and joining us. We said, 'Okay, let's go back to the island, round up more people, and come back.' "

They turned and marched off the bridge, wound their way back through the streets, and soon enough had garnered close to two thousand people. "By this point we were getting pretty tired, and we decided to have another latte," he said. "But the shopkeepers wouldn't let us in. 'You're demonstrators,' they said. 'You're toxic!' Our fluffy demonstration had become serious." By the time they arrived back at Qasr al-Nil, they had swelled to three thousand.

"The problem was, we had no idea what was going on anywhere else in the city," Dr. Sabit said. "Mobile phones had been cut off. We thought we were the only demonstration in Cairo that day. We had no idea there were hundreds of thousands of people doing the exact same thing all over the city. Only later did we learn, 'Wow. We're not alone!' "

By close to 4 p.m., the crowd finally made its move toward the bridge. As they approached, they were hit with a wall of tear gas. Thousands of riot police had amassed on the east end of the bridge in thick, forbidding rows, blocking the entrance to Tahrir Square. The protesters gathered on the east side of the bridge. The two sides looked like anxious armies on a living chessboard. "I now know what a Roman legion looks like in full battle array, because I've seen it right here," Dr. Sabit said. "Six thousand riot police in rows. Ready. They slid their helmets onto their heads, pounded their shields, and charged. Only this time, we charged back."

For the next three hours, the two sides were locked in an old-fashioned ground war for control of the bridge. The police would take the roadway for a time, bringing in ugly green armored cars that looked like they came out of a *Star Wars* battle scene, from which half a dozen fire-hose nozzles would poke out without warning, gushing water in every direction like a spastic, pissing arachnid. But then the protesters would press forward, swarm the water cannons en masse, pull chunks of asphalt from the road and hurl them at the police, and simply overwhelm the authorities with their sheer bravado, discipline, and numbers.

"It was remarkably well organized," Dr. Sabit said. "There where referee whistles, captains calling out orders." These were the more experienced, professional protesters from the April 6 Movement and elsewhere, who suddenly got to experiment with the techniques they had been reading about for years. Put another way, for them it was as if the video game they had been playing suddenly jumped from their computer consoles to the streets of Cairo, like a virtual reality experiment that went shockingly, wonderfully right.

"A group of protesters would rush to the front of the line," Dr. Sabit said, "take the brunt of the cannons, the batons, and the tear gas, then retreat, and a fresh band of demonstrators would rush forward to replace them." Everyone else was chanting, taking videos with their iPhones, and carrying the wounded to makeshift clinics. The police would regroup and make their surge, and the protesters would retreat, reconfigure their ranks, and press forward once more. The most poignant scene, Dr. Sabit said, was a group of one hundred protesters who made their way to the deadliest part of the bridge, stood face-to-face with a fearsome assault from the water cannons, dropped to their knees in silence, bowed to the ground, and prayed.

"By early evening it was Armageddon," he said. "Overturned police vehicles were on fire; smoke and tear gas curdled the air; the dreaded ruling party headquarters at the edge of Tahrir was in flames. By this point ten thousand people clogged the bridge; we were packed liked sardines. I was worried about a stampede. If the police had flooded the bridge, a lot more people would have died."

But then, just as suddenly as the police had amassed, they fled. They turned and started retreating toward their barracks. As night fell on the Friday of Rage, the people had won the battle for the river. And as it had been since the days of the Fertile Crescent ten thousand years ago, the Nile again proved critical for Egypt. The consensus quickly emerged in Cairo that the battle for Qasr al-Nil was the pivotal event in the entire revolution. A cheer rose up; the victors rushed forward in jubilation and sprinted toward their destination. Tahrir Square would be theirs that night. Freedom would once more take root along the Nile.

I asked Dr. Sabit what he felt when he got to Tahrir. "That

the regime was finished," he said. "We've won. When the population has risen, to that degree, you can't stop them. I know Egypt. When the fuse has been lit, you can't dampen it down. It was only going to get brighter and brighter."

"And the fact that the decisive battle took place along the river?"

"It's part of a historical continuum," he said. "The Nile once more emanating its influence on this country. It's always been the main artery to the heart, and on January twenty-eighth it was again."

III

THE VOICE OF FREEDOM

Moses and Revolution

The view looking up from the bottom of the pyramid is chilling. The stones seem to climb at an impossibly sharp angle. Each block is about the size of a refrigerator-freezer. And the prospect of having my hand or foot slip on the crumbling limestone, sending my body tumbling down the jagged face of this 4,600-year-old sanctum of death, is irresistible to imagine. For a second my mind wonders how many layers a falling body would traverse. My breathing is labored. My heart is racing. It's not too late to turn back. Climbers have not been allowed here for decades; too many were dying each year.

"Are you ready?" my guide asks.

"Let's go," I say.

On a chilly winter morning in 2005, I gripped the bottom layer of the second-tallest pyramid in Giza and began the tense process of pulling, pushing, and clambering my way to the top. I had come with special permission in hand to consider a question that has bedeviled lovers of the Bible for thousands of years: Did the Israelites build the pyramids? The question was part of my ongoing quest to understand the ancient world's impact on contemporary life.

Even as late as the 1970s, when Israeli prime minister Menachem Begin made a state visit to Egypt as part of the Camp David peace process, he stood with Anwar Sadat at the pyramids and boasted, "Our forefathers built these." The Egyptian president, dumbfounded, replied, "I don't see this." Aides came scurrying, but Begin brushed them away. In the Middle East, tradition is sometimes as important as facts.

The first few steps of the climb were harder than I expected. I had to search for tiny handholds on the rocks, look for corresponding footholds, then lever my body upward as if climbing the face of a cliff. I didn't have special equipment. I wasn't tethered to ropes. I began to wonder if I would make it to the top. A friend told me that a BBC reporter had gotten halfway up the side, then froze in fright. He had to be pried from his position.

A few layers up, I began to find a rhythm—grip, step, pull, push. The key was to climb the corner of the pyramid, because it presented the largest area to stand on, and to concentrate on the rocks immediately in front of your face. No looking up, and certainly no looking down. A pyramid without a view.

After about forty-five minutes, each layer became higher and narrower, and I could feel the tug from the top. My pace quickened. I ignored the ache in my thighs. And finally I bounded up the last few rocks to the top and raised my hands like a victorious prizefighter. I had reached the summit of one of the oldest tombs in the world. I had surmounted my fears. And before I collapsed in exhaustion, I peered over the edge and saw nothing but the knife's blade of stone descending to the ground.

"You mean now I have to go down?"

That climb was with me five years later when I returned to the pyramids during Egypt's revolution. The grounds were empty this time; no tourists were braving the city. I can safely say the pyramids seemed unaffected by the hullabaloo over Facebook and Twitter. This ain't the first revolution they've seen. For me, this visit had a deeper meaning, because this trip was the first I had taken out of the United States since the year I spent fighting bone cancer in my left femur. I vowed to take my rebuilt leg and grit my way a few layers up the side. But no sooner had I gone two levels up than a security officer scurried over. I did not have permission, and he asked for a bribe.

My companion snapped at him. "This is the new Egypt. You can't do that anymore!"

The officer slunk away into the sand.

Poor Egypt, the past hangs over it like a triangle cloud. Everywhere you go, you encounter some manifestation of the country's erstwhile glory. The hundred-pound note has the Sphinx on its face. EgyptAir's logo is the eagle-headed god, Horus. Even Qasr al-Nil Bridge now has two obelisks behind those bronze lions. For every time an American encounters the Founding Fathers in the course of a week, an Egyptian confronts twice as many reminders of ancient Egypt—every day.

Part of this is simply a matter of branding. The trophies of Egypt's past are the country's most recognizable symbols. Related to that, part of it is economic. Tourism provides 10 percent of the country's gross domestic product and supports at least 20 percent of the population. If you do what Mom says and put your best face forward, Egypt's best face is the Sphinx. Another part is pride. Egypt was the great superpower of antiquity, and a little reminder of that erstwhile grandeur helps boosts the ego when you're driving on dirty streets and breathing dingy air. The entire Middle East performs this kind of retroactive confidence grab, from the Saudis with Mecca to the Jordanians with Petra to the Iranians with Persepolis. After the Iranian Revolution, an ambitious general tried to raze the ruins of Cyrus the Great because they were pre-Islamic. Even Ayatollah Khomeini stopped him. Any mark of past glory holds out hope that future glory is possible.

Considering this presence of the past, I was not surprised when Hosni Mubarak was compared to a pharaoh during the revolution. Many posters in Tahrir Square made the connection. Headline writers beat the analogy to death. Even Noor Ayman Nour casually remarked to me that the president's powers were "pharaonic." In July 2011, the *Economist* used the image on its cover, putting Mubarak's face on the Sphinx, slowly being covered by sand.

But there's a deeper, even darker legacy to this connection, one that goes beyond glib sloganeering and has more lasting consequences. In his book *Moses the Egyptian*, Jan Assmann, one of the preeminent Egyptologists in the world, wrote that the biblical story of the Exodus, in which Moses leads the Israelites in a "revolution" against the pharaoh, created what Assmann calls the "Mosaic distinction" in history. In this view of history, Assmann insists, it doesn't matter whether the events actually happened as described in the Bible and Qur'an. What matters is how the story influenced history. And in that regard, the verdict is clear: "Egypt" in history stands not only for idolatry, but also for a past that has been rejected. "Exodus is a story of transformation and renovation, of stagnation and progress, and of past and future," Assmann wrote. "Egypt represents the old, while Israel represents the new."

Nowhere was that more true than in the Egyptian Revolution of 2011, in which Mubarak was tagged the pharaoh. He represented everything old, bloated, and outdated in the world. In other words, he was "Old Egypt," which even in "New Egypt" was considered an insult. It got so bad that my friend, Dr. Gaballa Ali Gaballa, the former secretary-general of the Supreme Council of Antiquities in Egypt and the chief expert we featured in the Egypt portions of *Walking the Bible* on PBS, said he grew offended. "The pharaohs weren't half as bad as Mubarak!" he told me one morning in his home. (And he should know; he was appointed by the deposed president.) "If they were, I would have quit my job. I kept thinking, *Don't insult the pharaohs by comparing them to this dictator, for goodness sake*."

"So what lessons should the youthful vanguard of New Egypt take from Old Egypt?" I asked.

"I would tell them the ancient Egyptians were good at their work," he said. "They were serious. They were creative. They were innovative. Their system of government was not good for us, but their values were admirable: Do your work properly, embrace innovation, and protect your country.

"My generation is the cowardly generation," he continued. "We were the ones who created this mess, and we lived in fear. I never imagined that these young people could bring down with their hands one of the most notorious regimes in the Middle East. It was a miracle, I tell you. Exactly the kind you read about in the Bible. But they were prepared to face death. They didn't learn the old-fashioned rules that they were supposed to respect their elders. They broke out of our shell, because they had this wider world that is strange to us. And now, the country is going to be theirs, which is good, because we are the past, and they are the future."

In other words, for the first time in history, the story was flipped: This time Pharaoh is the one who was kicked out of Egypt. Moses is the one who stayed.

———

The idea that Moses could inspire revolution is hardly confined to Egypt. If anything, it's one of the most underappreciated outgrowths in the Bible's history. This link was especially influential in America, a place that owes much of its revolutionary rhetoric to the Bible's greatest prophet. For several years after returning from my travels across the Middle East I made a similar journey across the United States, examining the connection between Moses and the story of America, a link completely unknown to me before. From the pilgrims to the Founding Fathers, the Statue of Liberty to Martin Luther King, Moses was America's most enduring champion of freedom. The fact that this story was born in the Middle East, imported so effectively into America, then reimported, so to speak, back to the Middle East in the twenty-first century, encouraged me to make this latest trip. How had one story inspired so many people to fight for freedom across so many centuries?

Before attempting to answer that question, let's take a step back and review the basic story. The Moses story opens in the thirteenth century B.C.E. with the Israelites enslaved in Egypt. After the pharaoh orders the slaughter of all Israelite male babies, Moses is floated down the Nile by his mother, picked up by the pharaoh's daughter, and raised in the palace. An adult Moses murders an Egyptian for beating "one of his kinsmen," then flees to the desert, where a voice in a burning bush recruits him to free his ancestors. After briefly claiming he is not a leader and is not qualified for this mission, Moses accepts God's challenge. He becomes the champion of freedom.

Moses marches back to Egypt and confronts the pharaoh, his surrogate grandfather. "Let my people go!" The pharaoh refuses, but after a protracted battle during which God sends the ten plagues, he finally relents. Moses then directs the Israelites across the Red Sea and into the desert, where they will eventually receive the Ten Commandments and prepare themselves to conquer the Promised Land. Though there will be many hardships, setbacks, rebellions, and retributions during the Israelites' forty years in the desert, Moses is still best known for leading the Israelites out of slavery into freedom. This secures his reputation for all time. He is the world's first revolutionary hero.

At least you would think so. Though Moses is by far the leading prophet in the Hebrew Bible, the only one God meets "face-to-face," he was largely overlooked by the religions that followed. Jews downplayed Moses in favor of God in their tradition; he's even completely ignored in the Passover service, for instance, which ostensibly celebrates his accomplishment.

Christians downplayed him even more, saying Jesus was a "new Moses," who supplanted the first. Muslims did largely the same thing when their time came along. Though Moses is called the "confidant of God" in the Qur'an and is mentioned in a quarter of the chapters, he is less central in the Islamic understanding of the story than the pharaoh, who's been called "the chief villain of the Qur'an." The outline of the story is largely the same, but the central theme of the Islamic version is that the pharaoh was unjust, rather than Moses being just. In Islamic tradition, the "pharaoh of Moses" epitomizes the swaggering, arrogant, blasphemous despot.

The downplaying of Moses began to change around the time of America's founding. Protestants naturally gravitated to Moses because he inspired them in their fight with the Catholic Church. Early American settlers, many of them breakaway Protestants themselves, identified with the Moses story because they felt subjugated by existing institutions in Europe. When the Pilgrims left England in 1620, they described themselves as the chosen people fleeing their pharaoh, King James. On the *Mayflower*, they compared themselves to Moses. When they reached America, they thanked God for helping them cross their Red Sea.

By the time of the American Revolution in 1776, the theme of beleaguered people standing up to a tyrant had become the go-to narrative of American identity. The Liberty Bell has a quote from Moses on its side. George Washington was often called America's Moses. And on July 4, after signing the Declaration of Independence, the Congress asked Thomas Jefferson, Benjamin Franklin, and John Adams to propose a seal for the United States. Their recommendation: Moses leading the Israelites across the Red Sea. In the eyes of America's Founding Fathers, Moses was our real founding father.

This connection grew in the coming decades. In the nineteenth century, "Go Down, Moses" became the national anthem of slaves. Abraham Lincoln was likened to Moses for freeing the slaves. Even the Statue of Liberty had a connection. Sculptor Frédéric Bartholdi chose the goddess of liberty as his model, but he enhanced her with two icons from Moses: the nimbus of light around her head and the tablet in her arms, both from the moment Moses descends Mount Sinai with the Ten Commandments.

As Americans grew increasingly secular in the decades that followed, Moses never disappeared as an icon of freedom. Superman was modeled partly on Moses. He, too, was put into a vessel and launched into an unknown world where he was summoned by a higher authority to save humanity. Charlton Heston quotes the Liberty Bell at the end of *The Ten Commandments*. And Martin Luther King invoked Moses the night before he died. "I've been to the mountaintop," he said. "And I've looked over. I've seen the promised land. And I may not get there with you, but I want you to know that we as a people will get to the promised land." Every president from Franklin Roosevelt to Ronald Reagan to Barack Obama has likened himself to the biblical prophet.

So, were Americans the only ones making this comparison? For a long time, the answer was yes. But in the twentieth century, the idea that Moses was a paradigm for oppressed people standing up to an oppressor spread to others—from Catholics in Latin America to Christians in Eastern Europe to Jews in the Soviet Union to blacks in South Africa. Still, most observers felt the idea was confined to Jews and Christians. The intellectual historian Michael Walzer, in his influential book *Moses and Revolution*, credits the Hebrew Bible with inventing this formula for revolution. "Since the late medieval or early modern times, there has existed in the West a characteristic way of thinking about political change," he writes. "This story has roughly this form: oppression, liberation, social contract, political struggle, new society. We call the whole process *revolutionary*." But he quickly adds this caveat: The story isn't told everywhere. "It belongs to the West, more particularly to Jews and Christians in the West."

Well, so much for that idea.

The 2011 uprisings in Tunisia, Egypt, Libya, Syria, Bahrain, and Yemen, all within a few weeks of one another, have clearly shown that Muslims know their scripture—and the formula for how to run a revolution—as well as Jews and Christians. And in terms that Professor Assmann might appreciate: They know they don't want to be on the pharaoh's side anymore; they want to be on the side of Moses. The "Mosaic distinction" Professor Assmann wrote about so eloquently has clearly been overturned. Egypt doesn't just represent everything old and outdated now. Egypt is the cutting edge of new.

And it was Moses, ironically, who helped get them there. As it turns out, the Muslim world has been developing this attachment to Moses for some time. Even before these latest events, the Moses story had been gaining traction in the Islamic world, in part because the region was so dominated by those swaggering, arrogant dictators the Qur'an so demonizes. This link was especially potent in Egypt, whose dictators were among the most swaggering. Sayyid Qutb, the leading theologian behind the Muslim Brotherhood in the 1920s, drew the parallel between the authoritarian leadership in the Arab world and the blasphemous conduct of the pharaoh in Egypt. He even likened President Nasser to the pharaoh. (Nasser returned the compliment by having him killed.) When Nasser's successor, Anwar Sadat, was assassinated by an Islamist in 1979, the assassin shouted: "I have killed Pharaoh, and I do not fear death."

But the most avid exploiter of Moses's revolutionary potential was none other than Ayatollah Ruhollah Khomeini. As early as 1944 the Shia cleric aligned himself with the Hebrew prophet. "It is rising for God when Moses with this staff defeated the Pharonians," he wrote in an essay about bringing about change. Later, in a message to the Iranian people, he explicitly compared the shah to the pharaoh and interpreted the Qur'an as an injunction to Muslims to confront the strongman. "Hopefully, like Moses, who was brought up in the household of the pharaoh [but] put an end to his oppression, you too will one day under the command of a righteous officeholder cut off these wicked hands and root out corruption and oppression." By the time of the 1979 revolution, posters depicting Khomeini as the "Moses of the Age" were widespread in Tehran.

If nothing else, my journey back to the Middle East helped me understand a profound similarity among Jews, Christians, and Muslims. We're all capable of being inspired by the same stories. And though it's admittedly odd that Moses can be deemed a hero by figures as varied as Benjamin Franklin and Ayatollah Khomeini, Martin Luther King and the Tahrir Square protesters, the connection gives me a reason to hope. It reminds us that Jews, Christians, and Muslims, instead of living on opposite ends of some uncrossable divide, have a shared scriptural heritage and a mutual language of revolutionary change.

————

But what role had Moses played in the revolutions of 2011? Was he more inspiring to the young, futuristic demonstrators or to the more traditional, religious ones? And was this a spiritual event anyway, or a secular one?

To help answer that question, I drove one night to the heart of Cairo's biggest bazaar. Amid the brassy, smoky crush of camel-leather stools, constellations of gold necklaces, and abundant belly dancing outfits, chess sets, and mounds of saffron, I walked into an open-air café. It had worn wooden chairs, a cheap linoleum floor, blinding fluorescent lights, and all the mysticism of a thirty-year-old Dairy Queen.

But leaning up against the wall with an ample belly and a walrus mustache, and wearing a brown cardigan sweater, was one of the more mystical men I have met in some time. His name was Ali Darwish, and he is something of a Sufi sage, a writer, an utterer of cryptic pronouncements, a political gossip, and a St. Nicholas–like hero to the poor. Over the next few hours, as he drank multiple cups of tea, rubbed wooden beads, and ignored his buzzing phone, he doled out dozens and dozens of coins, ones, twos, and threes, to bent-over beggars, men with no teeth, and kids with missing legs. It was an extraordinary display of generosity. Within minutes of sitting down, I was reaching for coins in my pocket and unfolding bills from my wallet just to refill even a small trickle of what poured from his outstretched hands.

"Fifty percent of my income I give to the poor," he said matter-of-factly. "Honestly, this is what I can do. If there is poverty around you, and you have some money, could you refrain from helping them? It's against my belief as a human being, and as a Sufi."

Sufism is the forgotten third wheel of Islam, the more internal, more spiritual, more inclusive offshoot of the faith, more focused on repairing the world and connecting with God than its sometimes more legalistic, more dogmatic cousins in the Sunni and Shia branches. Darwish bluntly called Sufism "wiser," and said practitioners enjoy more freedom and display more tolerance. He estimated that around 10 percent of Egyptians are Sufi.

I asked him whether he thought Egypt's revolution was a political or a spiritual event. He didn't actually rub his belly as he contemplated his answer, but given his tone and demeanor, he might as well have.

"Most Sufis believe this was an impossibility for Mubarak to fall," he said. "The collapse of the system is a miracle, in every dimension. The man had absolute power. He had the army; he had the Republican Guard; he had the intelligence service. He had everybody. Yet within two weeks there was no Mubarak, and the system was finished. This, for us Sufis, is the doing of God. He is the one who gives power, and if you mishandle it, he is the one who takes it away. This is exactly what happened in Egypt."

"When you see a miracle like this, what does it remind you of?" I asked.

"In the Qur'an, they narrate the story of Moses and the pharaoh," he said without my prompting. "Moses was asked by God to go and meet the pharaoh and tell him, 'You are on the wrong track. You are not a god.' And the pharaoh said, 'No, I am a god.' Then the pharaoh fell. He drowned and died. Moses lived. When I see what just happened here, I think Mubarak was the pharaoh, but I think the whole Egyptian people were Moses. Not one figure, but all the young people who came out and said, 'We want equality. We want opportunity. We want freedom.'"

He spread out his arms with incredulity. "The people were asking for the minimum," he continued. "They weren't saying, we want to be rich. Just equal opportunity and a better standard of living."

"So what's the lesson of the story of Moses and the pharaoh?"

"You should never make yourself a god. Pay attention to what's happening around you, care for the needy, and don't neglect the poor. The pharaoh treated the Israelites in a terrible manner; they were slaves. Mubarak was the same. He had no sympathy for the poor; he made most people poorer. We have a saying among Sufis: 'The poor and the weak are the children of God.' Only the pharaoh thinks he's greater than God."

"But what about the people who say this was a secular revolution, not a religious one?" I asked. "All these young people on Facebook, Twitter, and Skype who don't care about God. All they want is a better life, no?"

"If there was no religious meaning," Darwish said, "why did they pray in the square? Why did they hold noonday prayers and Sunday Mass? Why did they kneel in front of the water cannons and issue blessings on top of the tanks. There was certainly a spiritual dimension to what happened. If anything, I am worried that it might become too spiritual."

I looked at him. "What do you mean?"

He took a deep breath. "I'm worried about the future," he said. "I believe the revolution had a religious dimension, but some people appear to think it had an exclusively religious dimension. The man behind the assassination of Sadat was just on television spewing hatred. He was trying to sound moderate, but I don't trust him. The Muslim Brotherhood in this country are very cunning. Their intentions have yet to be revealed. If they come to power, they will kill the Sufis. They will close shrines. They will make life miserable for a lot of people."

"There seems to be a debate for the hearts and minds of young Muslims," I said. "On the one side are the extremists—Al Qaeda, Hezbollah, Hamas, the Wahhabis. On the other side are the futurists—the Twitterers, the Facebookers, the You-Tubers, the digerati. Which side will young people go with?"

"If the economy continues to be bad, they will probably go with the extremists," he said. "I will tell you the fundamentalists' technique. Let's say you're a young man approaching thirty years old. You have no job and no chance to get a wife. They come to you and say, 'Do you want to work? Do you want to get married? We'll do that for you.' They get you a job in a shop; they get you a young woman who believes as they do; and they indoctrinate you."

"So let's say I am that young man, and I come to you for advice. What would you tell me to do?"

For the first time all night, he squirmed in his chair. He paused for a long time. "I would tell you, 'There is only one way forward. Egypt for all Egyptians. Opportunity for all. If you try to make everyone believe the same thing, you risk becoming the pharaoh all over again.' "

"And if I went to back to the extremists and told them what you said, what would they say?"

"I don't know," he said. "You'll have to ask them."

———

The headquarters of the Muslim Brotherhood is located in a surprisingly posh area of Cairo. The residential street is crowded, pleasantly leafy, and lined with white, concrete, mid-last-century buildings eight to ten stories tall. After identifying the proper address, I stepped into a tiny elevator and nearly leapt out of my shirt as a loud Arabic chant—like the electronic call to prayer, only peppier and more jarring—blared from a speaker. The tune continued all the way to the third floor, then abruptly stopped as the doors opened.

"It's the prayer for transportation," explained the attendant who greeted me. "It thanks God for all means of transporting from one place to another, like an airplane, a bus, or a train."

"Or a revolution?" I added, gamely trying to lighten the mood.

He tilted his head, unsure how to respond. "That's transportation of another kind," he said, then showed me into a room. I noticed immediately there were no women around.

The conference room of this eighty-five-year-old organization looked like the conference room of any eighty-five-year-old organization. It had a large wooden table, green leather chairs (Aha! Muslim influence), a dead houseplant, and a TV showing Al Jazeera. A large Arabic banner hung on the wall: DIALOGUE FOR EGYPT #5. I don't know what I was expecting. A cave, maybe? But it certainly wasn't the kind of place you'd expect to find a terrorist crawling out from under a rock. If anything, the most notable thing about the room was the thirteen chairs and the *nine* boxes of Kleenex.

The Muslim Brotherhood may be the Middle East's most pivotal organization in the second decade of the twenty-first century. How it chooses to act in the coming years—with violence or nonviolence; Islamic exclusivity or partnership with other faiths (and those of no faith)—may go a long way in determining the future of freedom in the Muslim world.

The Society for Muslim Brothers was founded in 1928 by scholar and teacher Hassan al-Banna. From the outset, its goals were clear: to use any means necessary to instill the Qur'an as the "sole reference point" for individuals, families, and the state. Its original motto: "God is our objective; the Qur'an is our constitution; the Prophet is our leader; Jihad is our way; and death for the sake of God is the highest of our aspirations." The organization built its popularity by deftly deploying social services, such as constructing hospitals, pharmacies, and schools, along with forming strategic alliances. Through a partnership with Nazi Germany, for example, the Brotherhood distributed copies of *Mein Kampf* and *Protocols of the Elders of Zion*. By 1948, it had more than two million members.

In 1954, the government of Gamal Abdel Nasser, fearing the Brotherhood's growing clout, banned the organization and for the next decade and a half systematically tortured Brotherhood leaders. This period was captured in a prominent book, *Return of the Pharaoh*. In the 1970s, the group suddenly shifted course, renounced violence, and vowed to seek change through existing institutions. In recent years, the Mubarak regime arrested tens of thousands of members, yet the Brotherhood still managed to capture 20 percent of the parliament in the 2005 election. Its younger members, meanwhile, took to the blogosphere and social networks, and partnered with the April 6 Movement and other revolutionary groups.

After Mubarak's fall, the Brotherhood quickly rushed into the void, pushing its slogan: "Islam is the answer." But the organization emphasized that it did not seek to control the country outright. On its website, in books, and in op-ed pieces in

English in the *New York Times* and elsewhere, the Brotherhood claimed to be moderate, committed to a civil state, even pluralist in its vision. The question hanging over the world: Is their promise believable?

Muhammad Biltagy strolled into the conference room looking every bit the politician he is, with a drab brown suit, a green tie, deep-set, sleep-deprived eyes, and a cell phone affixed to his ear. The only sign of his religiosity was the dark brown calloused prayer bump just above his eyes, which Muslims call the *zabiba*, or raisin, from touching the forehead to the ground so assiduously during the five daily prayers. I told a friend in Cairo that I would be meeting Dr. Biltagy, a medical doctor by training and a former member of parliament who now runs the political arm of the Brotherhood, and my friend visibly shivered. "Ooh, he's one of the mean ones."

I asked Biltagy about his upbringing and why he had joined the Brotherhood. Almost exactly my age, forty-seven, he was born outside Alexandria as the sixth of seven siblings, and is the only Brotherhood member among them today. He joined when he was seventeen. "I was searching, and still am searching, for a national movement that works on the development of the country and the *ummah*," he said, using the Arabic word for the pan-Islamic nation. "As a force, I found the Muslim Brotherhood effective." He had been detained a number of times by the government, he told me, but was luckier than his colleagues, many of whom had served lengthy prison terms.

"I notice you still have your fingernails," I said, referring to the well-known torture technique of removing the fingernails of political prisoners.

He nodded knowingly. "That wasn't really happening so much in recent years, though much worse happened in the 1960s. It was more that we were deprived of our political rights; our careers were affected because we were in prison so much; our families suffered. I was unable to get a job for five years, until I got a court order."

He was clearly nervous speaking with me, and was watching his words carefully. He listened closely to the translator and thought before answering each question. But he was also noticeably unflappable. He had sat across from more menacing interlocutors.

"You seem very calm," I said. "I'm curious: If I had met you before the revolution, were you angry?"

He chuckled. "We were always looking for peaceful methods of change," he said. "We rejected the violent techniques put forward by other groups. We channeled our anger into activities that would push Egypt toward peaceful change."

And finally their luck changed. Muhammad Biltagy had been the public face of the Muslim Brotherhood during the revolution, and one of the protests' most visible organizers. But he and his colleagues were careful to try to conceal their role. "We were keen to participate in the revolution but not at the forefront," he told me, "because we knew the government would use our presence to scare people away. The first statement made by the Ministry of Interior spoke about the Brotherhood as being the hands behind the movement."

But everyone I spoke to emphasized that when the uprising turned ugly in its second week, the Brotherhood played a central role. They were well organized, disciplined, and experienced in handling crackdowns. After January 28, a kind of euphoria settled over Cairo. The emboldened protesters felt increasingly confident in their demands, which escalated from their original calls for the resignation of the interior minister to a full-throttled call for the president's resignation. On Saturday, January 29, President Mubarak sacked his cabinet but remained out of sight; on Sunday, opposition figurehead Mohamed ElBaradei addressed the protesters in the square, saying, "What we started can never be pushed back."

But the following Tuesday the pushback began. Mubarak gave a speech saying he would not run for reelection, but refused to step down. "I will die on Egypt's soil," he said. The next day, Wednesday, February 2, he sent in a rented army of thugs on camelback and horseback, wielding machetes and pistols. The sight of camels, who despite their romantic Hollywood image are actually ornery beasts, galloping menacingly into the heart of downtown Cairo like some Lawrence of Arabia fantasy gone mad, enraged the protesters. (As Gigi Ibrahim, one of the leaders of the youth movement, told me, "My first thought was, 'Oh, crap, we're stuck with the stereotype of the camels. Damn, Mubarak for making that stereotype stick—even in the midst of our revolution!'")

Dr. Biltagy and his comrades joined demonstrators who gathered near the Egyptian Museum, throwing Molotov cocktails and stones at the mercenary madmen as they slashed their way through the throngs. Dozens were bloodied, injured, or killed. The revolution seemed to be stalling.

"In moments like that," I asked Dr. Biltagy, "did you rely on your faith?"

"I believe that one of the main pillars of Islam, as much as prayer, is freedom," he said. "There are many verses that say that. But we decided not to use Qur'anic verses during those moments, because they would be divisive. We relied on them only for our internal feelings."

"And when so many died around you, was it worth the price?"

"I expected the price to be much higher," he said. "In 2006, an Egyptian ferry sank in the Red Sea; fourteen hundred people died. That was just one day under the regime of Hosni Mubarak. To lose eight hundred martyrs to achieve the dream of all Egypt, that was worth it."

We turned to the future—and to the controversies surrounding the Brotherhood.

"If 'Islam is the answer,' " I said, "what is the question?"

"That's not what's on the table right now," he said. "What's on the table is how to work with all the other political movements to achieve the demands of the revolution, which are democracy, freedom, and social justice."

"But one of the questions," I said, "is what will the role of Shariah law be in the future of the country." Shariah law, from the Arabic word for path, is the widespread Islamic code of conduct adapted from the Qur'an and other sayings from

Muhammad. For decades it was identified as *a* principle of the Egyptian constitution, but in 1980 it was changed to *the* principle. A big debate had broken out about what role it would play in the future.

"When the constitution was changed from *a* to *the* in 1980," Dr. Biltagy said, "it didn't change much in the practical lives of Egyptians over the last thirty years. That clause seems to reflect more of the cultural identity of the country than anything practical."

"But there are certain aspect of Shariah law, if I might push a little," I said, "like honor killing, violence against anyone who converts to Christianity, certain rules about homosexuality, that can become law in this country if Shariah is the foundation of the constitution."

"But Shariah has been the main source of legislation for three decades and none of what you fear has happened."

I asked him what he thought happened on 9/11.

"It's not my job to investigate what happened, but the fact that Islamists took part helped to join Islam with terrorism for the past ten years. I think it was a despicable act."

"Some of those violent Islamists live in Egypt," I said, "including the ones involved in the assassination of Sadat. Many were released from prison after the revolution. Do you believe they will join the Brotherhood?"

"That is not possible. We have always been critical of those people. We condemn violence and call for peaceful change. They have to figure out their own future, but we believe that they harmed Egypt and harmed Islam, both internally and externally. We don't agree with their ideology at all."

Now it was my time to lean forward. "Part of the challenge the Muslim Brotherhood faces, it seems to me, is that you have Islam and terrorism clearly united together in groups like Al Qaeda and the leadership of Iran. But there aren't a lot of examples of Islam and democracy living side by side."

"I think there is the example of Turkey," Dr. Biltagy said. "The ruling party is from an Islamic background, yet they have managed to have real democracy in Turkey. They are accepting of other religions. They are reaching out to the world in ways they haven't before. That would be an example that Egypt could follow."

Our time was coming to a close, so I decided to do a sort of lightning round where I asked him about a number of long-term issues in the new Middle East. Was he in favor of closer ties with Iran? "I believe in the closeness of human groups, regardless of differences. I don't believe in the conflict of civilizations." Could he imagine an Islamic caliphate from Iran to Morocco? "The European Union is a good example of similar countries cooperating on different levels, whether African, Arab, Euro-Mediterranean, or Islamic. And it doesn't have to be in historical relationship with the caliphate." What about peace with Israel. Does he support Camp David? "We have a comprehensive peace between the people, but not necessarily with the head of state. In principle we support all international peace treaties that Egypt has signed to date, but we also have the right like any people to renegotiate. Unless the issue of Jerusalem is resolved, a continuous, comprehensive peace in the region will be difficult to achieve."

Altogether, I was impressed that Dr. Biltagy, like other, more junior members of the Brotherhood I met (and unlike a number of the more ragtag members of the opposition I met), was focused, comprehensive, and, as the political consultants in America like to say, "on message." But was he being truthful, or just offering spin? There were plenty of signs in postrevolutionary Egypt that the Brotherhood and other Islamists were expanding their ambitions. They have heightened calls for Egypt to be declared an Islamic state and rallied supporters to defend the constitutional foundation of Shariah law; some have even called for the government to employ "morality police," as Saudi Arabia and Iran do. But other signs suggest they are following through on their more moderate platform. The Brotherhood said it would field candidates for only 50 percent of parliament, would not run a candidate for president, and repeatedly distanced itself from more flamethrowing Islamists on the right.

Still, I never felt I was seeing the man behind the carefully constructed mask Muhammad Biltagy presented me. That is, until I asked him again about his personal feelings during the revolution, and what story from the Qur'an most resonated with his experience. Suddenly his mood softened, his eyes moistened, and he told me a story.

"In 2006, it had been fifteen years since students in uni-

versities in Egypt held open elections for the Student Union,"
he said. "I was the head of the Student Union in the 1980s, and
I was invited to give a talk to the students before their vote. I told
them the story of the dialogue Moses has with the pharaoh in
the Qur'an. When Moses comes to the pharaoh and asks him
to follow the true path of God, the pharaoh reminds Moses of
the endless kindness, the food, and the security his adopted
family had shown him. And Moses says, 'That all means nothing if there is no freedom for the Israelites.' "

"Why did you tell them that story?" I asked.

"To tell the students that freedom is more precious than
anything. They should not compromise their dreams. Instead,
they should use whatever means possible to achieve them."

Sure enough, here was more proof that Egypt never escapes
its past. It never outruns the shadows of its great combatants,
Moses and the pharaoh. It doesn't matter that the Israelites had
nothing to do with the pyramids; they were constructed 1,500
years before the descendants of Abraham, Isaac, and Jacob
would have lived anywhere near the Nile. It doesn't matter that
in all likelihood God did not turn the Nile into blood or kill the
firstborn sons of Egypt.

What matters is that the stories changed the world. And
they still do. The stories that came from this land have animated people—from the banks of the Nile to the decks of the
Mayflower to the streets of Selma, Alabama, and now back
again to the Nile. For almost three millennia, they have inspired people in pain to stand in the face of their foes and say,

"Let my people go!" Freedom is the theme of those stories, and now we know there's no distinction in who craves it.

I said good-bye to Dr. Biltagy, and we shook hands. Then I stepped back into the elevator and made my way down, with prayers for safe passage echoing firmly in my head.

IV

FREEDOM TO BELIEVE

Abraham and the Road to Reconciliation

The smell of a burned-out church is a haunting, memorable stench. I have experienced it several times in my life. In east Tennessee in the mid-1990s after a string of attacks on predominantly black churches. In Lower Manhattan after the 9/11 attacks, at the Chapel of St. Paul's at Trinity Church, which wasn't destroyed when the towers fell but was covered in a layer of soot and debris. And I smelled it again not long after the fall of Hosni Mubarak, at the Church of the Two Martyrs (St. Mina and St. George), 130 miles southeast of Cairo, in the small city of Soul, in Helwan Governorate.

One afternoon I drove through the scorching, empty desert, passed through a bleak antechamber of cactus and vegetation, and finally arrived in this still-tense city of sixty thousand, which had suddenly erupted in sectarian violence in the days after the revolution and found itself thrust into the crosscurrents of one of the most pressing questions of the modern world: Can members of different religions live alongside one another without killing one another? At that moment, the answer appeared to be no.

The streets of Soul are not exactly paved with dreams. In fact they're not even paved at all. They're packed with a dense chocolate-colored dirt; they're bumpy, ridged, potholed, occasionally muddy, and lined with trash, donkey dung, and squatters, who tuck themselves between the motorcycles and car repair shops, waiting for prayers, trouble, or, as the world had unfortunately just discovered, love. About 80 percent of Soul's residents are Muslim, and fairly traditional Muslims at that. The rest are Copts, members of Egypt's leading Christian sect and, at around 10 percent of Egypt's 85 million people, the largest Christian denomination in the Middle East. The community traces its roots to the apostle Mark, who introduced Christianity to Egypt in the first century during the rapid spread of the so-called Jesus movement around the Mediterranean.

For several recent months, a forty-year-old Christian man named Ashraf Iskander had been having a romantic relationship with a Muslim woman. Some Muslims disapprove of such interreligious dating, and the woman's cousin confronted her father, demanding that he take her life to protect the family's reputation. Such in-family murders, not unknown around contemporary Egypt, are called honor killings. The father refused. The cousin promptly shot and killed the father. The man's son—the brother of the woman in the relationship— then retaliated by shooting and killing the cousin.

Two murders. One day. Both Muslim-on-Muslim.

The victims were buried on a Friday. Following the funeral and noonday prayers, the crowd became agitated. They went looking for the Christian man at the heart of the relationship and were told he had sought refuge in the church. Four thousand angry Muslims then marched en masse to the house of worship, a four-story sanctuary and neighboring community center located down a tiny alley in the back of town. The crowd exploded five or six gas cylinders inside the building, pulled down the cross and other icons, and watched as the entire building was burned to a shell.

The episode rattled Copts across the country, who were already agitated in the wake of a New Year's Eve church bombing in Alexandria that killed twenty-one and wounded dozens more and a shooting on a train ten days later that killed one Christian and wounded five. Inspired by techniques made popular during the revolution, two thousand Christians staged a sit-in outside the state television studios in Cairo, claiming the event was not sufficiently covered in the news. When word of the burning and the protests spread, riots broke out in a hilltop neighborhood of the capital famed for housing Christian garbage workers. Thirteen more people were killed and 150 wounded.

The number of people killed in sectarian violence during a six-week span was in the hundreds. The dream of a unified Egypt, revived by the revolution, seemed to be slipping away as fast as it had been created. It was exactly the sort of violence that Mubarak had warned about for years. Keep us in power or all hell will break loose. Egypt will disintegrate.

But then, just as quickly as this situation flared, something unexpected happened. A group of outsiders descended on Soul. What this group had in mind could alter the interreligious dynamic in the New Egypt virtually overnight. But could it succeed?

———

Just after nine on the morning of September 11, 2001, I got a call from my brother: "Look outside your window." It had rained the night before, and the view from the sixteenth floor of my apartment building in lower Manhattan was spectacular. The sky was as blue and clear as I could ever remember. You could see forever. As soon as I saw the plumes of dense black smoke rising from the World Trade Center, I reacted as I often do to cataclysms around me: I was drawn to it. I grabbed my camera and began hurrying down Sixth Avenue in the direction of the fires. At one point I stopped and considered the unthinkable. *What happens if those buildings fall? They could topple into each other. Tens of thousands of people might die!* I quickly dismissed the idea as science fiction.

Two hours later I was back home and watched from my window as the first tower fell. The second tower followed soon after. In the days to come, as my neighborhood was overwhelmed with the steady cry of emergency sirens and the stomach-turning smell from the smoldering metal and rubble, we began to hear the questions: Who are they? Why do they hate us? Can't the religions get along? For years we had been told that the big showdown in the coming century was the clash of civilizations between the Islamic world and the Judeo-Christian world. Was this the moment?

And in that conflagration, one name resonated. One figure stood at the nexus of all three religions: Abraham. The great patriarch of the Hebrew Bible is also the spiritual elder of the New Testament and the grand holy architect of the Qur'an. Abraham is the father—in some cases the biological father—of every Jew, Christian, and Muslim alive. Yet he is virtually unknown.

In the weeks after 9/11, I decided to return to the Middle East to figure out whether Abraham was just a hopeless fount of war or whether he could possibly be a vessel for reconciliation. I arrived in Jerusalem during an eerie, auspicious week. The city was empty of visitors. They had been scared away by a recent round of terrorist bombings there and by the start of the U.S. war in Afghanistan. It was also a rare, calendric coincidence: It was the last Friday before Christmas, the last Friday of Hanukkah, and the last Friday of Ramadan. Early that morning I went to the Old City and climbed a perch overlooking the Temple Mount. That fulcrum of history is the spot where Solomon built the Temple, where Jesus walked, and where Muhammad ascended to heaven. It's also the place where Abraham went to sacrifice his son.

Jerusalem on this day was a living embodiment of the challenges facing the three monotheistic religions. Thousands of Muslims streamed through the flagstone streets to gather atop what they call the Haram al-Sharif, or Temple Mount, the home of the third-holiest mosque in Islam. Down below, hundreds of Jews gathered at the Western Wall, the holiest spot in Judaism. Up above, Christians mingled on the Mount of Olives in the spectacular churches that mark Jesus's last steps. In Jerusalem, any prayer made in the direction of one of these holy sites will by geography encompass another of these sites. You can't separate the religions.

By midday, several hundred thousand Muslims had gathered on the plaza, and they rose for the holiest prayer of the month. Bending, kneeling, touching, standing, bending, kneeling, touching again. The tidal effect was awesome. More people praying in one place than live in my hometown. In their white tunics, they looked like giant waves of milk. At the same time, hundreds of Jews just beneath them were nodding, bowing, tucking notes into the wall. And at exactly noon, two dozen of the holiest churches in Christendom all burst into Christmas carols. It was the most joyful sound of faith I had ever heard. Then, just as quickly, the bells went quiet, the praying stopped, and the city held its breath. What would happen now?

———

The story of Abraham as it appears in the Bible is remarkably inclusive. When we first meet Abraham he's seventy-five years old, married, and living in Mesopotamia. He can't have a child. In a story about creation, he cannot create. He is the anti-God. God, meanwhile, is something of an antihuman. He has been looking for a human partner since the beginning of time. He first tries Adam and Eve, but they disappoint him. Fourteen generations pass before God tries again with Noah. That, too, fails, when Noah takes to drinking. Fourteen more generations pass. Then God tries again with Abraham. In effect, Abraham and God need each other.

So God offers him a deal. If Abraham goes forth from this native land to the land God shows him, God will give him a son. But God also promises to give him much more: "All the families of the earth shall bless themselves through you." The breadth of this offer is astonishing: Everyone who ever lives will consider you a blessing. Abraham takes the deal, forging a partnership with God that has never been undone. For Jews, Christians, and Muslims to receive God's blessing, they must trace their lineage through Abraham.

The story of Abraham in Genesis reflects this broad diversity. Indeed, it's a perfect tableau of the Fertile Crescent. Abraham is born in Mesopotamia, and his first wife, Sarah, comes from there. They travel down to Egypt, where Sarah takes a handmaid, Hagar. When no heir arrives, Sarah suggests that Abraham try to conceive with Hagar, who soon gives birth to Ishmael. Abraham finally has a son! But as soon as Ishmael is born, Sarah gets pregnant and gives birth to Isaac. Suddenly we have two sons, rivals for the father's legacy, rivals for the same land. In the same way that Mesopotamia and Egypt jockeyed for millennia over who would maintain political and cultural control over Canaan—the area the Bible calls the Promised Land—Abraham's descendants would continue a similar rivalry for thousands of years. Faith, geography, and politics have been part of every struggle in the Middle East.

The women in Abraham's life, faced with this standoff, take matters into their own hands. Sarah forces Abraham to kick Ishmael into the desert. Abraham doesn't want to; Ishmael is his firstborn son. But God comforts him. "Do not be distressed over the boy," he says of Ishmael. "I will make a nation of him, too, for he is your seed." Ishmael, too, will carry God's blessing. This moment represents the split between Jews and Christians and Muslims. Jews and Christians consider themselves descended from Isaac; Muslims from Ishmael.

But what's striking is that while Isaac appears to be the "winner" of the battle for Abraham's lineage, the text bends over backward to treat Ishmael well. Abraham expels Ishmael from the land, but not from his love. Isaac, who stays behind, is nearly slaughtered by his father in the very next scene and is largely mute for the rest of the story, even though he gets to live in the Promised Land. The narrative has remarkable balance. Neither son is a pure victor, nor a pure loser. God blesses Abraham and blesses both of his children. At the heart of the story is a message of two separate but equally legitimate traditions.

Or is there?

Though these stories appear in the Bible, there has never been any historical or archaeological evidence they really took place. This detail would appear to be problematic for the religions, but what actually happened is the opposite—the absence of any historical evidence helped the religions, because it allowed them to throw out the original story of Abraham and make up their own Abraham. Nearly every generation for the last 2,500 years has rewritten the story of Abraham for itself.

Judaism was the first to do this. Early Jews proclaimed that Abraham was a universal figure, but over time, as Jews began to feel oppressed, they began to take possession of Abraham for themselves. Commentators suggested Abraham was the reason God created the world; Abraham invented Passover; Abraham kept kosher—none of which is true about the original patriarch. Jews, in other words, turned Abraham into a Jew.

Christianity did something similar. Early Christians, who

also felt oppressed, wanted to use Abraham as a universal figure, one whose blessing was opened to Jews and Gentiles alike. But over time, as Christians grew more powerful, they started using Abraham as a figure to exclude Jews. God didn't call Abraham to go forth, commentators argued; Jesus did. God didn't promise the Land to descendants of Abraham but rather to followers of Jesus. Just as Jews made Abraham a Jew when he wasn't, Christians made Abraham a Christian, when he wasn't that, either.

Then came Islam. Sure enough, in the religion's vulnerable early years, Muhammad stressed that Muslims, Jews, and Christians worshiped the same God and had the same prophets, such as Abraham. But over time, as Islam grew more powerful, Muslims argued that Abraham cared more for Ishmael than Isaac, that he called for Muslims to make the pilgrimage, and that he built the shrine that all Muslims worship during the hajj. Muslims turned Abraham into a Muslim.

Much of my journey to understand Abraham was about trying to untangle this knot: How did the universal figure of Genesis, whom God chooses to spread his blessing to the world, suddenly become the object of bloody battle among his children? At first I thought this was nothing but a willfully ignorant rivalry, but later I came to see it as an opportunity. If every generation could create its own Abraham, why can't we? What would our Abraham look like? He would look a lot like us. He would surf the Internet, he would need to lose ten pounds, and he would struggle to balance science and faith.

More to the point, he would understand we live in a time in which religious-based terror is deadlier than ever, but in which the idea that one religion can become the world's only religion is deader than ever. Above all, he would know we face a choice: figure out a way to coexist, or descend into an unwinnable war.

My book *Abraham* was published on the one-year anniversary of 9/11, at a time when Americans seemed particularly eager to learn more about Muslims and how we might improve interfaith relations. Suddenly I found myself thrust into the middle of a robust and contentious conversation about the meaning of religion in the twenty-first century. I didn't know much about the interfaith movement before 9/11. If I'd thought about interreligious dialogue, I imagined it was probably little old ladies sipping lemonade and making themselves feel good with niceties like "You love butterflies; I love butterflies; see, we're just the same!"

What I quickly discovered was a vibrant, and growing, international effort to rethink the foundations of exclusivist theology and design a new model for religious inclusion. In seminaries across the United States, administrators were rewriting their curricula; in churches, synagogues, and mosques, clerical leaders were throwing out old sermons. Laypeople, in particular, were often leading the way. In Portland, Oregon, the Episcopal Cathedral initiated a two-year citywide study program called the Abraham Initiative. In Portland, Maine, the Children of Abraham Down East created a statewide program to curtail violence. In New York, the Chautauqua Institution began a three-year Abrahamic Program of concentrated study. Groups in London, Jerusalem, and Alexandria started similar efforts.

Time magazine picked up on this trend and in September 2002 put Abraham on its cover. "Jews, Christians, and Muslims all claim him as their father," the magazine said. "Can he be their peacemaker?" The effect was electrifying. Suddenly interfaith relations became Topic A around the world. And suddenly Abraham, four thousand years after he would have been born, became a rock star.

Many people were skeptical of this movement, of course. Some people I encountered simply didn't know believers of other faiths, or didn't trust that the ones they did know were genuinely interested in exchange. I heard from plenty of Jews, Christians, and Muslims who believed unequivocally that their faith offers the exclusive claim to truth. Still others doubted that change was really possible. I replied that not only is such change possible, but it's happened in our lifetimes. When I grew up in Georgia in the 1960s and '70s, Jews were still systematically discriminated against in business, politics, and society. In less than half a century, Jews and Christians have completely rewritten the way they relate to one another. The current status may not be perfect, but who can deny that it has improved?

That process is just beginning with Muslims. Most of us didn't learn until 9/11 that we were even supposed to include

Muslims in this conversation. While the term *Judeo-Christian* first became popular in the United States in the 1950s, the term *Abrahamic* didn't even enter the lexicon until 2001.

Despite the barriers, the movement did seem to gain traction for about five years after 9/11, when it suddenly hit a wall. The United States got bogged down in two wars in the Muslim world. Iran escalated its nuclear program and began saber rattling against Israel and others. The world slipped into a punishing recession. This tension seemed to boil over in the summer of 2010, after a Muslim group led by Sufi imam Feisal Abdul Rauf announced plans to build a Muslim community center and interfaith facility, called Park51, less than a mile from the site of the World Trade Center. At first the plans generated little interest. Six hundred thousand Muslims live in the New York City area, and they are served by nearly two hundred mosques, including half a dozen in lower Manhattan.

But a pair of bloggers who ran a group called Stop Islamization of America deftly dubbed the facility the "Ground Zero mosque," and a backlash quickly erupted. Mayor Michael Bloomberg, scores of local officials, and all the appropriate zoning boards approved the facility. Most Americans agreed that the group had a legal right to worship wherever they wanted. But a wide and diverse coalition, including cable news personalities, politicians, and 9/11 families, strongly objected to the move, claiming it was aggressive, insensitive, and yet another sign of Muslim incursion into the inner sanctums of American identity. In no time, three-quarters of Americans were against the idea.

The entire episode came to a head on the eve of the ninth anniversary of the original attacks, when Imam Rauf returned from the Middle East (where he was appearing on behalf of the U.S. State Department) and appeared live on CNN. He said that if he had known the planned facility would have caused pain, he wouldn't have done it. But he refused to relocate it, saying that doing so would be buckling to radicals and would harm the United States' position in the Muslim world. "The more that the radicals are able to control the discourse on one side," he said, "it strengthens the radicals on the other side. We have to turn this around."

I was backstage at CNN that night, waiting to join a panel after the interview. Next to me was Rosaleen Tallon, who lost her fireman brother in the Twin Towers. She clutched a photograph of her brother and was clearly still grieving. Next to her was Andy Sullivan, a fireman who had worked on the rescue effort, and who wore a helmet in tribute to his fallen colleagues. As Imam Rauf spoke, all three of us knew his defense was not as strong as it might have been and had little chance of reversing the widespread opposition. Sullivan leapt to his feet, pumped his arms in victory, and thrust his finger at the monitor. "We won!" he shouted.

I never believed the Park51 Community Center would be built on the proposed spot. As I said on the air a few minutes later, I always believed a compromise would be struck. But I still felt the episode was a positive opportunity for the interfaith movement. It elevated the conversation about interreligious cooperation to center stage in America. It reminded

Americans that throughout our history, we have welcomed the outsider and befriended the stranger, sometimes first with anger and hostility, but ultimately with acceptance. The discrimination many Muslim Americans experienced in the twenty-first century was no different from what Jews faced in the twentieth century and Catholics in the nineteenth. Eventually, it, too, would pass.

But that hopeful future seemed far away on this night. The opposition had clearly won. When Anderson Cooper asked Andy Sullivan if Imam Rauf had done anything to change his mind, Sullivan grinned confidently. "Actually, he has done more good for my movement tonight than a hundred demonstrations have done," he said. "He shot himself in the foot so badly. You are not going to be able to chisel the smile off my face." Asked to explain, Sullivan said Imam Rauf's remarks about how our reaction would be taken abroad were a warning that Muslim extremists would attack us if we didn't build the center. "It was a veiled threat." Tallon agreed. "Isn't that really scary, that if we don't build this mosque, as the old expression says, there will be hell to pay?" An interfaith center built by Muslims didn't belong in the United States at all, she said; it belonged in the Middle East. "The people in the Middle East are the ones that attacked us at Ground Zero. Why don't they learn to be tolerant?"

Backstage a few minutes later, I was despondent. Suddenly everything gained in the last decade seemed lost. I telephoned my wife. "We've hit a wall," I said. "We've gone as far as we can go." Afterward, I sat by myself. *The only way we're going to make progress,* I thought, *is to be met halfway by the other side.* We needed some voice from the Muslim world that offered some promise of moderation, some hint they share the same belief in freedom—including freedom of religion—that Americans hold so dear.

———

Two armored personnel carriers and a tank were stationed at the top of the narrow alley that led to the Church of the Two Martyrs in Soul. This part of the town was even more dilapidated than what I'd seen earlier. A goat was wandering up a short stairway into a house that had no door. Twin girls in diapers were toddling in the mud. A young soldier in forest fatigues and a red beret stopped me from entering the roadway and asked for identification. In the days since the church was destroyed, reporters had been unwelcome here. A female reporter from *Time* described being surrounded by young men in Muslim robes, who shouted, "Leave! Leave now! You are not allowed to pass." Another added, "Are you Christian?" before grabbing her notebook, ripping out several pages, and forcibly marching her out of the village.

Having been warned of this hostility, I had come prepared with special permission from the Ministry of Information back in Cairo. But while the young soldier here in Soul went to confer with his superiors, I, too, was suddenly surrounded by a group of around sixty men, all wearing cotton robes, slip-on shoes, and eager expressions. Afternoon prayers had just ended, and the assembly materialized almost instantly. I was trying to gauge their mood, which I took to be a mix of curiosity, skepticism, and hostility, when one of the men, who was around sixty, with neatly trimmed salt-and-pepper hair and rimless eyeglasses he kept adjusting nervously, elbowed his way through the crowd and came uncomfortably close to my face.

"I am the principal of a secondary school," he announced proudly. "I have been a teacher of English. I am very happy to meet you."

He identified himself as Muslim, and I asked him to explain what led to the church burning. "We consider this a shame," he said. "We are farmers in this town. Muslims and Christians have been living together very well here." The boy who committed the original murder, he explained, who later became the second victim, was beloved in the town. "When the people came from the cemetery, they were very angry. A number of us tried to stop them from going to the church. I myself tried to stop them. But they were too many."

He said the mob walked up the street we were on, turned down the alley, and approached the building. "When they got to the church, they found papers indicating that the Christians were doing magic inside. They were casting spells on Muslims. This made everyone very angry, and they destroyed the church."

"But isn't this against the teachings of Islam?" I asked. "How does the Qur'an say you should treat Christians?"

"Islam teaches us to protect Christians," he said. "Even if

somebody came here and tried to attack a Christian, Islam orders us to stand side by side with him. In the January twenty-fifth revolution, Egyptians raised the crescent and the cross together. It was a mixed revolution."

"But then this church burned," I said, "and riots in Cairo killed more people. Many people fear the revolution will bring a time when Muslims will attack Christians."

"You are putting this the wrong way," he said. "The revolution was for Muslims and Christians together. We are united, believe me. Go see for yourself."

I said good-bye to the assembled men, and the young army officer ushered me down the alleyway, which was about ten feet wide. Tanks couldn't have made it down here, but every wheelbarrow, donkey cart, and reed basket within a ten-mile radius was there. Hundreds of people were milling about the alleyway, lugging bricks, hammers, burned-out pieces of wood, and a steady stream of materials. I stumbled on a mound of cement bags. Each one was decorated with a drawing of the three pyramids. How lucky, I thought. If you need a logo for your Egyptian cement company, why not use the longest-standing buildings ever constructed!

The Church of Two Martyrs is not the kind of grand, freestanding institution you might see on a town square in Europe or in a rural town in America. It's more confined, like the kind of facility you'd see squeezed into the old city of some ancient capital. It was built of red brick, about the size and style of a small high school gymnasium. I stepped inside the sanctuary, which was mostly exposed beams and some metal joists at the moment, and that's when I was hit by the sweet, acrid smell of charred wood. Maybe it was all the incense infused in Coptic services, but the ruins smelled fruity and sad at the same time. I rubbed my finger along a blackened wall and rubbed ash on the back of my hand. It was dense, and a little moist.

By far the most striking thing about the church was not its appearance—it's how crowded it was. There were dozens and dozens of men—of all ages, social classes, and faiths—laying bricks, running electrical wire, and hammering studs. Though only a week or so had passed since the fire, a massive rebuilding effort was already under way. This was clearly the miracle of Two Martyrs—how this town on the brink of religious war suddenly became a model for religious cooperation. Who pulled this off during a revolution? Or rather, was it *because* of the revolution that it happened in the first place?

The person most qualified to answer that question was Dr. Hany Hanna Aziz Hanna, and I went to see him in Cairo after leaving the church. His business card is made of shiny, see-through, onionskin paper. It lists the following titles for him.

- Member of Front Support of the Egyptian Revolution
- Member of the Council of Trustees of the Revolution and Member of the Peer and Editing Commission on the Preparation of Its Decisions
- International Expert in Conservation and Restoration
- Professor, Higher Institute for Coptic Studies in Cairo
- Writer, Egyptian and International Newspapers

And that's just the first five items. The card also has his photograph, which shows a serious man in the manner of a *Dragnet* agent, forty-five, with heavy black-rimmed glasses, dark hair, and a practical suit. Yet when I stepped into his parlor, this man who carefully considers his appearance was unshaven, droopy-eyed, and slumped. But as I soon discovered, he had good reason. All those titles on his card really communicated one thing: He was the highest-ranking Copt in the leadership of the revolution, which means he was the person most responsible for putting an end to the violence.

Which is exactly what he had done—at least for now.

Dr. Hanna was a midlevel conservator in the Supreme Council of Antiquities when he got drawn into the youth movement for change in the years before the revolution. Like everyone I met who was part of the leadership, he was so consumed by its passions that it had altered his identity and sense of self. During the peak of the revolution, he spent a week at a time in Tahrir, without going home to visit his wife or three young children, who were three, eleven, and twelve. When I asked him why, he said, "Because I'm a martyr."

"What does that mean?"

"It means since I left home for the revolution, I—and my family—consider myself a dead person. I can be killed at any time. Because I was one of the key people who organized the revolution, I would be among the first to be killed if it failed."

"Why not go home and live your life?"

"Because we started something. And I am not the kind of person who starts something and stops before completing it."

Once the regime fell, the leaders of the revolution turned to spreading its values—particularly the searing experience of Christians and Muslims marching, planning, and praying alongside one another—to the larger society beyond Tahrir. They got their first test with Soul.

When word of the fire at the church reached beyond Soul, the media portrayed it as rank sectarian strife. And who could blame them: A raging group of Muslims destroyed a Christian church. But those involved in the revolution—including the protesters and the army—knew better. They viewed it as a stunt by the old regime to stir up interreligious conflict, thereby justifying a counterrevolution that might return the old elite to power, albeit minus Mubarak and his sons. Dr. Hanna put this view to me directly, as had Dr. Mahmoud Sabit before him.

"After Mubarak fell," I said at one point in our conversation, "there was an outbreak of sectarian violence here—"

He cut me off. "These were not sectarian incidents," he said. "These were political incidents. The Mubarak regime was used to dividing people. These are Muslim Brotherhood, these are not. These are Copts, these are not. It was a game to make people nervous about others so they would believe they needed a strong government."

"So how did this work in Soul?"

"I have the story from the people involved," he said. "A boy and a girl had sex. In Egypt, like any country in the world, thousands of boys and thousands of girls have sex. This happened four times in this town in the last few years. So why now this incident? Why did this suddenly become an honor killing? The answer is that some members of the old regime sent provocateurs to Soul. Their goal was to take a trivial problem and turn it into a huge sectarian problem."

Only this time, there was a new sheriff in town, namely the military, the leadership of the revolution, and the liaison committee that bridged the two. Dr. Hanna was the key Copt in that equation, and within twenty-four hours he helped organize a massive delegation made up of Muslims, Christians, and military brass to descend on the otherwise unsuspecting town of Soul and stabilize the situation. It was Shock and Awe 2.0, only this time the bombs were packed with cooling-off sessions instead of TNT. Visitors included Dr. Biltagy from the Muslim Brotherhood, Sheikh Mohamed Hassan from the even more fundamentalist Salafi sect of Islam, and Amr Khaled, one of the most popular preachers in the Muslim world.

The delegation hosted a garden party at a local dignitary's house, where Muslim and Christian representatives from each district in Soul mingled and discussed a path forward. Authorities then set up a thousand chairs in the heart of town, along with a stage, microphone, and bunting, and the visitors all made speeches to the crowd. Sheikh Khaled, often called the "Muslim Billy Graham," admonished the residents: "My message here today for Muslims and the Christians is: Let's be one hand. Each one of the people here in Soul has to do something. First we must each stop this problem in our own homes." Visitors responded to Khaled's message by chanting slogans calling for unity. By the end of the event, the military brass promised to rebuild the church in its original location. Work began the next day.

As Dr. Hanna was telling me this story, I almost didn't believe it. It was too good to be true. It reminded me of the Christmas Truce along the Western Front during the First World War, in which German and British soldiers swapped seasonal greetings and songs, even walked across the battlefield to exchange gifts with their enemies. Now, with sectarian blood on the streets of Soul, some of the busiest religious, political, and military leaders in the entire country had left their posts and traveled two hours south into the desert, to the Egyptian boondocks, to turn a bloody eye of interreligious tension into a shimmering rose of the revolution. Even Hollywood would tone down this story because it sounds too saccharine.

When I asked Dr. Hanna to explain this reaction, he lifted his hands to the sky. "This is the revolution!"

"But a revolution can't change attitudes overnight," I insisted.

"Why not? Did you ever hear about a revolution in which people overturned a government and the next day cleaned the streets?"

He was referring to the day after Mubarak fell when hundreds of protesters returned to Tahrir Square and swept up their own mess.

"This is us," he continued. "This is Egyptians. That night I went on state television and told the country what happened."

"I go on television, too, from time to time," I said. "And if I tell the story of what happened in Soul, there will be someone sitting next to me who will say, 'You are so naïve. The Muslim extremists are just waiting quietly, being very nice, until the proper time comes and then they will pounce, just like in Iran. This type of violence will come back, and the dream of this revolution will die.' How would you respond to that?"

"I would say to that other person, 'Okay, you have a point. But what's your advice? You suggested a problem, what's your solution?' Seriously, I don't think we're that weak. We're not Iran. We're not Afghanistan. We're not Gaza. We are Egypt. We have ten million Christians living in this country. Not five hundred, or fifteen hundred. Ten million. Who is going to kill ten million people? We're very well organized. We have history. We have culture. We have a civilization that has been here for two thousand years. We've spent hundreds of years living under rules by Islam. So what? If the Muslim Brotherhood takes control of Egypt, we will still live."

"How worried are you that this will happen?"

"I have no fear of anything," he said. "Whatever the Muslim Brotherhood were to bring, we already had Mubarak. I can't believe they'll be worse than him. The only thing I fear is if the army itself is destroyed."

And therein lies the future. The real story behind the church in Soul is the underlying truth behind the short-term prospects for civil society, religious coexistence, and even economic opportunity in Egypt, and with it other places in the region. The military agreed to rebuild the church, which sent the message that they wanted to maintain the movement toward a unified Egypt. They were building on the themes of the revolution, of course. It was the revolutionaries who adopted the symbol of the 1919 revolution—the union of the Muslim crescent and Christian cross—and made it a symbol of the revolution. But until democratic institutions have time to develop, that vision requires a guarantor. In Egypt, that guarantor is the military, the most dominant institution in the country. It was no surprise when Dr. Hanna told me his greatest fear: "That the army doesn't stick by the goals of the revolution. They will either develop the country, or they will destroy it."

But when I asked his greatest hope, he expressed a desire that would be familiar to people of different faiths all over the world. Its roots are in the Ancient Near East, at the time when Abraham came here four thousand years ago, creating two different sons and two different traditions that are still struggling to coexist. At the end of Abraham's life, in a little-known scene in the book of Genesis, Abraham's sons, Ishmael and Isaac, rivals since before they were born, leaders of opposing nations, come together for the first time since they were torn apart as children and bury their father. Abraham achieves in death what he could never achieve in life: a moment of reconciliation between his two sons, a peaceful, communal, side-by-side flicker of possibility in which they are not rivals, warriors, Jews, Christians, or Muslims. They are brothers, They are mourners. And the message of that moment is as powerful today as it was forty centuries ago: Maybe it's not the parents who will make peace.

Maybe it's the children.

"I would like to see a new Egypt," Dr. Hanna said, "with its true values and its true place in the world. I think we can be an example to other countries where Muslims and Christians live side by side. Even places where Christians are a minority. It can be done. We're doing it in Egypt, and we have been for thousands of years. I always say, 'Oh, Egypt, return to your noble origins. Contribute, as you once did, to the great achievements to humanity. And remember, that you are truly beautiful.' "

V

GENERATION FREEDOM

Who are they? What do they believe?
How will they change the world?

S he didn't want to go. She'd attended too many of these demonstrations. She'd stood on the Journalists' Syndicate's steps too many times. She'd been disappointed on too many occasions. But something happened on January 25, 2011, that hadn't happened in the previous six years of protests. Her daughter said she was going and asked her mom if she'd like to come along.

"Everything in my life seems to revolve around my children," said Ghada Shahbender, forty-nine, a filmmaker, human rights activist, and divorced mother of four. We were sitting in Tahrir Square on a relatively quiet Friday morning when a mere ten thousand people had gathered to express displeasure over the progress of the revolution. An unexalted public space, Tahrir Square is as much a roundabout as it is a glorious invitation to reimagine urban life. It was created in the early twentieth century when modern Cairo took its current form, and the place earned its name, Liberation Square, after the Nasser revolt in 1952. Only with the protests of 2011 did Tahrir Square assume the sacred stature of, say, Tiananmen Square. Within weeks, young protestors in other Arab cities were nicknaming their otherwise undistinguished meeting spots "Liberation Square."

"I was sitting with my daughter on the night of the twenty-fourth," Shahbender said, her voice slow and artful, as if direct-ing a pivotal scene in a film. "She's twenty-seven, a psychologist, and she says to me, 'Are you going tomorrow?' I told her I didn't want to have my heart broken again, but she looked so heart-broken herself, I said, 'Okay. Better be a good role model.'"

The following morning they dressed in practical shoes, baggy pants, and loose-fitting sweaters. Shahbender, like every-one else, has a dedicated wardrobe for fighting dictators. "My main concerns are ease of movement and modesty," she said. They drove to the Syndicate headquarters, and Shahbender in-stantly noticed that something was different. "There were all these young people, particularly in their teens," she said.

I asked her why she thought they had come. "Over the past few years, many parents were complaining their children were not going out," she said. "They were spending all their time in Internet cafés. But now we know what they were doing there: They were practicing freedom. On the Net, they could chat with anyone they wanted, express any opinion they wanted, explore themselves sexually. They had a space to do that—cyberspace—and now they wanted to have it on the streets."

January 25 would be their day, Shahbender realized, so after a few hours of marching, when she saw her daughter slip past the barricades and into Tahrir Square, she returned home. But by 10 p.m., when she could no longer reach her daughter or sons by mobile phone, she decided she needed to return. She grabbed some woolen shawls and went to the market to pick up painkillers, tangerines, bananas, juice, and water. She paused in front of the candy section, carefully picking out a Kit Kat for her daughter and Galaxy bars with hazelnuts for her sons.

"Wait," I asked her. "You were about to go back into the violence of Tahrir Square, and you had the wherewithal to stand in front of the candy bar section and say, 'This child wants one with hazelnuts and this one wants one without'?"

"Mommy is going over to the square where her kids are demonstrating," she said, "so Mommy better take food for her kids. They need energy!"

History, I was reminded, is made by people, and these people have mothers and fathers.

Shahbender arrived in Tahrir Square just as the riot police had lost patience and were launching a vicious counterattack. Sound bombs were exploding; volley after volley of tear gas was flying. "Suddenly the ten thousand people on the square started running in my direction," Shahbender said. "People were pushing and shoving and everyone was scared." She found herself shoved into a building with a dozen young people. "They were all suffocating, crying, scared. I gave them all baby wipes and told them to cover their noses and mouths and breathe. Then I started handing out the tangerines, the bananas, the juice, and the water. I probably provided some comic relief."

The group sought refuge on the roof, and a young man came and sat down next to the only mother figure in sight. "I work as a butcher," he told her. "And I'm just looking for a better life. I'm not political. Everyone told me this would be a peaceful demonstration. Had I known it would be so violent, I would have come with knives."

After a while, Shahbender decided she should go out and see if it was safe for everyone to leave. "I'm an older woman," she said. "They won't harass me." The young butcher volunteered to accompany her, to keep her safe. "If they ask, I'll just tell them you're my mom," he said.

As soon as they stepped out of the building, a police officer hurried over and pushed Shahbender aside. "I'm small, so it doesn't take much effort to fling me across the sidewalk." She ended up at the base of building. "Then he took the young boy from me, threw him to the ground, and started kicking him. Soon five other soldiers appeared and started beating him on the head with batons and kicking him all over. And I could not speak. I could not utter a word. I got up off the ground and starting staring at the officers. The only thing I could say was 'Why? Why? Why are you doing this?' I just kept saying, over and over, 'Why? Why? Why? Why?' "

The officers started screaming, "Lady, get out of here!" and chased Shahbender away. She never heard what happened to the boy. She never learned his name. He could easily be among the 850 people killed in Egypt between that night and the fall of Mubarak.

Shahbender wandered in a daze toward the square. She didn't know where her children were or if they were safe. This was the satanic hour, the time when Noor Ayman Nour and many others were rounded up in paddy wagons and whisked off to the covert shadows of Arab repression. "The square was nightmarish," Shahbender said. "Every few meters there was a boy, lying on the ground, and five, six people kicking at him, beating him. The lights in Tahrir are quite yellow, and there was a lot of tear gas."

Her voice was deliberate and drenched with emotion. She described the scene as a screenwriter would—the visual display of a society being ripped open. A slight, imperceptible breach between what was and what just might be. The birth pangs of a newborn world. "There was fog in all of downtown Cairo," Shahbender said. "And the only sound you could hear were the batons—they make a very ugly clacking sound when they hit bones or skulls—and the screams from the boys on the ground."

Why? Let's turn Shahbender's question on its head. Not "Why would the police beat that boy?" But "Why would he—and so many like him—come out in the first place?" This was the first of three questions I came to answer: Who are these young people? What motivates them? Why did they suddenly rebel?

Let's begin by naming them. In recent years, many in the West looked at the twenty Muslim countries across the Middle East and North Africa and tried to decipher some unifying message. What they saw was largely the portrait of anger and aggression—the coldhearted terrorist, the raging jihadist, the fuming "Arab street." But the uprisings of 2011 generated a unifying message of an entirely different order. It's one forged by the young out of frustration, fear, desire, and aspiration. It's built out of an appreciation for how bad things have been and how much better they can be. It stretches deep into the well of the region's past and reaches far into its future. It's the common identity of an ascendant population.

It's Generation Freedom.

So what can we say about this generation? For starters, they surprise you with what they know, and with what they don't. One young woman in a veil quoted Abraham Maslow's hierarchy of needs to me, but a man in a suit had never heard of World War II. With schools so spotty and much of their knowledge garnered online, they have surprising blind spots. But they are very style conscious. The West is used to inhaling endless images of monotonous worshipers in white cotton robes but that misses the mark. Arab and Persian bazaars brim with tailored leather jackets, low-cut dresses, and shining rows of knock-off products from brands as varied as Louis Vuitton and Abercrombie & Fitch. And while Western women view the veil as repressive, I've met many single Arab women who decorate theirs with jewels, broaches, and sparkles that would make my six-year-old daughters jealous. My wife once went to a gym with a group of young women in Tehran and said she's never seen such elaborate preening. And in every Muslim country I've been in, regardless of the degree of Islamist rhetoric emanating from the men in charge, the young people drink, sleep around, and smoke. Boy, do they smoke.

Altogether, Generation Freedom can be captured in four attributes. I call them the Four Ps.

Plentiful. Any conversation about young people in the Middle East and North Africa must begin with their sheer size.

One-third of people living in the region are between the ages of fifteen and twenty-nine, a total of one hundred million individuals. In the United States, by contrast, the figure is 20 percent and in Western Europe 18 percent. When you expand the range to include *all* people under the age of thirty, the number balloons to 60 percent. This demographic engine, while slowing somewhat, is still chugging along. Today's growth rate in the region is 2 percent, which is 60 percent higher than the global average. The reasons for this so-called Youth Bulge are not particularly hard to identify. Beginning in the 1970s, improved medical care meant greater numbers of babies survived, even though the number of babies being conceived did not change.

Baby booms have surprising consequences. Scholars, for example, have found a direct correlation between population bulges and social unrest. A study by Population Action International found that between 1970 and 2007, 86 percent of all outbreaks of conflict occurred in countries where 60 percent of more of the population was younger than thirty. The West knows this, too. The peak of the post-World War II baby boom reached young adulthood in the 1960s, a period of vast social and political upheaval in the United States and Western Europe.

In some ways, these figures should bring comfort to the West. The country in the Middle East with by far the largest Youth Bulge is Iran, where 34 percent of the population is between the ages of fifteen and twenty-nine. The Iranian baby boom is particularly pronounced because in addition to improve childhood mortality, Ayatollah Khomeini urged all Iranians after the revolution to have babies in the name of Allah. They listened, creating a huge engine for change today. The overwhelming impression I took from two trips to Iran in the last decade is that young people, fed up with the pain of the last revolution, are just waiting for the right time to act. As Ragui Assaad, a professor at the Humphrey School of Public Affairs at the University of Minnesota, said of these young Iranians, "These are the young people who were fueling the protests in 2009 in Iran, and they're going to continue to fuel protests for quite some time. We haven't seen the last of youth unrest in Iran."

Even more important, this Muslim baby boom is not limited to the Middle East and North Africa. A United Nations study in 2009 concluded there are more than 780 million Muslims under the age of twenty-five living around the world. Expand that bracket to include people under thirty and the number balloons to more than one billion. If you want to understand the importance of religious coexistence in the twenty-first century—specifically, finding a way to integrate Muslims into a productive, cooperative relationship with non-Muslims—spend a minute contemplating this simple fact: One in seven human beings today is a Muslim under thirty. No matter what we may think of their religion, their heritage, or their culture, we must find a way to live alongside this next generation in the global economy of tomorrow.

Pinched. Any search for the underlying causes of the Arab Spring of 2011 always seems to return to the Great Squeeze:

the painful gap between the enormous size of the young Arab population and the meager opportunities that await them. First among these is economic. Unemployment in the Middle East and North Africa is the highest of any region in the world. Youth unemployment is particularly acute: 26 percent in the fist decade of the 2000s, compared with 18 percent in sub-Saharan Africa, and even less in Latin America and Southeast Asia. In many countries, youth unemployment is four times the rate for people over thirty. And this problem shows no signs of abating. King Abdullah of Jordan has said the Middle East must develop 200 million jobs by 2020.

To satisfy these needs, countries in the region need 6 to 7 percent sustained annual economic growth. Excluding oil, the current rate of expansion is 3.6 percent. A core demand of the protestors has been a reworking of the basic economic equation that created this morass. As Dr. Assaad and others have noted, Arab autocrats struck an implicit bargain with their people. They would give the middle class subsidized employment (in the government or government-controlled industries), subsidized housing, and subsidized commodities. But in return, the middle class agreed not to question the authority of the dictators. Now, young people have begun saying, "If we're not receiving our end of the bargain, we might as well have a voice in choosing the government."

Deepening these economic challenges is the quagmire of bad schools. On the surface, school enrollments across the region have skyrocketed in recent decades, reaching the totals of the powerhouse Asian Tigers in the 1980s. Primary education is nearly universal and the crippling gap between boys' and girls' enrollment has shrunk to near zero in most countries. Regional literacy now stands at 91 percent. (Egypt is a marked exception to this trend, with a literacy rate of only 75 percent, placing it 164th in the world, largely because of the legacy of gender bias.) But beyond teaching basics, Middle East schools are sorely lacking in teaching problem solving, cognitive reasoning, research methods, and communication skills—in other words, all the tools needed to survive in a global economy. A similar problem extends to higher education. The region that first translated Plato and Aristotle, bringing these writers for the first time into the Dark Ages, now lives almost entirely in the dark with regards to contemporary knowledge. A U.N. study found that ten thousand books were translated into Arabic in the last one thousand years. The equivalent number is translated into Spanish every year.

The lack of opportunity also stifles the social lives of young Arabs. Who wants to marry a man with no economic future? Fifty percent of Arab men between twenty-five and twenty-nine are unmarried, compared with 31 percent in Latin America and 23 percent in Asia. The financial burden of getting married, from securing housing to purchasing furniture to paying for the ceremony, contributes to the delay. In Egypt, where the groom's family pays for the bulk of a wedding, the average cost of a wedding equals forty-three months of the earnings of both the groom and his father. Among the poorest workers, the groom and his father must save for seven years. The bride might be expected to kick in more than the one-third of costs her father contributes, but women have been largely excluded from the private sector workforce in Egypt. In Saudi Arabia, women are not even allowed to work for themselves. The easiest way to improve the stagnant economies of the Arab world would be to eliminate the lingering stigmatization against allowing women meaningful work.

Plugged in. With such widespread cultural bias against women, up-to-date learning, and outside knowledge in general, it's no wonder young people in the Muslim world have flocked to the Internet. Google doesn't care what you search for. Wikipedia doesn't care what you study. Flickr doesn't care if you're a woman. (In fact, it was cofounded by a woman.) Data from Nielsen shows that in 2010, just under 30 percent of the Middle East population has access to the Internet, a full percentage point higher than the rest of the world. Usage was highest in the Gulf states of Bahrain, the United Arab Emirates, Qatar, Kuwait, and Saudi Arabia. Evidence suggests women are particularly active users of social networking, blogging, and other services, as the keyboard doesn't require you to cover your head or be accompanied by a man.

The best way to understand the impact of technology on the Middle East and North Africa is to draw the analogy with cell phones. Countries that bypassed traditional telephone lines and went straight to mobile phones are called leapfroggers, because they "leapfrogged" an entire century of technology. With their sudden access to the free flow of information in the early twenty-first century, the Arab world is poised to leapfrog an entire millennium of ignorance, poor leadership, and intellectual stagnation. If the current uprisings are any indication, young Arabs appear to have learned more about freedom, democracy, and equal rights before their wedding nights than their parents, grandparents, and great-grandparents did in their entire lives.

But while everyone agrees new technology was a factor in this generation's sudden change of outlook and assertiveness, did the technology actually *cause* the transformation? Are the popular terms that surrounded the uprisings, like "Twitter Effect" or "Facebook Revolution," justified? Put more directly, Can technology create freedom? There is heated and important debate about this.

On one side are what's called the "cyber-utopians." This group, led by Clay Shirky, a professor at New York University and the author of *Here Comes Everybody*, argues that social networking technology was pivotal in recent uprisings, from the Philippines in 2000 to Egypt in 2011. Sites like YouTube and Tumblr helped protestors coordinate their planning, enjoy real-time, shared awareness of events on the ground, and provide a vital pipeline to the outside world. After the student-led protests in Iran in 2009, some even called for Twitter to earn the Nobel Peace Prize. As Shirky observed, "We have historically overestimated the value of access to information and underestimated the value of access to one another." This group attracted a marquee supporter in Wael Ghonim, who said he hoped to meet Facebook creator Mark Zuckerberg one day to thank him. While Ghonim is not exactly neutral (he was employed by Google, the world's leading Internet company, after all), he memorably told CNN, "The revolution started on Facebook."

On the other side are what's called the "cyber-skeptics." This group, led by Belarus native Evgeny Morozov, a visiting scholar at Stanford and the author of *The Net Delusion*, argues that dictators are as adept as using modern technology as protestors are. Totalitarian regimes use the digital paper trail Facebook and Twitter provide to grant them more sophisticated ways to surveil, censor, propagandize, and abuse their own people. The skeptics attracted their own marquee supporter in Malcolm Gladwell, who wrote a lengthy article in *The New Yorker* titled "Small Change: Why the Revolution Will Not Be Tweeted." Political activism is a "strong-tie" phenomenon, Gladwell wrote; Twitter and Facebook are "weak-tie" phenomena. He pointed out that Martin Luther King, Jr., organized a year-long bus boycott in Birmingham, Alabama, in 1954 without so much as a cell phone. Even Twitter cofounder Biz Stone threw his weight behind the doubters. Asked by an interviewer, "Do you believe Twitter overthrew the Egyptian government?" he replied, "No. People did that."

The back-and-forth between these two sides was unusually fierce and personal, unfolding over a hyperquick tit-for-tat of articles, blog posts, retorts, and name-calling. In the West, at least, the cyber-utopian side seemed to be winning. But as is typical for these kinds of arguments, one thing was missing from the debate: the view of the people on the ground. So what do the activists themselves think of this debate? Quite a lot, actually, and not at all what you might expect. Every single person I met in Egypt thought the influence of technology has been overplayed in the West, and many were openly offended by the idea, considering it a conspiracy by outsiders to downplay Arabs' sophistication and give the West credit where it didn't belong.

"The Internet was just a tool," said Noor Ayman Nour. "Facebook helped to organize people; Twitter to give people live updates. They complemented each other. But if they weren't there, the revolution would still have happened. The perfect example was when Mubarak cut off the Internet for four days beginning the night of January twenty-seventh. The strongest demonstrations were on days when there was no Internet."

Gigi Ibrahim, a twenty-three-year-old graduate student, concurred. "I really disagree with the whole sentiment of Revolution 2.0," she said. With her spiked hair, ubiquitous tweets, and heavily eyelined, oversized eyes, Ibrahim became one of the more visible members of the revolution's leadership. "It really undermines the history of mobilization that started with the Second Palestinian Intifada in 2000," she said. "This came after a decade in which people didn't go into the streets. The movement continued with protests over the U.S. invasion of Iraq, and really escalated in Egypt in 2006. Anybody who was watching in the last few years could see we were heading to this threshold.

"The Internet played a role," she continued, "but so did the fax in Tiananmen Square and the telegraph back in Russia. Many credit smuggled audiotapes of Ayatollah Khomeini with building support for the Iranian Revolution in 1979. But nobody called those the Fax Revolution or the Telegraph Revolution."

Perhaps the most persuasive critique I heard came from Ahmed Maher, who did as much as anyone to insert social networking into the heart of the revolt. "I personally reject the title the Facebook Revolution," he told me. "January twenty-fifth was the result of an accumulation of effort, fear, and a desire for change that had been growing since 2005." Why does he think the label has stuck? "I've heard a million explanations," he said, "including that the American government was complicit in supporting the Mubarak regime, so they wanted to credit American technology with bringing him down. I would say this was a purely Egyptian revolution."

To be sure, the technological innovation of Egyptian technogeeks was brilliant, a model for the world. In January 2007, for example, a young Egyptian initiated a campaign called "President Mubarak, you've got mail," in which he solicited users to post hostile, obnoxious, or amusing messages to a website. Whenever someone typed "Mubarak" into a search engine anywhere in the world, they would get mini Google ads made from these converted posts. In another instance, when the Internet was cut off in the midst of the revolution, some young Egyptian programmers jerry-rigged a system in which protestors could call a landline on three continents—in the United States, Italy, and Bahrain—and leave short messages, which others could then dial in to hear or (if they were elsewhere and still had access to the Web) read by visiting speak2tweet on Twitter.

The point is, technology did play a role in the youth uprisings, but not because of the innovation of the technology itself. Rather, it was because of the innovation of its users. That savvy is a hallmark of Generation Freedom and has ramifications far beyond Tahrir Square.

Proactive. This generation's final quality is the least remarked upon but may be the most significant. They took matters into their own hands. They responded to decades of sclerosis, stasis, and stultification and overnight decided, "We've had enough! We're going to act!" In the process, they created something that had been almost entirely dormant in the Middle East in the last forty years: political activism.

"I think what distinguished my generation is a sense of social responsibility that didn't exist before," said Ethar El-Katatney. A twenty-three-year-old multiplatform megastar, El-Katatney embodies all the whiz-bang mash-ups of Generation Freedom. She was raised in a privileged, private-school environment where her schooling was entirely in English and Islam was an afterthought. But she made the choice to become a learned, devout Muslim and wear a veil, and had just become engaged to a traditional man, a car salesman. She also tweets more than anyone I know, has written two books (one about Yemen, the other about Islam in China), is an anchor on Egyptian state television, is getting two master's degrees, and was on an Arab reality show called *The Renewers,* a knock-off of

The Apprentice, in which the host was a charismatic Muslim televangelist and sixteen contestants from nine different Arab countries competed in volunteer programs to see who could be more charitable. She came in third. (A week after we met, she announced by tweet that her engagement had broken off.)

"We had the French and the British here, then a succession of military rulers," El-Katatney said. "Everyone just kind of atrophied. In the last thirty years in particular, the Egyptian population had become like a child, where you feed it, you clothe it, but you don't ask it to think or make any decisions. 'Oh, Hosni, you're just like a father to us.' "

Organized Islamists across the region were the one group willing to offer an alternative to the stagnation and political infantilizing, she noted. Fundamentalism became a fallback. In a land with no political parties, no dissent, and no free expression, the mosque became the only place to discuss politics. Religion became the language of opposition. As the Egyptian-born scholar Fouad Ajami wrote, "The fundamentalist call has resonated because it invited men to participate . . . [in] contrast to a political culture that reduces citizens to spectators and asks them to leave things to their rulers," Ahmed Maher told me that growing up he found it hard to find friends who would talk about politics. Most just wanted to keep their heads down and study.

"But it just became too difficult to be an ostrich with your head in the sand," said El-Katatney. "If I would use one word to capture the conversations of my community, it would be *awakening.* We would have these tweet-ups, where we sat around and chatted on Twitter, and the feeling you had was a mixture of passion and hope. For me, the biggest surprise of this awakening is that people realized, *We don't simply have to always submit. We have to stand up for our rights. We have to stand up for ourselves.*

"So many of us have traveled and been exposed to other cultures," she continued. "You see what it can be like. What our country could be like. What our personal lives can be like. To me, that's what characterizes my generation. We have that spark to improve things. And if you look around the region today, that's exactly what we're doing. The dinosaurs are finally becoming extinct. There's a new way of living."

These Four P's—*plentiful, pinched, plugged in, proactive*—capture the fundamentals of who this generation is. But what about their religion? This was the second question I hoped to answer. What are their beliefs? And what will their uprising mean for the future of faith?

To help answer that question, I went to see one of the savvier young people I met. His name is Hossam Bahgat, and he is his own mash-up of unlikely qualities. Thirty-one years old, with closely cropped hair, trendy, dark-rimmed glasses, and a trim, almost lithe frame, he wore a fashionable white shirt unbuttoned just so. He brought a relentless, analytic intensity to a subject more often given to emotion and fear—sectarian violence. He is the founder and executive director of the Egyptian Initiative for Personal Rights and one of the most decorated human rights activists in Cairo.

"Had you asked me about the religious beliefs of young people before the revolution," he said, "my answer would have been completely different. Egypt the last few years was a ticking time bomb, where sectarian violence was getting much worse. But now, as a result of this young generation, we are seeing an entirely different situation and, for the first time in a long time, a real opportunity for change."

Trying to make sense of the innermost beliefs of a billion people across multiple continents is obviously a dangerous, foolish errand. Religion is deeply connected with national history and political circumstance. Sunnis and Shias are locked in mortal combat within certain countries, for example, yet cooperate within borders (and across borders) in others. Christians ostracize Muslims in many countries north of the Mediterranean, while being ostracized *by* Muslims south of the Mediterranean. Jews lived for centuries under Muslim rule in the Middle East more freely than they did under Christian rule in Europe, but are now almost nil in the region outside of Israel. Religion is also connected to quality of life. As the economic, education, and health-care gap between the Muslim world and the West has widened in recent decades, Islamic groups have rushed in to fill the gap and salve the pain. Religion is also connected to information. Much of the Arab world has been trapped behind a veil of ignorance for sixty years, the most explosive period in the history of knowledge. The true impact of the Internet on faith—specifically, what unlimited access to rival points of view might do to religious orthodoxy—is just beginning to be felt.

But drawing some conclusions is possible, even necessary. First, Islam may be the one religion of Abraham that has grown stronger in the last half a century. The Pew Global Attitudes Project does annual surveys on religious identity, and the willingness of Middle Easterners, including young people, to embrace Islam is much higher than how Western populations embrace their faiths. The number of Muslims who said Islam should play a "large role" in politics was 95 percent in Egypt and Indonesia, 88 percent in Pakistan and Nigeria, and more than 50 percent in Lebanon and Jordan. A poll taken after the revolution in Egypt found that two-thirds of Egyptians thought laws should "strictly follow" the Qur'an and another quarter thought they should follow the "values and principles" of the Qur'an. While these numbers may strike many in the West as uncomfortably high, we simply have to get used to the fact that even a more youth-oriented, free Middle East will continue to have a strong Islamic identity.

But *Islamic* doesn't necessarily mean "Islamist." The second characteristic of Islam today is that violent extremism is on the defensive. Even before the death of Osama bin Laden further eroded the credibility (and functionality) of the world's leading extremist organization, when Muslims were asked which side they identify with in the struggle between modernizers and fundamentalists, 84 percent in Lebanon said the modernists, along with 74 percent of Turks, 61 percent of Pakistanis, and 54 percent of Indonesians. In Egypt, the modernist camp is so strong, 80 percent don't even recognize a struggle. Eight in ten Muslims, meanwhile, say suicide bombing and other acts of violence against civilians to defend Islam are never justified;

majorities in Turkey (77 percent), Indonesia (61 percent), and Jordan (54 percent) agree.

Third, a washed-out, nondoctrinal, Islam-in-name-only is on the rise. In his landmark 1950s study *Protestant-Catholic-Jew*, Will Herberg wrote that true religion in the West was being replaced by what he called a watered-down "faith-for-faith's-sake" attitude, where "familiar words are retained, but the old meaning is voided." This is the religion of Christians who attend church only on Christmas and Easter, and Jews who go only to High Holiday services and a Passover Seder. A half-century later, a similar brand of Islam seems to be taking root in the Middle East, especially among young Muslims. As Ayman Nour described himself, "I am a Muslim. I might not practice as efficiently as I should, according to many people. But I do identify myself as a Muslim." He then went off arm in arm with a woman to rehearsal for one of his four bands. Feel-good Muslims even have their own gurus, a group of "satellite sheiks" who pedal their liberal, modernist philosophy on popular television shows and social media. The most prominent of these is Amr Khaled, the "Dr. Phil of Islam," who favors Hugo Boss shirts and coexistence with the West and made vocal attacks on Osama bin Laden. He was the host of the show on which Ethar El-Katatney was a semifinalist.

In recent years, this greater emphasis on Islam, however it's practiced, has been detrimental for interreligious relations. That's exactly what Hossam Bahgat found in Egypt. Beginning in 2007, the Egyptian Initiative for Personal Rights began an unprecedented series of quarterly reports of Muslim-Christian sectarian incidents. For the first two years, they found an average of two incidents a month, a situation that only worsened in subsequent years. "It got so bad we were starting to doubt our ability to live together in peace," Bahgat said.

But then came the revolution, and an unimaginable breakthrough.

"Suddenly the moral threshold shifted, and Egyptians were no longer tolerant of intolerance," Bahgat said. "Suddenly everyone, including the Muslim Brotherhood, was saying, 'Of course, Egypt is for all Egyptians. Of course, there should never be discrimination. Of course, we are all Egyptians first then Muslims or Christians second.'" A poll taken after Mubarak stepped down showed that 84 percent of Egyptians thought it was important that Copts and other religious minorities be able to practice their religion freely.

"Now this could be discursive or the heat of the moment," he said, "but the fact that the public discourse was cleansed of bigotry, and that anyone who was an advocate of a more isolationist, alarmist discourse became too embarrassed to voice this view in public, was a complete reversal of what I personally have been studying for five years."

Where did this attitude come from?

"It's hard to say. It wasn't exactly nationalism, and it wasn't exactly patriotism. I felt kinship in Tahrir Square. It was as if everyone had been members of the same organization for many years and had been attending meetings and strategizing for this moment. And not only did they start working together, but they cared for one another in genuine, emotional ways.

You had the locking of arms to protect others in prayer. You had a Christian woman carrying a big cross pouring water for Muslims doing their ablutions.

"On January twenty-ninth," he continued, "tanks entered the square. It took us about two minutes for Egyptians to get used them. Then we jumped on top of them and wrote anti-Mubarak graffiti. I remember standing in the middle of the square, watching this tank with about thirty young men on it, moving around the square, with everyone chanting, 'Muslims or Christians, we are all Egyptian!' And I remember thinking, 'Wait a second. Where am I?' There was no reason for them to choose this chant, but they did."

"And how did you feel at that moment?"

"I teared up. I felt we could have spent many years working against sectarianism, and it wouldn't have shown the impact I saw right in front of me."

"So you've seen the worst," I said. "You've seen this period of idyllic fantasy. Which will prevail?"

He took a long time before answering my question.

"We're going to become a normal country," he said.

"All this for that modest result!?"

"No, that's the best-case scenario," he said.

"What do you mean?"

"Take America. We're going to have a crazy preacher announcing a Qur'an burning one day, and we're going to have a social outrage against it. We're going to have people who are for the Ground Zero mosque and those who are against it. We're going to have reactive and regressive forces competing against progressive and equality voices. Some battles we're going to win. Some battles we're going to lose. But we're not going to be the first country on the planet that has zero bigotry. That country doesn't exist, and we're not going to be it."

"And if you succeed, what will the impact be?"

"It will change the world. Not just the region, the entire world." I asked him to elaborate. "We will serve as a moral model," he said. "We will be a counter to the influence of the Wahhabis and other extremists. We will become an advocate for freedom of religion and other rights-based policies on the global scene. And we will be a final nail in the coffin of the clash of civilizations and those who believe Muslims cannot handle tolerance."

"And you believe this will happen?"

"It could go either way," he said. "First it has to be imagined, and that's what happened during the revolution. Now it has to be constructed and defended. Just like the opposite philosophy. But I am one who believes that with a lot of hard work, perseverance, and constant nurturing, good can prevail over evil."

On my last day in Egypt, I drove two hours east of Cairo to Ismailia, the administrative headquarters of the Suez Canal and a resort town on the shores of Lake Timsah, which many believe is the likeliest candidate for the Sea of Reeds, the body of water the Israelites are said to have crossed on their way out of Egypt 3,200 years ago. This episode represents *the* moment of freedom in the Bible, the liminal gap between the children of Abraham's oppressive past and their liberated future. In other words, it is the moment for self-congratulation, second-guessing, successful planning, or severe missteps—exactly where the Arab Spring was right now. Were there any lessons to be learned from the first time this place went through this kind of transition?

Ismailia, like other places in Egypt, still seemed in shock from the abruptness of the change. A number of people had died in clashes with riot police in this small city. The office building of the old ruling party was a burned carcass, a mirror of the party headquarters alongside Qasr al-Nil Bridge that was also a scarred shell. The fish shacks and rental boat outfits along the water were starving for business. Few people seemed in the mood for a holiday.

I rented a small fishing dingy and set out onto the water with the fisherman, Kamil. Tufts of bullrushes dotted the perimeter. A handful of men in other boats were casting for their daily haul, mostly gray mullet, perch, and what the locals call "Moses fish," a flounder that's black on one side and white on the other and that earned its nickname from the idea that when Moses split the sea he chopped this specimen in half, thereby creating its flat shape.

We passed under a small bridge and were suddenly in open water. No spot in Egypt better embodies the country's complex relationship with the region and the world. About a mile in front of us was a line of enormous tankers and container ships making their way through the Suez Canal, which bisects the lake. Beyond it was a memorial to those killed in the 1973 war with Israel. The memorial was built in the shape of an AK-47 bayonet and is called a "victory monument," even though Egypt didn't exactly win the war. To the south was a shrine on Mary Mountain, named for a spot where the Holy Family is said to have stayed when they fled Bethlehem with their infant son Jesus. To the right was a hideaway hotel for police named "The January 25 Resort." "I guess they'll have to change the name," Kamil said dryly.

While he was speaking, a speeding pontoon police boat emerged out of nowhere and headed directly toward us. I held my breath. The officers pulled up alongside us, gripped our bow, and alternatively interrogated Kamil and barked questions over a walkie-talkie. It seems we were getting too close to the Suez Canal and were perceived as a threat. Within several minutes, they saluted us and sped off. Kamil couldn't believe it. Normally, he said, they would have detained him, taken his catch, and generally roughed him up.

"So after the revolution, everyone will be nice all the time?" I asked.

"Now they even salute me!" he said.

As he knew, this kind of harmony would not last forever, which is one of the great themes of the Moses story. When I first came to this lake years earlier, I quickly realized I had been missing a major element of the Israelites' crossing of the Red Sea. I always viewed the story as one of exhilaration. "We're escaping slavery! We're becoming free!" But while the Israelites were clearly excited, they must also have been deeply afraid. They were leaving the world they knew, for a world that didn't yet exist. Indeed, the next forty years were marked by a series of setbacks, rebellions, and counterrevolutions that amounted to a never-ending struggle between the Israelites' better angels and their deepest demons. The clearest lesson of freedom to emerge from its earliest telling is that freedom is never easy. It does not come freely; it does not come naturally. It must be earned.

Many people across the Middle East were already drawing the same conclusion about this generation's rebellions. As Ethar El-Katatney told me, "I'm afraid Egyptians will lose their way. They'll lose their clear-cut vision of change and their willingness to endure and work for it. My fear is that people will eventually start to convince themselves that it was better before the revolution, especially because economically people are going to suffer a lot before their lives improve. This attitude is something we have generally in our culture. The idea of looking back. All I can say is, 'I hope we're up for it.' "

Given this insecurity, how should the rest of us react to these events? One reason the West's response to the uprisings was so inconsistent—supporting regime change in some places but not in others; intervening militarily in response to some crackdowns but not to others—is that their implications for the world depend so much on their outcome. The Arab middle class wasn't the only one to strike uncomfortable bargains with their ruling regimes; Western governments—along with Israel—did the same. In addition, the pace of reform was proving to be vastly different for different countries. The miraculous eighteen-day revolution in Egypt was never going to be the model for everyone, not least because that golden fortnight was preceded by years of underground preparation that other countries have not necessarily undergone. Also, tyrants who are prepared to fire on their own people cannot be easily dislodged, though they can't buck history indefinitely, either. As the Egyptian pharaohs, Roman emperors, Ottoman pashas, French monarchs, and British majesties discovered over the years, no one rules these sands forever.

But over three millennia, going back to the original Fertile Crescent, Egypt has had an outsized influence on the region. As the area's most populous country, as well as its cultural and political heart, it still does. As one diplomat told *Time*, "What happens in Libya stays in Libya. What happens in Egypt affects the entire region." Historian Mahmoud Sabit put it even more colorfully to me during our trip on the Nile. "When I lived in the States, they had these Dean Witter ads," he said. "A Dean Witter advisor would be talking in a restaurant and everyone would stop to eavesdrop. The slogan was, 'When Dean Witter talks, people listen.' The Middle East is the same way. 'When Egypt talks, people listen.' "

So what exactly is Egypt saying? What messages, however preliminary, can be drawn from the Arab Spring? This was my final question: What do these uprisings—coupled with the demise of the region's most visible terrorist—mean for the world?

The answer, I believe, can be summarized with five lessons.

1. THE ISLAMIC INCLUSION. In his otherwise nuanced and foresighted book *The Future of Freedom*, Fareed Zakaria titles his chapter on the Muslim world "The Islamic Exception."

The idea behind this term is that sixty years of thuggish, dictatorial rule across the Middle East and North Africa—enabled by the compliance of its people—raises the serious possibility that Arabs cannot handle freedom. As Zakaria noted, two-thirds of the world's Muslims, from Indonesia to India, have lived in free societies for decades, but democracy has been stubbornly absent from the region that gave birth to civilization.

The Arab Spring has eliminated this misconception. As David Brooks wrote in a *New York Times* op-ed piece criticizing Samuel Huntington's *Clash of Civilizations*, subscribers to this view committed the "Fundamental Attribution Error," ascribing to culture qualities that are actually determined by context. "It seems clear that many people in Arab nations do share a universal hunger for liberty. They feel the presence of universal human rights and feel insulted when they are not accorded them." Even before 2011, two-thirds of Muslims across the region told pollsters democracy was preferable to other forms of government, and those numbers started rising soon after the autocrats started falling. Whatever else comes out of the Middle East uprisings, they have forever shown that Islam is compatible with the deepest yearning for human freedom. The Clash of Civilizations has given way to the Convergence of Civilizations.

2. THE NEW WAY TO FLY. When I was sitting with Ghada Shahbender in Tahrir Square, her cell phone rang. Her ringtone was the chant that went up on Tahrir Square on January 31 when F-16 fighter jets flew over the crowed of one hundred thousand protestors. "For about ten seconds, I was

thinking, 'Oh, my God, the criminal is going to bomb us.'"
She was recalling the incident in which Hafez al-Assad of Syria
bombed and otherwise savaged his own people in 1982, killing
up to ten thousand. "But in Tahrir, it took about thirty seconds
for the people to start chanting, 'Hosni's lost his mind! Hosni
has gone crazy!' And then there was an outburst of laughter."

For the last century, flight has represented everything bold,
innovative, and futuristic about the intersection of human beings, technology, and imagination. From the Wright Brothers
to Charles Lindbergh to Amelia Earhart to Neil Armstrong to
Sally Ride, some of America's most wondrous heroes have been
aviators. In recent years, meanwhile, Middle Eastern aviators
have been known for two things: flying their planes in circles
and occasionally bombing their own people, or flying their
planes into buildings and slaughtering innocent civilians. For
Arab youth, these rival flight paths were the leading suitors for
their imagination.

The uprisings of 2011 were like a cockpit warning light
that these strategies were failing. Autocrats were put on notice they must adapt or die, while Al Qaeda was discovering
that their appeals were falling short. In every Muslim country
where polling is available, Al Qaeda had been losing support
precipitously in recent years. Confidence in Osama bin Laden
fell 42 percentage points in Jordan between 2003 and 2010,
34 points in Indonesia, and 28 points in Pakistan. In Turkey
his approval rating went from 15 to 3; in Lebanon from 19 to 0.
Hitler would poll higher. The death of bin Laden, coming in

the middle of the Arab Spring, will surely hasten this precipitous drop in support for his organization and way of life.

At their heart, extremist groups were offering Arab young people an invitation. "Come with us. We'll improve the world together." Terrorism has never been an end; it's a means to an end. And that end has been a better life for your family, your country, the broader Muslim nation, and, in its wildest formulation, the entire non-Muslim world as well. "You may have to kill yourself to achieve those ends," the recruiters say, "but you'll get a direct pass to heaven and help the people you leave behind get one step closer to paradise on earth."

Though he wasn't the only purveyor of that philosophy (and surely won't be its last), Osama bin Laden was always its most visible and successful face. His downfall, at a minimum, makes the extremists' invitation less appealing to young Muslims. The fact that his death came at the precise moment a rival invitation was capturing the imagination of the region's youth makes his departure even more impactful. A decade after 9/11, both despotism and terrorism are in retreat in the Muslim World. And now Generation Freedom has offered the Arab Street a new way to fly: forward.

3. THE FIFTH FREEDOM. On January 6, 1941, President Franklin Roosevelt delivered a State of the Union address in which he articulated "four essential human freedoms": freedom of speech, freedom of worship, freedom from want, and freedom from fear. These "four freedoms" became the foundation behind the United Nations Declaration of Human

Rights. More than five decades later, at a town hall meeting with students in China, President Obama responded to a question submitted over the Internet—"Should we be able to use Twitter freely?"—by stressing that people should also have free, unfettered access to the Internet and that the more freely information flows, the stronger societies become. Invoking Roosevelt, Secretary of State Hillary Clinton later deemed this notion the "freedom to connect," the idea that "governments should not prevent people from connecting to the Internet, to websites, or to one another."

The idea of extending human freedoms to the Internet had been around for a while, but it hadn't exactly captured the public's imagination. Until now. In coming decades when people single out the tipping point for the idea that access to the Internet is a fundamental human right on par with freedom of expression or freedom of religion, they will likely point to the Middle East uprisings of 2011. Regardless of whether these events are deemed Facebook Revolutions, they were clearly marquee moments for the power of social networks in political life. The Arab Spring secured a permanent place for the "freedom to connect" as humanity's "fifth freedom."

4. THE WINDOW IS NOW OPEN. Dr. Iman Bibars is an economist and the vice president of Ashoka, a global organization of social entrepreneurs. Based in Cairo, she took her fourteen-year-old son to the protests, and everyone kept saying to him, "You're part of the 'lucky generation,' the ones who will be around when schools are better, when entrepreneurship is encouraged, when you can get loans from banks without bending to corruption, when you don't need to be the son of an elite to start your own enterprise."

For all the downsides of the Youth Bulge, there is one tremendous advantage: There's a demographic bonus that follows the bulge. When the ratio of those who don't work (those under fifteen or over sixty-five) to those who do work shrinks, greater productivity and income is possible. Economists call this windfall, often around forty years, the demographic "window of opportunity" for growth. Both Japan and the United States benefited from similar periods of economic expansion when their baby booms reached prime earning years. (And they're both about to experience the backlash that follows when they reach retirement age.)

In order to reap the rewards of this window, countries must adapt their educational, social, and political institutions to the coming needs of the population. The political changes unleashed by the uprisings are a necessary first step, but they are only a first step. School reform, health-care reform, and human rights reform must follow. So must a flourishing of the private sector, and here the region has something of a head start.

My wife runs an organization called Endeavor that helps young business entrepreneurs around the world access the mentoring, networks, and capital necessary to build a vibrant middle class. After a decade in Latin America and Africa, Endeavor expanded to the Middle East and now runs offices in Turkey, Egypt, Lebanon, Jordan, Saudi Arabia, and the UAE. "A decade ago there was no word for 'entrepreneurship' in Arabic," she said. "People feared failure and had trouble thinking big." Now a new class of entrepreneurs, most in their late twenties, is emerging, from computer gamers to fashion designers to biometric engineers. They've even coined a new word for themselves, *riyadah,* which is Arabic for pioneer. One such pioneer, from Jordan, invented eye recognition technology so powerful it's being used to protect U.S. borders. A company based in the Middle East is providing technology to U.S. sheriffs to help protect Americans in part from . . . terrorists from the Middle East. That's as good an emblem as I know of the post-9/11 Middle East.

For Generation Freedom, the challenges they have unleashed are clear. Beyond the complex and ongoing process of trying to change leaders, constitutions, and political systems, the real and, arguably, greater burden they face is to take advantage of the economic opportunities their numbers provide to build a sustainable future. The window is now open. It won't stay so forever.

5. THE G2G MOVEMENT. And the burden is on the West, too. How will we react to this outstretched hand? In his inauguration speech, President Obama addressed the Muslim world, saying, "We will extend a hand if you are willing to unclench your fist." The Arab Spring is surely an unclenched fist. But I would go further. To me, it's a direct plea to the Western countries to switch our allegiance from dictators who serve our need for stability to young people who share our dreams. And while it may be too much to expect Western governments to abandon long-term allies overnight—after all, many of these protestors are unknown and untested as leaders—it's not too much to ask young people in the West to form a generational alliance with their counterparts behind the Green Curtain of the Muslim world.

After Sputnik, Americans responded to the threat from the Soviet bloc by redoubling our efforts in math and science and generally working on our own house as well as fighting theirs. After 9/11, in response to the threat from Islamic extremists, Americans have done our share of fighting, but have we worked on our own house? This effort could mean anything from reducing our dependence on Middle Eastern oil, to advancing peace between Israelis and Palestinians, to studying Arabic, traveling to the region, or sitting down with Muslims in our own communities. In the that way Americans movingly said after 9/11, "We're all New Yorkers now," we need to tell young people across the Middle East on occasion, "We're all Khaled Said, too."

Instead, not only do we lack a national commitment to reach out to the Muslim world, we have the opposite problem: a growing hostility toward them. A magnet school in New York City focusing on Middle Eastern studies was so roundly criticized it was forced to close; a program in Texas to give twenty minutes of voluntary Arabic classes a day was shot down after the school board was accused of brainwashing students; states across the country introduced measures to ban Sharia law, as if the two and a half million Muslims in America were at risk of overwhelming a population of 308 million. And my favorite example of post-9/11 craziness: In 2009, a twenty-two-year-old student at Pomona College in California was interrogated, handcuffed, and detained by security officials at the Philadelphia airport. The reason: The physics major was studying Arabic and had Arabic language flash cards in his backpack. Our pioneers have become our enemies.

It's hard not to conclude that our leaders have failed us, too, and maybe it requires our own young people, the generation just reaching maturity now, to form an alliance with their counterparts. From business, to schools, to social networks, to sports (the Middle East will host the World Cup in 2022 and no less an authority than International Olympic Committee president Jacques Rogge expects the region to host its first Olympics after that), we must reboot our efforts to have people-to-people contacts with the one-seventh of humans who are young Muslims. In the same way that B2B came to describe the direct communication from business to business in commercial transactions, we could call this direction communication from generation to generation, G2G. It's time for the G2G movement.

On the night I arrived in Cairo, I logged onto Facebook and found a notice recommending that I "friend" a certain person with whom I had many friends in common. There was only one problem: This friend was an ex-friend with whom I had had a painful falling-out in college. That night I lay in bed thinking about whether the Facebook algorithm might be sending me a message. Was it time to salve that twenty-five-year wound? And that's when it struck me. What a perfect analogy to what was happening out my window in Tahrir Square. The cries of those young people in squares across the Middle East were their own Facebook friend request to the rest of the world. And like all such requests, you don't really have to be close to the other person to accept. You just have to have a positive, warmly inclined, friend-like relationship, where you wish them happy birthday, keep up with their musings, their status changes, their photos from the beach, and occasionally "like" what they have to say or offer a witty retort.

Maybe the Middle East uprisings were a Facebook Revolution after all. They were a massive, generation-wide Facebook friend request from a people as enamored of freedom as we are that arrives in our inbox looking for support at exactly the moment we had all but turned up our noses and turned our backs on anyone from their neighborhood. And in that way in which the Internet tries to make things easy, this request comes with two helpful options: CONFIRM or NOT NOW. The choice is ours: Which will it be?

ACKNOWLEDGMENTS

I am extremely grateful to the vast network of people on multiple continents who themselves cooperated via Facebook, Twitter, Skype, telephone, mobile phone, fax, courier, and good old-fashioned late-night editing sessions to make this book possible under sometimes challenging conditions. Special thanks to Ahmed Ezzat, Romany Helwi, and particularly Nagwa Hassaan for their assistance in Egypt. At HarperCollins, I have innovative and fast-moving colleagues in Michael Morrison, Liate Stehlik, Carrie Kania, Sharyn Rosenblum, Amy Baker, Jennifer Hart, Danny Goldstein, and especially the tireless and high-minded Henry Ferris. Special thanks to Stuart Emmrich, Laura Marmor, Ben Sherwood, Joshua Ramo, and Chadwick Moore.

David Black shared this journey alongside me. Andrew Feiler read every page of the manuscript and improved it immeasurably. Linda Rottenberg added her grace to the words and ideas, but even more provided the confidence and enthusiasm that made the entire project possible in the first place.

Eden and Tybee Feiler got great belly-dancing outfits out of the deal, and we all got a memorable birthday dance from them in return. But I am most indebted to the quiet wisdom and gentle hands of Dr. John Healey, who at exactly the moment it seemed as if I might never walk again, gave me back the gift of walking. This book is dedicated to him.

For more information about this and other projects,
and to join the conversation, please visit
www.brucefeiler.com,
where you can email me directly.
You can also follow me on Facebook at
www.facebook.com/brucefeilerpage
or Twitter at
www.twitter.com/brucefeiler.
If Generation Freedom can do it, why can't we!

MEET BRUCE FEILER

BRUCE FEILER is one of America's most popular voices on religion, the Middle East, and contemporary affairs. He is the best-selling author of ten books, including *Walking the Bible*, *Abraham*, and *Where God Was Born*. He also writes the "This Life" column for the Sunday *New York Times* and is the writer/presenter of the PBS miniseries *Walking the Bible*. His last book, *The Council of Dads*, tells the uplifting story of how friendship and community can help one survive life's greatest challenge.

Bruce Feiler's early books involve immersing himself in different cultures and bringing other worlds vividly to life. These include *Learning to Bow*, an account of the year he spent teaching in rural Japan; *Looking for Class*, about life inside Oxford and Cambridge; and *Under the Big Top*, which depicts the year he spent performing as a circus clown.

His recent work has made him one of the country's most

respected authorities on religion. *Walking the Bible* describes his perilous, 10,000-mile journey retracing the Five Books of Moses through the desert. The book was hailed as an "instant classic" by the *Washington Post*. It spent more than a year and a half on the *New York Times* bestseller list, has been translated into fifteen languages, and is the subject of a children's book and a photography book.

Abraham recounts his personal search for the shared ancestor of Jews, Christians, and Muslims. "Exquisitely written," wrote the *Boston Globe*, "100 percent engaging." The book was featured on the cover of *Time* and inspired thousands of grassroots interfaith discussions.

Where God Was Born describes his year-long trek retracing the Bible through Israel, Iraq, and Iran. "Bruce Feiler is a real-life Indiana Jones," wrote the *Atlanta Journal-Constitution*. *America's Prophet* recounts his unprecedented journey through American history—from the pilgrims to the Founding Fathers, the Civil War to the Civil Rights movement—exploring how the story of Moses helped shaped America.

In 2006, PBS aired the miniseries *Walking the Bible* that received record ratings and was viewed by 50 million people around the world. "Beguiling," wrote the *Wall Street Journal*. "Mr. Feiler is an engaging and informed guide."

Bruce Feiler has written for numerous publications, including *The New Yorker*, *The New York Times Magazine*, and *Gourmet*, where he won three James Beard Awards. He is also a frequent contributor to National Public Radio, CNN, and Fox News. He has been the subject of Jay Leno jokes and a

JEOPARDY! question, and his face appears on a postage stamp in the Grenadines.

The Council of Dads is the international sensation that describes how he asked six men from his life to form a support group for his young daughters. The book was profiled in *People*, *USA Today*, *Time*, and the *Washington Post*, was included in *O! The Oprah Magazine* Reading Club, and was the subject of a one-hour special hosted by Dr. Sanjay Gupta on CNN.

A native of Savannah, Georgia, Bruce Feiler lives in New York with wife, Linda Rottenberg, and their twin daughters. For more information, please visit www.brucefeiler.com.

Have You Read?
More by Bruce Feiler

WALKING THE BIBLE

Feeling disconnected from the religious community he had known as a child, Bruce Feiler set out on a perilous ten-thousand-mile journey across the Middle East to discover the roots of the Bible. Traveling through three continents, five countries, and four war zones, Feiler is the first person ever to complete such an adventure in an attempt to answer the question: Is the Bible just an abstraction, some book gathering dust, or is it a living, breathing entity with relevance to contemporary life? From Turkey to Israel, the Sinai to the heart of Egypt, Feiler explores how geography affects the larger narrative of the Bible and ultimately realizes how much these places—and his experience—have affected his faith.

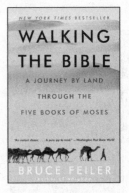

"Ranks among the great spiritual autobiographies."
                    —*Washington Post Book World*

ABRAHAM

Both immediate and timeless, *Abraham* tells the powerful story of one man's search for the shared ancestor of Judaism, Christianity, and Islam. Traveling through war zones, braving violence at religious sites, and seeking out faith leaders, Bruce Feiler uncovers the defining yet divisive role that Abraham plays for half the world's believers. Provocative and uplifting, *Abraham* offers a thoughtful and inspiring vision of

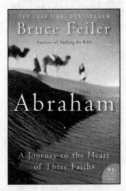

unity that redefines what we think about our neighbors, our future, and ourselves.

"An exquisitely written journey."

—*Boston Globe*

AMERICA'S PROPHET

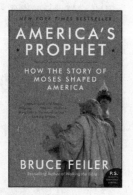

For four hundred years, one figure has inspired more Americans than any other. His name is Moses. Traveling through touchstones in American history, bestselling author Bruce Feiler traces the biblical prophet's influence from the *Mayflower* through today. Meticulously researched and highly readable, *America's Prophet* is a thrilling, original work of history that will forever change how we view America, our faith, and our future.

"Audacious. . . . Classically Feiler."

—*USA Today*

WHERE GOD WAS BORN

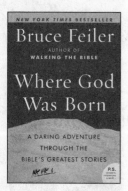

Continuing the gripping journey he began with *Walking the Bible*, Bruce Feiler travels ten thousand miles through the heart of the Middle East—from the Garden of Eden to the rivers of Babylon—uncovering the little-known origins of Western religion. Combining the excitement of an adventure story and the insight of spiritual exploration, *Where God Was Born* offers a rare, universal vision of God that can inspire different faiths into a shared dialogue for hope.

"Breathtaking. . . . Goes from cover to cover, from one eye-opening story to the next, without letup."　　　—*Boston Globe*

THE COUNCIL OF DADS

When Bruce Feiler was diagnosed with cancer in 2008, he instantly worried what his daughters' lives would be like with him not around: "Would they wonder who I was? Would they wonder what I thought? Would they lack for my approval, my discipline, my voice?" The Council of Dads is the inspiring story of what happened after he decided how to give his daughters that voice. Bruce reached out to six men from all the passages in his life and asked them to be present in his daughters' lives. And he would call this group "The Council of Dads." This is a touching, funny, and ultimately deeply moving book on how to live life, how the human spirit can respond to adversity, and how to deepen and cherish the friendships that enrich our lives.

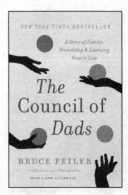

"*The Council of Dads* . . . reminds us of which values we value most, and helps us make sure we transmit them."   —*Time*

WALKING THE BIBLE:
A PHOTOGRAPHIC JOURNEY

Featuring Bruce Feiler's own photography as well as his selections from professional collections, *Walking the Bible: A Photographic Journey* brings together breathtaking vistas, intimate portraits, and fascinating panoramas, providing firsthand access to the inscrutable land where three of the world's great religions were born— and finally puts a face on the stories

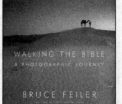

that have long inspired the human
spirit.

"Beautifully depicts the dramatic land
that gave birth to three of the world's
great religions." —*USA Today*

DREAMING OUT LOUD

Country music has exploded across the
United States and undergone a sweeping
revolution, transforming the once
ridiculed world of Nashville into an
unlikely focal point of American pop
culture. In writing this fascinating book,
Feiler was granted unprecedented access
to the private moments of the revolution.
Here is the acclaimed report: a chronicle
of the genre's biggest stars as they
changed the face of American music.
With intimate portraits of Garth Brooks,
Wynonna Judd, and Wade Hayes, Feiler
has written the defining book on the new
Nashville.

"Penetrating and insightful."
  —Elvis Mitchell, *New York Times*

UNDER THE BIG TOP

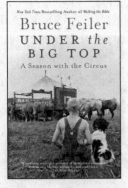

It's every child's dream: to run away
and join the circus. Feiler did just that,
joining the Clyde Beatty–Cole Bros.
Circus as a clown for one year. This is
the story of that crazy, chaotic,
heartbreaking ride, a book that will
remind you of how dreams can go
horribly wrong—and then miraculously
come true.

"A stunning collective portrait."
  —*The New Yorker*

LOOKING FOR CLASS

An irresistible, entertaining peek into the privileged realm of Wordsworth and Wodehouse, Chelsea Clinton and Hugh Grant, *Looking for Class* offers a hilarious account of Feiler's year at Britain's most exclusive universities, Oxford and Cambridge—the garden parties and formal balls, the high-minded debates and drinking Olympics—and gives us a eye-opening view of the often romanticized but rarely seen British upper class.

"A trenchant, witty, and engaging critique of the English establishment."
                    —*San Francisco Chronicle*

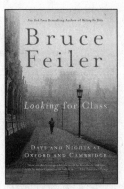

LEARNING TO BOW

Feiler's first book, *Learning to Bow*, is one of the funniest, liveliest, and most insightful books ever written about the clash of cultures between America and Japan. With warmth and candor, Feiler recounts the year he spent as a teacher in a small rural Japanese town. Beginning with a ritual outdoor bath and culminating in an all-night trek to the top of Mount Fuji, Feiler teaches his students about American culture, while they teach him everything from how to properly address an envelope to how to date a Japanese girl.

"Incisive, often hilarious, and presents a rounded portrait of the modern Japanese."   —*USA Today*

The Cubs
Fan's Guide
to Happiness

The Cubs
Fan's Guide
to Happiness

GEORGE ELLIS

TRIUMPH
B O O K S

The Library of Congress has catalogued the previous edition as follows:

Ellis, George, 1977–
    The Cubs fan's guide to happiness / George Ellis.
        p. cm.
    ISBN: 978-1-57243-936-8
    1. Chicago Cubs (Baseball team)—History. 2. Chicago Cubs (Baseball
    team)—Humor I. Title.

GV875.C6E45 2007
796.3570977311—dc22
2006037831

This book is available in quantity at special discounts for your group or
organization. For further information, contact:

Triumph Books LLC
814 North Franklin
Chicago, Illinois 60610
www.triumphbooks.com

Printed in U.S.A.
ISBN: 978-1-60078-940-3
Design by Patricia Frey
All photos courtesy of AP Photos unless otherwise indicated
Illustrations by Vito Sabsay

Contents

Acknowledgments... vii

Introduction ix

A New Edition of This Book: Why??? xi

Chapter 1: There's Always Next Year (TANY).. 1

Chapter 2: If Not a Championship, Beer Will Make It Better!™ 11

Chapter 3: Everybody Needs a Scapegoat (Or Even Just a Goat).......... 19

Chapter 4: It's Not Over until You're Mathematically Eliminated.......... 27

Chapter 5: Winning Really Isn't Everything.. 35

Chapter 6: Loyaltiness Is Next to Godliness 43

Chapter 7: At Least You're Not a Sox Fan 49

Chapter 8: The Power of Low Expectations 57

Chapter 9: To Boo or Not to Boo 65

Chapter 10: Sabermetrics? No, Cubbiemetrics!..................................... 73

Chapter 11: A Renovated Ballpark, A Renovated Future 79

Conclusion: What Does All This Mean? 91

Appendix A: 15 Habits of Highly Happy Cubs Fans............................... 97

Appendix B: A Century of Losing: 100+ Years, 100+ Frustrations....... 115

Appendix C: Frequently Asked Questions... 195

Cubs Fan's Glossary 201

About the Author... 209

The Heckler

Acknowledgments

This book would not have been possible without the help of so many people, none of whom work, root, or play for the St. Louis Cardinals. First I'd like to recognize Brad Zibung and everyone that makes *TheHeckler.com* the finest satirical sports website in the world, or at least the finest satirical sports website that's based in Chicago.

Thanks to talented illustrator Vito Sabsay for providing drawings I could never do on my own, no matter how hard I tried. His illustrations bring this book to life, which is good, because nobody wants to buy a dead book, especially one written about the Cubs.

Thanks to Brian Summerfield, who helped research and write much of the 100 Frustrations list. Despite being a White Sox fan, Brian's writing is surprisingly coherent and engaging.

Thanks to Alec MacDonald and Danielle Egan-Miller for helping get this project off the ground and into the hands of the people at Triumph Books.

Thanks to Drew Wehrle, whose idea and research gave birth to the Goin' Deep sidebars, ensuring this book's success in academic circles.

Thanks to my wife, Deborah, for putting up with my late-night writing sessions, to my mom for being a Cubs fan, and to my dad (even though he's a Sox fan) for not forcing me to root for the South Siders.

Last but not least, there are some people and entities I would specifically *not* like to thank: the 1969 New York Mets, Steve Garvey, Will Clark, the 2003 Marlins, Ronnie Woo-Woo, and any Hall of Fame member responsible for keeping Ron Santo out of the Hall until after he passed away.

Introduction

The brain of the average Cubs fan works like the brain of the average human, except for one little detail: it has no concept of reality.

Normal people buy lottery tickets thinking they might get lucky. Cubs fans buy lottery tickets expecting to win because they've lost so many times before. And when they lose yet again, it breaks their heart. After enduring this experience 100+ times in a row, you'd think Cubs fans would learn their lesson. But that's what's so tragically amazing about these folks—they don't. They just keep hanging on to hope.

The following is your guide to feeling like you just bought the winning lottery ticket, even though you haven't and most likely never will. Because who knows? Maybe if more people lived like Cubs fans, the world would be a better place. Probably not, but there's a chance, right?

The Heckler

A New Edition Of This Book: Why???

Originally published in 2007, *The Cubs Fan's Guide To Happiness* was meant, in part, to help Cubs fans cope with the strain of their team failing to win a World Series for nearly 100 years.

Seven years later, things have changed dramatically.

Well, not the World Series part.

But the team *is* (probably) getting a JumboTron. And who could forget those delicious Bison Dogs? Even more importantly, the Cubs are no longer owned by the Tribune Company, and their current owner, Tom Ricketts, is a life-long fan that brought in Theo Epstein (who helped the Boston Red Sox break their own curse in 2004) to finally right the ship.

Progress has been slow thus far.

Still, there's a new optimism about the franchise that simply didn't exist back in 2007. The point of this updated edition is to examine that strange new vibe in Wrigleyville and try to understand why Cubs fans think a giant video board and an organizational focus on stats like Walk Per At-Bats Divided by Strikeouts Times Pinstripes on the Jersey (WPABDBSTPOTJ) will equal success in this new Cubs era.

The Heckler

There's Always Next Year (TANY)

Or next week. Or next whatever. That's the beauty of having the Cubs fan mentality. What happened last time around has no bearing on what could happen in the future. It's like waking up every day with a completely new start. No matter how horrible today was, tomorrow is sure to be better. Take love, for instance. Maybe you've never had a meaningful relationship in your entire life. Conventional wisdom says you probably won't have one next year, either. Screw conventional wisdom. Let's not forget that this is the kind of wisdom that said man couldn't go to the moon and dogs couldn't talk. One of those things has already occurred, which means it's just a matter of time before Butch can ask you about your day when you get home from work.

Unlike conventional wisdom, Cubs wisdom says anything is possible. Sure, the Chicago Cubs haven't won a World Series title since 1908. And yes, that's more than a century. But instead of focusing on the annual letdown, Cubs fans look to next season to find solace. If they ever actually dwelled on the drought between championships, they'd probably jump off a Wrigleyville rooftop with notes that have the words "I give up" scrawled on them attached to their shirts.[1]

Cubs fans have come to depend on TANY, and never was this more evident than in November 2003. The Cubs were just weeks removed from the most agonizing collapse in team history—which is saying something, considering this team's history—having blown a 3–1 National League Championship Series lead to the Florida Marlins. The turning point of the series came in the eighth inning of Game 6, when infamous Cubs fan Steve Bartman interfered with left fielder Moises Alou, causing him to drop a foul pop off the bat of Marlins second baseman Luis Castillo. Whether the ball was actually catchable will never be known (replays suggested it was), but one thing is clear: something happened when that baseball ricocheted off Bartman's outstretched hands. A shroud of silence rolled over Wrigley Field, and it seemed Cub Nation knew it was about to be left at the altar yet again.

Castillo ended up walking, and the dramatic shift in momentum sparked an eight-run Marlins rally from which the Cubs would never recover. The North Siders had entered the inning up 3–0, with their ace Mark Prior on the mound. By the time Castillo popped to second for the third and final out of the frame, the Cubs were down 8–3. After dropping Game 6, they were pounded 9–6 in Game 7. The Marlins went on to beat the New York Yankees in the World Series.

---

1. Given the brutal 2013 Cubs season, it's possible that someone will have actually offed himself in this manner by the time this book is printed. Apologies in advance to any affected relatives.

The headphoned Bartman bungled his way into Cubs lore on that fateful night in October 2003.

The Cubs went home.

What should have followed was mass suicide. Under brand-new manager Dusty Baker, the Chicago Cubs had come within five outs of the promised land, only to have their hopes dashed once more. The fragile hearts of Cubs fans had been pushed to the brink and then ground to a pulp. Immediately following the 2003 season there was plenty of the inevitable commiserating and talk of the big "what if," but that kind of defeatist thinking was gone by November, when TANY hit Wrigleyville like a 1960s Christian revival.

Goin' Deep:
The Philosophy of Next Year

When it comes to TANY, Cubs fans have solid support in the annals of great thought. Scottish philosopher David Hume thought it erroneous to assume that since something has always happened the same way that it will continue to do so. Just because the sun has risen every day since the beginning of the earth, it doesn't necessarily follow that it will rise again tomorrow. There's simply no proof, no definitive way to be sure, that the sun will rise.

Now, let's apply this notion to the Chicago Cubs. It might sound naïve, but I challenge anyone—especially Rick Morrissey or Ken Williams—to prove the Cubs will not win all 162 games next season. Sure, it seems easy. After all, the average Cubs roster is filled with guys who wouldn't even crack most Triple-A lineups. But because the future is not bound to the past, it's entirely impossible to prove the Cubs won't go undefeated Next Year. You can't even prove the Cubs bullpen will continue to suck, despite an established history of consistent suckage.

Of course, it should be noted Hume did believe that to ignore all these sorts of connections would be downright silly. He would likely assert that while the Cubs' legacy of failure isn't causing their continued troubles, we should keep an open mind in "conjoining" these consecutive years of disappointment.

But in fact, it doesn't stop with Hume. Cubs fans can also take consolation in one of the central dictums of the philosophy of this very subject—that is, correlation does not imply causation. For instance, say that a bell in a Chicago

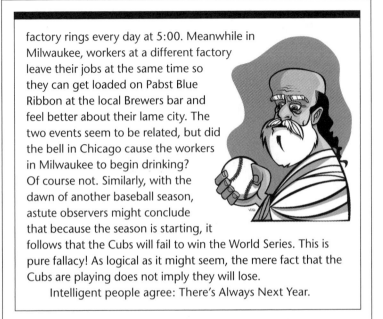

factory rings every day at 5:00. Meanwhile in Milwaukee, workers at a different factory leave their jobs at the same time so they can get loaded on Pabst Blue Ribbon at the local Brewers bar and feel better about their lame city. The two events seem to be related, but did the bell in Chicago cause the workers in Milwaukee to begin drinking? Of course not. Similarly, with the dawn of another baseball season, astute observers might conclude that because the season is starting, it follows that the Cubs will fail to win the World Series. This is pure fallacy! As logical as it might seem, the mere fact that the Cubs are playing does not imply they will lose.

Intelligent people agree: There's Always Next Year.

Suddenly, Next Year was going to be the one all over again. Every Cubs fan was sure of it.[2] The 2003 team had collapsed in the playoffs because they were inexperienced. In 2004, with the same personnel, they would most certainly soar to their first pennant since 1945 and their first World Series victory since 1908. TANY didn't just make

---

2. A little story to illustrate the far-reaching effects of TANY: I have an extremely disconnected "granola" friend in Los Angeles. Up until 2003 he knew nothing about baseball, let alone the Chicago Cubs. He had never even heard of Sammy Sosa. That changed during the 2003 NLCS, when the Cubs suddenly became a national phenomenon for their great play—and ultimate demise. After they lost to the Marlins, my friend said to me, "This means next year is the year, right?" Which is a pretty remarkable thing to hear from a guy who couldn't tell you how many runs a grand slam scores.

Notable Quote

Question: What is it that makes Cubs fans different from other types of fans?

Telander: The one thing that separates them is a love for good times...and blind hope. I mean, I've never even met anybody that was alive when the Cubs last won a World Series.

—national sportswriter and *Heaven Is a Playground* author Rick Telander

it possible, TANY made it inevitable. The spread of TANY grew so much over the winter that even *Sports Illustrated* picked the Cubs to win the World Series in 2004. Next Year was finally here.

Well.

It wasn't, of course.

The club didn't even make the playoffs in 2004. But that only underscores the amazing power of TANY. Any person in his or her right mind should have known the Cubs would not be successful in 2004—that's what happened, after all—but TANY forced everyone to think differently, and it made for a more enjoyable season.

Likewise, just because you've been emotionally challenged every day of your life up until this morning, that doesn't mean things can't turn around. Tomorrow is a new day. And if you don't fall in love tomorrow, may I remind you of next week? Nobody knows what's going to happen a week from Tuesday, which means it's entirely possible love could happen. You could sit down on the bus next to the man or woman of your dreams. You just have to hope. What else are you going to hope for? Lonely nights? Sad holidays? Yeah, that's a great existence. Excuse you while

Cubbie Kid

you cry yourself to sleep on a huge pillow made of microwave dinner receipts.

In addition to nullifying past tragedies and providing for a hopeful tomorrow, TANY is a great excuse, so you should feel free to use it liberally in your everyday life. If you don't do a good job on your TPS Reports this year, just tell your boss they'll be accurate Next Year. When people ask why you live in a conversion van, simply remind them

Practical Application

Problem: You didn't get the big promotion at work.

Solution: Don't worry about it. If you had received the promotion today, you wouldn't have anything to strive for tomorrow. Remember: the thrill is in the chase, whether it be for a World Series title or a slightly bigger cubicle. Achieving your goal will only force you to come up with a new goal, and that can be pretty daunting. Just look at the Boston Red Sox. After finally winning the championship in 2004, and again in 2007, what's their goal now? To win it...again? Doesn't sound too exciting, does it?

Clearly, this all makes sense in the abstract, but you may be thinking it doesn't do you any good in real life. Hoping for the promotion Next Year won't get you more respect. It also won't give you the raise you need to afford a shiny new sports car. But neither will being sad about not getting the promotion this time around. Did you ever think about that, smart guy? So you can either get depressed about being passed over or you can look at the bright side and say, "Hey, maybe I'll realize all my dreams Next Year." At least you'll be in a good mood the next 12 months.

that life is a marathon, not a sprint. "There's Always Next Year," you could say. "I guarantee my home won't have wheels in 2015."

TANY can also help prepare you for the worst before it happens. In 2004

Did You Know?

Independent studies have shown that Cubs fans can deal with disappointment better than any other social group in the United States.

Cubs fans were already using TANY when the team was tied for the wild-card lead with just a week left in the season. The ballclub had been sliding precipitously, so instead of waiting for the Cubs to fall short of the playoffs, fans knew what to think: TANY. That way a playoff berth would have exceeded expectations, while a playoff miss (what actually happened) didn't hurt so bad. In short, TANY takes away the sting. But don't take a Cubs fan's word for it. Try it out yourself. This January, when you don't keep your New Year's resolution to drop 10 or 15 pounds, satiate yourself with a big éclair and a nice dose of TANY.

And it doesn't have to be TANY all the time. It could be TANJ, for when you lose your job to outsourcing. Or TANL, for when you need a liver transplant because you took chapter 2 of this book to heart.

Perhaps the most important aspect of this "next" philosophy is that it doesn't involve the "how" factor. If you tell a friend you're going to be a more attractive person Next Year, he or she may ask you exactly how you plan to achieve that. Who cares? The point is that you'll be more attractive, dammit. Cubs fans don't ask themselves how the team is going to assemble a World Series roster during the off-season. That would completely undermine TANY by creating doubts and concerns about the future. Besides, the "how" can be figured out later because Next Year is great for that, too.

Chapter 1

Quiz

1. You just found out your spouse wants a divorce. You should:
    A) Jump off a bridge
    B) Murder said spouse for insurance money
    C) Denounce all members of the opposite sex
    D) Hope for a more committed mate next time around

2. What's the best way to deal with mounting credit card debt?
    A) Declare bankruptcy
    B) Promise yourself that you'll pay off your bills Next Year
    C) Borrow money from a close friend or relative
    D) Rob a bank and/or convenience store

3. Which of these statements is accurate?
    A) Live for today
    B) Live for tomorrow
    C) Carlos Marmol was underrated

Answers
1. D; 2. B; 3. B

If Not a Championship, Beer Will Make It Better!™

Historically, the Cubs haven't exactly built a reputation as huge spenders. Over the past century of futility, long-suffering fans often blamed this lack of financial investment for rosters that have routinely flirted with 100 losses per season.

Then, in the early 2000s, something changed. Suddenly, the Cubs regularly boasted one of the top payrolls in either league, including contracts like the $136 million whopper to Alfonso Soriano, the fifth-largest deal in major league history at the time. To many people around Chicago, the bigger, bolder payrolls were a sign of better things to come: wins, division championships, maybe even a World Series.

But better things don't always happen in Wrigleyville, a place where pennant dreams go to die. Indeed, as every Cubs fan knows, there's only one surefire way to make things better: drinking beer.

This seems like an obvious one, but too many Americans ignore the magic of beer. Whether they've turned to prescription drugs like Prozac and Oxycontin or simply prefer to wallow through their misery as sober fools, they're underestimating just how good you feel when you're drunk. Even a slight buzz can turn the biggest frown upside down. Just ask former Cub Todd Hundley.[1]

A primary reason for the Cubs fan's fascination with beer is location. Chicago is a beer-drinking town, nestled in the heart of the Midwest. If ever there was a part of the country that could use a couple drinks to make things a little more interesting, it's a state like Illinois. Flat land can make you extremely thirsty. The same can be said for daily life in any of Chicago's suburbs, nice, boring places like Schaumburg and Naperville that have more shopping malls than residents per square mile. Of the 35 billion gallons of beer consumed annually in the world, roughly half of them are imbibed in the greater Chicago area, you gotta figure. In fact, it's not uncommon for some midwest-erners to have a few Bud Lights before heading off to work, or if it is uncommon, it doesn't seem so. Chicago is a lot like Boston, if Boston could handle its liquor.

But why?

Why does Chicago love beer so much? Theories abound. One suggests it's much easier to handle the ridiculous Chicago climate under the influence of alcohol. If you're over the age of eight, you simply can't be sober and happy in 10-degree November weather. Luckily, beer has a way of warming up the extremities. Some people even believe that Chicago's fondness for alcohol can be traced back to the 1920s, right about the time the Cubs began finding

---

1. If you think this is a cheap shot, you obviously never hung around Piano Man Lounge on Clark Street after Cubs home games in 2001 or 2002.

themselves on the wrong side of a winning record with unfortunate regularity. This seems the most likely scenario.

Did You Know?

When you black out, you don't remember anything, including all of your problems.

No matter the reason, the bottom line is that Chicagoans from 79th and Phillips to Sheffield and Armitage all enjoy downing a few pints every four or five hours. With the swilling gene already in them, Cubs fans have taken beer drinking to epic proportions. Part of it is recreational (nothing says baseball like a $6 Old Style, except maybe a $7 Budweiser), but the majority of the boozing is therapeutic in nature. Cubs fans have discovered one of life's irrefutable truths: Beer Will Make It Better!™

It doesn't even matter what *it* is. Who worries about a three-run deficit in the bottom of the ninth inning when

Practical Application

Problem: You feel old.

Solution: Try a drinking game. Nothing makes you feel young and immature like a good round of Quarters. If you're drinking alone, maybe the Hour of Power is more up your alley. The point is that just because you happen to be old, it doesn't mean you have to feel that way. Every drunk person in the world acts the same age: 18. The more beers you drink, the closer you get to that age. If you're 21, it only takes one or two. But if you're 43, it'll be a good eight or nine bottles of Miller Lite before you're running naked through Wrigleyville, wishing you were back in college.

Goin' Deep:
Plato Was a Lush for a Reason

Legendary Greek philosopher Plato is credited with perhaps the most inspired drinking quote of all time: "He was a wise man who invented beer."

Unfortunately, Plato didn't elaborate on this belief in any of his writings, suggesting he may have uttered the famous phrase moments before getting annihilated at the local bath house with a few of his students. Still, Plato clearly ascribed to the Beer Will Make It Better!™ philosophy, as the following fictional-but-entirely-probable dialogue demonstrates:

Final Lesson

Plato: Well if it isn't Aristotle, my favorite pupil. This is quite the rager you've thrown for my retirement.

Aristotle: I just hope we have enough beer.

Plato: Simple Aristotle. In this day of strife, persecution and abhorrent hygiene, can you ever really have enough beer?

Aristotle: No, I suppose not.

Plato: Indeed. Consider that my final lesson. You are now ready to be a great philosopher.

See? Even way back in the 4th century BC, the world's finest minds knew the magical qualities of beer. One can only imagine how drunk Plato would get if he was a modern day Cubs fan.

they've had 12 beers? It's enough to keep your eyes open at that point.

The following is what typically happens during a game at Wrigley Field. The opposing team scores more runs than the Chicago Cubs. This results in what baseball purists call "a loss." Losses can be depressing, especially if they are the kinds of losses the Cubs bring upon themselves. These involve mental errors, physical errors, blown saves, runners left in scoring position, strikeouts, missed signs, wild pitches, passed balls, double plays, injuries, managerial mistakes, poor relay throws, and awful base running. The cumulative effects of such blunders could ruin anyone's day. So why do Cubs fans always seem so happy after their team suffers yet another agonizing defeat? Booze.

There are approximately 1,924 pubs and taverns within a three-block radius of Wrigley Field, and each is stocked to the brim with ice-cold beer. From tallboys of domestic swill to Stella Artois on tap, Cubs fans have a myriad of options to lift their postgame spirits. It's pretty difficult to care about 1/162 of a season when you're sucking down the sweet nectar of the gods alongside a throng of cheerful yuppies—many of whom are scantily clad women you just know would be willing to go home with anyone with a pulse.

While beer might not be the long-term answer to all of life's problems, it's the perfect short-term solution to quite a few of them. This is not strictly a modern phenomenon. The ancient Egyptians, the first beer drinkers in recorded history, knew the benefits of a good brew. After all, nothing helps you unwind from a long day slaving at the pyramid like a nice, lukewarm jug of Tutankhamen's Best.[2] The Egyptians also drank beer to make themselves feel better about not having cable television and proper plumbing. In medieval times, the French were known to get sauced on a regular basis, probably to make up for a lack of women who shaved their armpits. Many people in France drink for similar reasons today. Likewise, beer can help you deal with your own daily annoyances. Maybe you aren't happy with your job, your car, or your spouse.

Not to worry. Beer will make them all better! Beer can turn your sad, rusty Chevy into a...well, you won't be able to see the rust, anyway. And when was the last time you heard a drunk guy complain that his lady wasn't hot enough for him? Never. Just like beer makes a blown save acceptable, it makes an ugly girlfriend or wife acceptable, too. The opposite also holds true: any average, balding Joe can be as smooth as George Clooney if you look at him after 60 ounces of Heineken.

---

2. Unless you preferred Sphinx Light, of course.

Top 5 Beers Cubs Fan Love

5) Bud Light—You can't get more American than the King of Beers, but you also can't drink 12 regular Budweisers in seven innings (it's way too filling), so Cubs fans often choose the Light version, which will get you just as drunk with half the calories.

4) Heineken—Cubs fans know the best way to impress the ladies is with a high-class foreign blend: a Mai Tai. The second-best option is an import beer, and this is the only one they sell at Wrigley—unless you count Guinness, which they probably give away free in the skyboxes to "friends of the Cubs" from companies like Boeing and Accenture.

3) Pabst Blue Ribbon—Sure, it might be the most bitter beer this side of Keystone Light, but at least there's a fancy blue ribbon on the can. That screams quality.

2) Old Style—It's local. It's bad. It even comes with instant "saloon breath." What more could 40,000 drunk fans ask for?

1) "The Special"—All other beers pale in comparison to whatever costs the least—or comes cheapest by the bucket.

"But how can beer actually make my life better?" is what you're probably thinking.

Technically, it can't. It simply creates the illusion of betterness. And illusion is the foundation of every Cubs fan's approach to life.

So drink up. That's what they do in the bleachers.

Chapter 2

1. You just got fired from your job as a bank teller. What's the first thing you do?
   A) Purchase a shotgun at the nearest Wal-Mart
   B) Tell your spouse
   C) Update your résumé
   D) Get so drunk you can't remember why there's a cardboard box with all your work stuff on the bar stool next to you

2. How many beers does it take for a 200-pound man to forget all his problems?
   A) 11
   B) 8
   C) 2
   D) 5

3. Which of these statements is accurate?
   A) Beer just makes things worse
   B) Not having beer just makes things worse
   C) Being sober is fun!

Answers
1. D; 2. A; 3. B

The Heckler

Everybody Needs a Scapegoat (Or Even Just a Goat)

When the Chicago Cubs didn't make the 2004 playoffs because of a 2–7 record over the final nine games of the season, it wasn't the fault of Sammy Sosa, Kerry Wood, or even LaTroy Hawkins, the team's combustible closer. Nor was it because easygoing manager Dusty Baker failed to press the right buttons down the stretch.

According to Cubs fans, it was all because of a billy goat named Murphy. If you believe the legend, this smelly, lovable farm animal has been behind every Cubs collapse over the past six decades, causing blown saves, botched ground balls, and various other forms of North Side choking.

And did I mention that this goat's been dead for more than 50 years?[1]

For all you non-Cubs fans who happen to be gleaning this book for valuable life lessons, here's the abbreviated story of what happened the last time the Chicago Cubs played in the World Series, from Wikipedia:

---

1. Presumably.

William "Billy Goat" Sianis, a Greek immigrant who owned a nearby tavern, had two $7.20 box seat tickets to Game 4 of the 1945 World Series between the Chicago Cubs and the Detroit Tigers and decided to bring his pet goat, Murphy, with him. Sianis and the goat were allowed into Wrigley Field and even paraded about on the playing field before the game before ushers intervened. They were led off the field. After a heated argument, both Sianis and the goat were permitted to stay in the stadium, occupying the box seat for which he had tickets. However, before the game was over, Sianis and the goat were ejected from the stadium at the command

The late Bill Sianis's nephew, Sam (left), and his son, Tom, bring a descendent of Bill Sianis's infamous goat to Wrigley Field prior to the start of a game on October 14, 2003. Don't believe in karma? The game played that night is now known as the Bartman Game.

Practical Application

Problem: You accidentally ran over the neighbor's gerbil.

Solution: Wow, that's a tricky one. On the one hand, your neighbor deserves the truth. On the other, it's not like anyone's going to launch a full investigation to see who did Mr. Puffles in. Here's what you do. First, you utilize a scapegoat to make yourself feel better. In this case, the obvious cause of the problem was the gerbil, who never should have been mingling around your driveway. Unfortunately, while blaming the rodent will improve your mood, it probably wouldn't do much for your neighbor's disposition, so now you'll need a secondary scapegoat. Not to worry. The answer is written all over the gerbil: tire tracks. Those tires could belong to any of the cars that have driven up and down the street today. So just put on a sympathetic face, knock on your neighbor's door, and calmly explain that you saw a large SUV hit their gerbil in the middle of the street (where you just finished moving the animal with a shovel). This way your neighbor knows his pet is dead, but the two of you can still be friends.

of Cubs owner Philip Knight Wrigley due to the animal's objectionable odor. Sianis was outraged at the ejection and placed a curse upon the Cubs that they would never win another pennant or play in a World Series at Wrigley Field again (Sianis died in 1970). The Cubs lost Game 4 and eventually the 1945 World Series; worse yet, following a third-place finish in the National League in 1946, the Cubs would finish in the league's second division for the next 20 consecutive years, this streak finally

A black cat was to blame for the Cubs' 1969 late-season collapse, so when Jeromy Burnitz spotted this feline at Wrigley Field in June 2005, the Cubs threw in the towel en route to a 79–83 season.

Notable Quote

Question: Do you believe in the Curse of the Billy Goat?

Mantegna: I don't believe there's a curse. There's an aura of defeat over the team. It's been there for nearly 100 years. It's tough. It makes a huge mental block. In terms of the Cubs, as close as they come, they get a crack in the dike, the trickle of water becomes a flood. You sit there and ask, "Can this be?" But it can be overcome. It's got to be. We wouldn't be Cubs fans if we didn't believe.

—celebrity Cubs fan Joe Mantegna

ending in 1967, the year after Leo Durocher became the club's manager. Since that time, the cursed Cubs have not won a National League pennant or played in a World Series at Wrigley Field—the longest league championship drought in Major League Baseball history.

As interesting as that may be, most people don't really believe some Goat Curse is keeping the Chicago Cubs out of the fall classic. But we're not dealing with most people, are we? We're dealing with Cubs fans, the same folks who blame their team's 1969 collapse on a black cat and the 2003 downfall on an overzealous fan in the stands. Should you ask them to clarify either of those debacles, the die-hard Cubs faithful would probably claim the goat was somehow behind both, haunting the franchise from the big petting zoo in the sky.

The point? It doesn't matter if the curse is plausible. All that matters is that Cubs fans are more than willing to

Top Five Cubs Curses You Didn't Know Existed

5) The Curse of Tommy John—Every year at least one Cubs pitcher must undergo (or be returning from) this very serious elbow surgery. Recent victims include Kerry Wood, Jon Lieber, Scott Williamson, Ryan Dempster, Rod Beck, Will Ohman, and Chad Fox. The curse has even affected nonpitchers, like former Cub Tony Womack.

4) The Ghost of Gary Scott—The most famous Cubs bust who's not named Corey Patterson, Gary Scott, is still alive, but his spirit has found a way to kill the future of every position player prospect who has dared to don Cubbie blue since the early 1990s.

3) Cell Phone Arm—One of the few curses that afflicts the fans, Cell Phone Arm forces seemingly normal people to flail like wild monkeys when they're told (by the person they're on the phone with) that the WGN cameras have found them.

2) The Cash-Cow Curse—As long as the Cubs continue to be a limitless piggy bank for their owners, with the fans filling Wrigley Field rain or shine, nothing will change. Except maybe the amount of advertising sold in the ballpark.

1) Wrigley Field Goggles—Beer goggles have nothing on their baseball-based cousins, Wrigley Field Goggles, which make 40,000 people watching bad baseball think they're watching good baseball just because they happen to be sitting in a historic ballpark.

believe in it, giving them the power to blame anything on a scapegoat. Which, in this case, just happens to be an actual goat.

You, too, can employ this tactic in your life. From your own shortcomings and mistakes to random acts of God, you'll soon be able to gloss over the real causes of your problems. The first step is to

Did You Know?

In the late 1980s, a popular Milli Vanilli song prompted many people to blame all their problems on the rain. It didn't work, and one of the guys in the duo ended up killing himself because of it. Lesson? Never blame it on the rain, just to be safe.

come up with a scapegoat. It can be a person, an inanimate object, or perhaps a memory from your childhood.[2] In a perfect world, the scapegoat would somehow relate to the problem, but it's not always necessary. If baseball outcomes can be blamed on a dead billy goat, surely your troubles can be blamed on...your overbearing boss.

You got in a car accident on the expressway? Well, maybe if you weren't so angry at your stupid supervisor at work you would have been able to focus on the road and avoid the crash.

Your wife overcooked the chicken? Of course she did. How was she supposed to know your boss would keep you at work so late? Call it the Curse of the Boss, and blame

---

2. Memories from your childhood should be saved for extreme circumstances, like when you're accused of murder. Because if you try to claim that your dad forcing you to hunt when you were 12 somehow caused you to run that red light back there...it probably won't work. But it'll make a lot more sense if you're accused of being a sniper.

him for your sudden weight gain, too. It might not fix the problem, but it sure will make you feel better about eating yet another chocolate cupcake for breakfast.

If it sounds silly or trite or just plain dumb, you're missing the point. Blame first. Ask questions later. Let's say you just got dumped. Would you rather face the fact that you and your aforementioned face are totally undesirable or blame the whole thing on the mirror you broke in the bathroom that morning?

Chapter 3

Quiz

1. You passed gas in the elevator. What do you do?
   A) Claim responsibility for that bad boy
   B) Start whistlin' "Dixie"
   C) Hit the emergency stop button
   D) Ask the guy next to you if he had burritos for lunch

2. If you get caught cheating on your spouse, you should:
   A) Blame it on evolutionary instincts
   B) Call it the Curse of the Broken Zipper, then shrug
   C) Denounce the devil for making you do it
   D) Any of the above—they're all great

3. Which of these statements is accurate?
   A) You have nobody to blame but yourself
   B) Everyone's a suspect but you
   C) Honesty is always the best policy

Answers
1. D; 2. D; 3. B

The Heckler

It's Not Over until You're Mathematically Eliminated

How long can you hold out hope?

If you're like a Cubs fan, as long as the numbers allow. For the past 10 decades, these people have been waiting until the last possible moment before declaring it time to get ready for Next Year. The Cubs could be 19 games behind the St. Louis Cardinals with just 20 games to go, but they've still technically got a shot to make the post-season. It's still mathematically possible, and that's what truly matters.

When I was a kid, I was a master of holding out hope. While all the White Sox fans in the family[1] were busy making fun of me for still believing in my beloved Cubs at the end of August (any August, unfortunately), I was diligently working the math.

---

1. Sadly, I come from a broken baseball home. My mom's side of the family is all Cubs, and my dad's side is all Sox. I was actually a White Sox fan until 1983, when I abruptly switched allegiances and decided to start rooting for the Cubs. This was due in large part to the fact that I was only six and had no rationale for doing anything. Much of the blame also belongs to WGN.

"If the Cubs win 20 in a row and the Cardinals lose 19 of 20, we would be in first place," I'd say. "Providing the Cincinnati Reds play at or below .500 for the next three weeks."

It might seem a little far-fetched to an outsider, but Cubs fans know the twisted logic only too well. Had I shared such calculations with other "believers," they probably would've given my formulas serious consideration. And why not? It all made sense on the page. By removing variables like players and injuries and poor coaching, all that was left were the numbers. Numbers that could be worked, massaged, and twisted to help my team reach the postseason.

Before you question my methods, consider my madness: if there's one thing Cubs fans understand, it's knowing exactly when their team has officially been eliminated from the playoffs. Years of evolution have made this an innate ability. As I write this very sentence, the Cubs are 19 games behind the Pirates (the stinking Pirates!) and 16 games under .500, and this year was supposed to be a step forward for the club. To some, the 2013 season is over. To the math, it's Central Division all the way, baby! There are still seven weeks left, which is plenty of time for the Cubs to make up 20 or 30 games, let alone a measly 19.

So how does this help you? How can the fuzzy math of being a Chicago Cubs fan change your life? Easy. It will give you hope. But not just a little bit of hope. You probably have that much already, even if you're a Milwaukee Brewers fan. I'm talking about a boatload of the stuff, enough to combat a lifetime's worth of insurmountable odds. Imagine a more confident you, a you that laughs in the face of failure right up until the moment you actually fail. The lesson here isn't to devise mathematical equations that will make it possible for you to land that perfect job. That really wouldn't work. The moral of the Cubs fan's story is to believe as long as possible, which in itself is a noble goal.

Let's say you're an unemployed investment banker, seven days removed from an interview with Goldman Sachs, and you still haven't heard back—even after you sent a brilliantly worded thank-you email. Two things are happening here. One: you really want the job. It's Goldman Sachs, the New York Yankees of the financial investment industry. And two: you are starting to worry. By any measure, a full week is a long time not to hear anything regarding your status. Prospective employers don't usually make their favorite candidates wait, so the odds of you sitting in a corner office in Manhattan anytime soon are pretty remote.

Screw the odds.

What have they done for you lately? Probably less than Janet Jackson, and clearly not enough if you're still

Practical Application

Problem: You're a 35-year-old female, and you're beginning to think you'll never get married.

Solution: Actually, you're pretty much mathematically eliminated at this point. Refer to chapter 2.

Goin' Deep: You Can't Mathematically Eliminate Logic

L et's take a detour into the world of logical possibility. Again, Cubs fans can breathe easier thanks to the work of thousands of philosophers who have dedicated their lives to thinking through these issues. This is a simple synopsis, but, in logic, philosophers break down propositions like this:

> **True propositions:** These are true in the actual world, the world we know (i.e., "The Cubs did not make the playoffs in 2013.").

> **False propositions:** These are false in the actual world, the world we know (i.e., "The Cubs won the World Series in 2013.").

> **Necessary propositions:** These are true in any world that we can imagine (i.e., "All unmarried men are bachelors.").

> **Impossible propositions:** These cannot be true in any world we can imagine (i.e., "Starlin Castro and Anthony Rizzo are both taller than each other at the same time.").

Now take the proposition, "The Cubs and the Brewers must each win the 16 games they play against each other if the Cubs are to make the playoffs." Ridiculous. In any world we can imagine, it cannot be possible that the Cubs and the Brewers each win the games they play against each other—it's illogical.

It's an impossible proposition.

> However, let's look at the proposition, "The Cubs will win the next 29 games, which will allow them to make the playoffs." Granted, this may be a false proposition—I mean it seems unlikely, after all—but it's not an impossible proposition. We can imagine a world in which it could be that this proposition is the case. So, you know...you never know.
>
> This world might also be one in which Starlin Castro pays attention for nine consecutive innings.

unemployed. But instead of giving up on Goldman Sachs, hold out some hope. Maybe all the top decision-makers are at another one of those corporate get-togethers in the Cayman Islands. Or maybe there's a bitter power struggle going on as the executives decide who to hire, with three people in your favor and just two holdouts left. While there's only one possible negative reason you haven't been contacted by your interviewer (you aren't going to be hired), there are literally thousands of possible positive reasons to hold out hope. In order to make room for your fabulous new salary, they could be dispensing with a few superfluous vice presidents and their huge bonuses. They could be preparing your office; marble floors take time to install. It's not entirely inconceivable that they have already hired you—you just don't know it yet. At least that's what you should be thinking, because your goal is to postpone giving up as long as you can.

That way, when your friends and family ask how the job search is going, you can honestly tell them you're awaiting good news from a certain company called Goldman

Bleacher Bum

Sachs. Maybe they've heard of it? Yeah, that's right. You bet they have. And what happens if another prospective employer calls two weeks from now? Normally, you wouldn't mention the fact you didn't get the last

Did You Know?

Unbeknownst to Cubs fans, Magic Number refers to the number of games you have to win to decide whether you'll be playing in October.

job you interviewed for. But if you think like a Chicago Cubs fan, you could say something like this:

"Oh, hello KPMG! I'd love to interview with you. I expect to hear back from Goldman Sachs about a recent meeting that went extremely well, but I've always been interested in talking with you guys. The timing couldn't be better."

You see? It's that easy.

Chapter 4

Quiz

1. It's been two whole days, and the jury is still out. You should:
   A) Decide whose "girlfriend" you want to be in prison
   B) Change your plea to, "Just sentence me already!"
   C) See if that involuntary manslaughter offer is still on the table
   D) Assume they're debating between not guilty and "way innocent"

2. Why hasn't your date from last week called you back yet?
   A) You smell funny
   B) Nobody wants a crazy person with a glandular problem
   C) You have all the personality of a rock
   D) He/she has been out of town on business and is bound to call any minute now

3. Which of these statements is accurate?
   A) It's not over until the fat lady sings
   B) Who cares about a fat lady?

Answers

1. D; 2. D; 3. B

The

Heckler

CHAPTER 5

Winning Really Isn't Everything

From overzealous NBA fans to angry Little League parents, America is officially obsessed with winning. These days, being a good sport isn't nearly as important as throwing batteries onto the field or knocking out the teeth of the guy whose kid just struck out your son to end the game.

While the rest of the sports world descends into a mess of riots, shouting matches, and obscene gestures, one group of folks is just happy to be at the game: Cubs fans. Oh, sure, there are a few bad apples in every bunch. But just because a couple hundred angry bleacher fans who aren't willing to put up with the constant losing decide to boo and throw empty beer cups onto the field, that doesn't mean it's representative of all the fans at Wrigley. They don't call it the Friendly Confines for nothing.[1] Most Cubs fans are way more accepting of failure, so they just sit there enjoying baseball, good or bad. And for the first time in recent history, the downtrodden are the only ones who have it right, because they're the only ones who are still

---

1. Actually, as you'll learn in the "Cubs Fan's Glossary" at the end of this book, "Friendly Confines" is probably a nickname given to Wrigley Field by opposing teams because it's so easy to win there.

35

having a good time, win or lose. Cubs fans understand there's more to baseball than winning.

Like eating an entire tray of cheese-drenched nachos in one inning. Or finding out the paunchy fan next to you has been to 184 home games in a row and has missed only nine contests in the last decade. That's interesting stuff, and it can make an otherwise sorry loss worthwhile. You might even get to hear firsthand about a game the Cubs actually won. Too many people think the final score determines the overall experience of the game, as if the Chicago Cubs losing 8–2 somehow turns a sunny day gray or negates the great time you had drinking Old Style with your friends all afternoon long.

Winning really isn't the only thing. It's a bonus.

Some people might argue that a fan who roots for a losing franchise isn't a very smart fan, but you have to

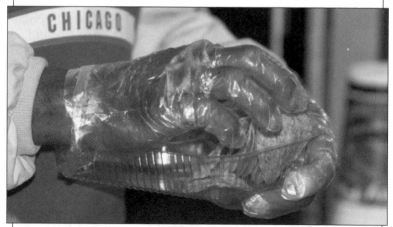

So what if the Cubs are losing again? You can't get nachos like these at home. *Photo courtesy of Getty Images.*

be pretty crafty in the head to continually enjoy Cubs baseball. The team goes out of its way to make the people in the stands miserable, and the fans keep finding ways

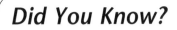

Did You Know?

Losing doesn't make you a loser unless you were a loser to begin with.

to enter and leave the Wrigley Field gates with smiles on their faces. Who do you think is smarter? The New York Yankees fan, who can't be happy just getting to the World Series, or the average Chicago Cubs fan, who can somehow manage to have the best summer of his life watching his team finish 17 games out of first place?

Which brings us to the statement you probably expected to see much earlier in this book: life is like baseball.[2] Just as people lose sight of what's truly important when it comes to sports, so, too, do they miss the point in everything else. What it means to "win" in life is different for everybody. For a person living in rural Ohio, it might mean keeping the farm in the family for one more generation. For a 21-year-old Northwestern graduate living in Wicker Park, it could be landing a job with IBM, Citibank, or some other stuffy company that pays exceedingly well. My friend is a good example, actually. For the purposes of this book, let's call him Jake. Jake wants to be a rock star. He's played the guitar since he was 11 years old in the hopes of someday jamming on a stage in front of 50,000 people. Then, after the show, he would love nothing more

---

2. If you were waiting for something hilariously negative about White Sox fans, you can find that in chapter 7.

Goin' Deep:
Is Struggling a Good Thing?

Even in the worst sorts of hell, shreds of solace can sometimes be found. Consider French existentialist author Albert Camus's take on the myth of Sisyphus. Sisyphus, a terrible murderer, was condemned to an eternity of pushing a giant boulder up a mountain only to have it roll back down each time he reached the top. Camus was using the analogy to describe modern life (he was discouraging suicide), but if this sort of fate doesn't adequately fit the futility of Cubs fandom, I'm not sure what does. I mean, you have a doomed soul, an eternal struggle, and a baseball-shaped object.

Anyway, despite Sisyphus's existential horror, in the end Camus argues that it's the process itself—the rolling the rock up the hill—that gives meaning to his life. So while the end result is meaningless (the rock is going to roll back down just as surely as the Cubs will crumble), the eternal struggle is the very point of it all. Which may explain

French existentialist writer Albert Camus gestures as if to say, "What's done is done, there's always next year." *Photo courtesy of Bettmann/CORBIS.*

why so many Cubs fans show up to games in September even when the club is 12 games out of the wild-card spot.

One cautionary note, however: Camus did think this angst-ridden existence was best kept to the back of our minds. While our day-to-day struggles may be the only point to life, it's probably not wise to contemplate them.

than to go backstage and have sex with eight or nine groupies.

Jake currently works part-time as a UPS package handler. In between night shifts down at the distribution center, Jake plays shows at local venues like the Elbo Room, Beat Kitchen, and the Cubby Bear. Now, Jake could let this get him down. To him, winning is playing the big stage with the postshow sexfest, and to the best of my knowledge, he's yet to sleep with groupie number one. By any stretch of the imagination, Jake is losing, or at least tied. If Jake were living life like a Yankees fan, he probably wouldn't be too happy. In fact, he might have ended it all years ago. Yet that's hardly the case. The last time I saw Jake, he was rip-roaring drunk and smiling from ear to ear. Why? Had he finally booked that gig at the United Center? Had The Lumineers personally requested that he open for them? Nope. He was just happy about the three-day weekend. It was a holiday, you see, and Jake likes to sleep in. It sounds trivial, but that's the whole point. While Jake could be busy hating his "losing" existence, he's having a ball. Jake's extra four hours of holiday sleep are the Cubs fan's tray of nachos.

Lincoln Park Trixie

To paraphrase a famous quote: it isn't whether you win or lose, it's how much you enjoy the game. If you're not careful, you could get so wrapped up in losing that you don't even appreciate the game itself. And by game, I really mean life, if you haven't figured that out already.

Chapter 5

1. That guy in the SUV beat you to the parking space. This means:
    A) You should give up now and drive home like the failure you are
    B) He's the only one getting groceries today
    C) Life has frowned on you
    D) You get to spend more time in your air-conditioned car

2. Which of these statements is accurate?
    A) If you don't win, you lose
    B) If you don't win, you're still drunk and/or have a belly full of cotton candy

Answers

1. D; 2. B

The Heckler

Loyaltiness Is Next to Godliness

Nobody likes a traitor. Whether you're an international spy who turns on your native country or a Chicago Cubs fan who decides to start cheering for the St. Louis Cardinals, there is absolutely no honor in switching sides. Sure, it would be nice to root for a team that actually wins more often than it loses, but changing allegiances is a serious offense that will ultimately leave you feeling hollow and dirty.

At the very least, it will alienate you from your friends. One day you're wearing Cubbie blue, and the next day you've got a Yadier Molina jersey on your back. What are your friends supposed to take away from that, other than the fact you clearly have no character and are completely untrustworthy. And for what? A cheap thrill? One of the biggest misconceptions in life is that the grass is always greener on the

The newlywed Burtons of Vincennes, Indiana, show that—although rare—mixed marriages can work.

other side. But sometimes it isn't. Sometimes it's covered with weeds and dog shit. Coincidentally, that kind of grass can often be found in Missouri. Now, obviously, there are clear benefits to being a Cardinals fan. The winning. The professional play. The joy of heckling lesser teams.[1]

But it's not all great. Much like Chicago White Sox fans, the people of St. Louis have their own stigmas. They are

---

1. Admittedly, this is one benefit that would almost be worth switching allegiances for—but only almost. In 2006, for example, the Cubs were the worst team in the National League. This meant North Side fans couldn't even heckle the Brewers or Pirates, and that's just sad.

Sad but True (but Really Fake) Loyalty Factoid

Unfortunately, according to an online survey done by theheckler.com, Chicago was home to 1,174 defections in 2005 following the White Sox's impressive march to and through the World Series. While the majority of Cub Nation remained steadfast in its loyalty to the one true Chicago franchise, some fringe fans were taken in by the surprising South Siders. The amazing offense, timely pitching, and couldn't-miss coaching were exactly what these North Side fans had been looking for in a team all their lives. Manager Ozzie Guillen's charisma alone was responsible for nearly 500 of the conversions. Conservative estimates suggest 80 percent of those defectors already regret their decision, but it's too late, as they are already covered in tattoos.

The unfamiliar glitter of a world championship was too alluring for more than 1,000 defecting Cubs fans in 2005.

Did You Know?

Treason is punishable by death in all 50 states, including Illinois. And Chicago is in Illinois.

seen (mostly correctly) as overweight yokels, and the only positive thing these overweight yokels have in their lives is the Cardinals franchise. Is it really worth a few more victories a season to be associated with these people? This Cubs fan doesn't think so.

Regardless, say you do make the change. After a particularly excruciating home losing streak against the New York Mets and Arizona Diamondbacks, you decide enough is enough already, and you buy a Cardinals hat. Congratulations, you're now an overweight yokel.

It gets worse, though, because breaking loyalty in one area of your life shows people what you're really made of: wishy-washiness.

Imagine the parents of your godchild trying to trust you with the care of their newborn baby, while at the same time wondering if you won't just find a better godchild instead, one that's cuter or doesn't smell so much like feet. Or imagine your spouse wondering if you'll trade him or her in the first chance you get. Or imagine your boss not giving you the big promotion because he just doesn't feel like he can trust you anymore.

If you live like a Cubs fan, however, you don't run the risk of alienating anyone, because you will embody loyalty in all its forms. So the next time you pledge your devotion to a loved one, you must honor that pledge, no matter how many times he disappoints you. You also won't turn your back on an alcoholic friend. Hell, you won't even

Wrigley Granny

turn your back on a friend who stole your lawnmower. That's how dedicated you should be. Remember, loyalty isn't always pretty, but it certainly beats the alternative: wishy-washiness.

Chapter 6

Quiz

1. You're thinking of becoming a St. Louis Cardinals fan. You should:
   A) Totally go for it, and buy some overalls while you're at it
   B) Reconsider, because being a Cincinnati fan is pretty sweet, too
   C) Buy a kitchen knife with a Cardinals logo on the handle, then stab all your friends in the back with it
   D) Have a few more beers. There's Always Next Year

2. Which of these statements is accurate?
   A) Friends don't let friends switch teams
   B) Friends are for suckers
   C) Friends are not nearly as important as Yadier Molina

Answers

1. D; 2. A

The Heckler

At Least You're Not a Sox Fan[1]

No matter how bad it gets for Cubs fans, it could always be worse. They could be White Sox fans. True, the White Sox won the World Series in 2005, ending an 88-year drought between championships and stomping all over the hearts of Cubs fans in the process. It was an exciting season for the South Siders as their team was in first place every day of the year, then went on to cruise through the playoffs with a 15–1 record. The pitching was sensational, with the Sox starters going deep into every ballgame and actually completing four games in the NLCS against the Anaheim Angels. This was especially difficult for the Cubs faithful to swallow; we were supposed to be the ones with the pitching. Unfortunately, the North Side is home to more pitching busts than Coors Field. So on the one hand we have the Sox, World Champs. On the other end of the spectrum we have the Cubs, who most certainly did not win the World Series in 2005. Or 2013. Or any other year since 1908. This should make it infinitely better to be a White Sox fan right now.

---

1. Zing!

Sox fan William Ligue had himself something of a Bartman moment when he inexplicably ran onto the field and attacked Royals first-base coach Tom Gamboa in 2002.

Not to be outdone, this Sox fan tried to bag a Royals first-base coach of his own the following season.

Only it doesn't.

There are three reasons for this. First, rooting for the Sox is not without its disadvantages. The moment you put on a White Sox jersey,

Did You Know?

The average Sox fan spends at least six months of his life in prison.

you must also put on the stigma that goes along with it. When you walk down the street, people in Chicago no longer think of you as a normal person. They think of you as a stereotype: poor, obnoxious, blue collar, uneducated, and ready to rush the field so you can attack a Kansas City Royals base coach.[2] You are a threat to society, capable of wreaking havoc at a moment's notice. Now, to be fair, not all Sox fans fit that profile. I once heard about a Sox fan who almost finished community college.[3]

See?

See that joke I made?

South Siders get no respect in this town, especially from North Siders like me. My own father is a White Sox fan, yet I have no qualms lumping him in with the rest of them (so long as he doesn't read this book—sorry Pops!).

The second reason it's no fun being a Sox fan is simple: only like five or six of them have been around since before October 2005. While Wrigley Field routinely sells out, U.S.

---

2. For more info, simply Google "William Ligue."
3. This Sox fan was named Joey Malonecki. Sadly, he was just two semesters short of graduating when he impregnated his girlfriend, Desiree, forcing him to quit school and get a full-time job at a local hardware store. On the bright side, he didn't have to worry about studying during the 2005 playoffs. He spent all his time gettin' ripped!

Cellular Field is one of those places where you can hear your voice echo, like in an empty hallway or a bathroom. Despite the fact that they were in first place the entire 2005 season, the White Sox rarely sold out the stadium, probably because so many people were worried about being associated with everyone else at the park. "Oh, I'm not that kind of fan," the casual White Sox fan often tells himself. "I'm different."

Unfortunately, they're the only ones who think that.

The last (and most important) reason it's tough being a Sox fan is that it means you can't be a Cubs fan. In Chicago, you are one or the other. Period. And while we've already discussed what a Sox jersey suggests about the person wearing it, a Cubs jersey suggests just the opposite: Cubs fans are seen as wealthy, well-mannered, white collar, and educated. And it's all true.

See?

There I go again.

Practical Application

Problem: Someone just stole your car.

Solution: The fact you even had a car in the first place means you're way better off than those people who ride bikes all over town and then claim they're doing it by choice. "I could totally afford a car if I wanted," one of those bikers might say. "I just prefer being sweaty when I arrive at work, home, or anywhere, really." So at least you're not a pathetic biker. Besides, you have insurance, right? So what's the problem?

But forget Sox fans. Let them write their own book if they care so much.

The point is that no matter how many losses the Chicago Cubs rack up, no matter how many games their bullpen blows, no matter how many times they send fans home wondering what could have been, no matter the final score, no matter the weather, no matter the history, no matter the fact it's July and their season is already over—no matter any of that and so much more, I can always take solace in my Cubbie blue. Because unlike the Sox fan, I have plenty of brethren. Millions of them across the nation. If I move to a new city, you can be sure there's a Cubs bar in town. Unless that new city is Cicero or Beverly, Illinois, the same can't be said for White Sox fans.

Question: Was there ever any doubt between being a Cubs or Sox fan?

Garlin: When I was a kid, I went to a game at Wrigley, and they wouldn't let me bring in my bottle of water. I got so angry that I burned my Die-Hard Cubs Fan Card, and I swore off the Cubs for the Sox. That didn't even last a month.

—*Curb Your Enthusiasm* star Jeff Garlin

Another good thing: nobody asks me if I drive a 1989 Chevy Camaro when I put on my Cubs jersey.

They don't expect me to appreciate their mullets, either.

Being a Cubs fan in Chicago is a little bit like being a handsome older brother. You get all the attention, while the mongrel eight-year-old gets all the dirty looks.

The lesson to be learned from this is simple. There's always someone out there who has it worse than you.

So you think you're a few pounds overweight? Just imagine what it must be like to be one of those people who has to purchase two seats on the airplane because they can't control their Kentucky Fried Chicken intake. At least you're not that guy. At least you're not the guy on the plane with halitosis, either.

Nine out of 10 psychiatrists do not endorse the "Sox fan comparison" as an official treatment for depression, but they should. If 10 shrinks ever actually heard about it, this Cubs fan has no doubt they'd get all their patients on board immediately. The following are just a few times when this technique can lift your spirits.

Top Five Most Common Sox Fan Baby Names

5) Hope
4) Randy
3) Staci
2) King
1) Destiny

If you think you're ugly, just be glad you're not Lyle Lovett.

Got no money? Hey, at least you have a house that isn't made of cardboard, like that guy in the alley next to Starbucks.

Just got fired? Yeah, well you could be Julie from accounting, who had to sleep with Dan "Back Moles" Borden to keep *her* job.

No matter how bad the situation gets, at least you're not a Sox fan.

Chapter 7
Quiz

1. You just got voted "Least Likely to Succeed" by your high school class. You should:
   A) Try to make the best of it by being the biggest damn failure ever
   B) Satiate yourself with a dozen codeine tablets
   C) Prove them wrong by applying to Harvard, despite your 1.74 GPA
   D) Be glad you weren't voted "Least Likely to Marry," like that loser Theodore Rosenblatz

2. You're the only one in the office who didn't get a raise. This means:
   A) You suck at your job
   B) You should really stop getting in at noon
   C) Your stupid boss has it in for you
   D) You should still be happy, because at least you aren't a nine-year-old Chinese kid blow-torching the soles onto Nikes for 50¢ an hour
   E) All of the above

3. Which of these statements is accurate?
   A) At least White Sox fans get to watch a winning team
   B) White Sox fans are too busy changing my oil to have time to watch the game

Answers
1. D; 2. E; 3. B

CHAPTER 8

The
Heckler

The Power of Low Expectations

A wise man once said: "When you hope for the best, anything less sucks."[1] That man was right, because the easiest way to make sure you aren't happy with a particular challenge in life, whether it be a baseball game or an SAT exam, is to place too much faith in a positive outcome.

Chicago Cubs fans know this, which is why they expect to lose every single game. Their team could be up four runs going into the ninth, but the seasoned fan knows a loss is still pretty damn likely, so he doesn't get his hopes up. It's called the Power of Low Expectations.

"Wait, wait, wait," you say. "That's not called the Power of Low Expectations. It's called 'the Cubs are awful.'"

Sure, if you're talking about any year since 1945, the Chicago Cubs may indeed be awful. But if you think that's why their fans have low expectations, you're missing the point. Any team can be bad enough to inspire a defeatist attitude, yet it is a uniquely Cubs phenomenon to trample a fan's hopes and dreams.

---

1. It's possible this has never really been said by anyone.

One of the hallmarks of being a Cubs fan is keeping the proverbial bar low. If you don't expect every routine ground ball or fly ball to be handled, you won't be so disappointed when one gets away.

Practical Application

Problem: The sex wasn't that great.

Solution: What did you expect? You think just because you're cheating on your spouse it's going to be a wild, passionate romp? Those kinds of things only happen in movies, not in room 12B of the Motel 6 on Roosevelt Road. Perhaps you should simply try to be happy about the fact that you still have the ability to pull off an affair without the help of Cialis.

Luckily, Cubs fans have learned to combat it. This problem is commonly referred to as optimism, and it's caused by everyone from Cubs president Theo Epstein to the oddsmakers in Las Vegas casinos. Every year, it seems, the Cubs purport to have a chance at winning a championship. All they needed was a consistent third baseman—and now they have him! Meet Gary Scott,[2] circa 1992. The Cubs finished that season in fourth place, 18 games out of first. All the Cubs needed was some playoff experience—and now they have it! Say hello to your 2004 Chicago Cubs, who finished in third place, 16 games out of first, despite just missing the World Series in 2003.

But it was no biggie, at least not for Cubs fans.

---

2. Hailed by baseball experts as a can't-miss prospect that would finally restore order to third base for the Chicago Cubs, Gary Scott played just 67 games in parts of 1991 and 1992. He notched a .160 batting average in 175 at-bats and was quickly demoted to the minors. He would never make it back to the big leagues.

Notable Quote

Question: If there were a big book of something based on the Cubs, what would it be?

Neyer: Big Book of Dashed Hopes. There's no reason why this team hasn't won more pennants over the years. The fan base is there.

—ESPN writer and *Big Book of Baseball Blunders* author Rob Neyer

We stopped believing the hype decades ago and have learned the Power of Low Expectations. It goes like this: never expect to win. Consider a simple example.

Pretend it's mid-June, and the Cubs are two games in front of St. Louis in the NL Central. (I know this is hard, but really pretend your ass off.) On this particularly pleasant summer evening, the Cubs are playing host to the Houston Astros, the punching bag of the major leagues. The grand old scoreboard in center tells us the Cardinals have already lost their game, meaning the Cubs can separate themselves from the Redbirds if they can just hang on to the three-run lead over the lowly 'Stros. Considering that—in this hypothetical situation—the Cubs have won their last eight games, one is tempted to expect a victory. Did I mention we're in the eighth inning already, and the Cubs pitcher has only surrendered two hits thus far?

You couldn't possibly imagine a better scenario for the Cubs, and that's exactly your problem. Instead of looking at the negatives, you've been caught up in the emotions of the moment and have allowed your expectations to be raised. You expect the Chicago Cubs to win. Over the last 90 years, how many times have the Cubs put distance between themselves and whoever was in second place?

Top Five Reasons to Be a Pessimist

5) By always viewing the glass as half-empty, you always have a reason to get another beer.

4) Sure, good things come to those who wait—in ketchup commercials.

3) If you expect to fail, then the act of failing could really be viewed as...success.

2) Optimism is so '90s.

1) Hope gets shot down all the time, but when was the last time you heard of someone's apathy being trampled?

What are the odds, given their history, that the Cubs starter or bullpen will nail this thing down? What are the chances of the Cubs winning nine games in a row? And finally, now that you're so sure of a victory, how much more will it hurt when they lose?

If only you had reined in your expectations. It's infinitely easier to watch the Cubs blow a game in the late innings when you kinda thought it was going to happen anyway than it is when you thought they were going to win. Both losses hurt, to be sure, but at least one doesn't leave you absolutely crushed.

The same can be said for your career.

After years of being taken for granted by your manager, the old bastard finally retired. With him out of the picture, you were so sure your new boss was going to make everything better. Yep, you'd finally have a chance to shine under this new guy, who gave a totally convincing and motivating speech to the department his first day in charge. But that's not how it worked out, is it? Instead, you got your hopes up for nothing, as the new boss turned out to be even worse than the old boss. Now look at you, more disgruntled than ever and you still have to photocopy tax receipts for a living.

Another great example of the dangers of unrealistic expectations is marriage.

We've finally reached the point in this country where over half of all marriages end in divorce. Let's all pause a moment, as Americans, and congratulate ourselves for

Being a Cubs fan is like getting married. If you go into it expecting a bitter divorce from the start, anything else feels that much more special.

yet another achievement in the field of pursuing our own happiness. The key words here are *our own,* as in not yours. It's gotten so bad you can't even depend

Did You Know?

Mitt Romney actually expected to win the 2012 presidential campaign. Ouch.

on parents to suffer through a rotten marriage for the sake of their children anymore. What's this world coming to?

With a divorce rate topping 50 percent, maybe it's time everyone just lowered their expectations a little bit and agreed to stay together until "something" do us part. You're really setting yourself up for failure if you mention the whole death thing. Surviving better, richer, and good health is a breeze, but if you think you'll make it through worse, poorer, and sickness just as easily, you need to lower the bar because it's not going to happen. Another thing that won't happen is you being able to cope with your divorce if you never thought it was going to occur in the first place.

Confused?

High expectations can do that to a person, leaving you dizzy with feelings of disappointment, failure, and angst. In the future, just expect nothing. You won't be disappointed.

Chapter 8

Quiz

1. The asking price for your Wrigleyville condo is $320,000. This is:
   A) Exactly as much as you paid, and therefore appropriate
   B) Only half of what you could get if you played your cards right
   C) Ridiculous—they could buy three condos for that in Cicero
   D) Going to be really disappointing when you only get $280,000

2. Which of these statements is accurate?
   A) Expect the world
   B) Be happy with stale beer and a kinda-okay spouse

Answers

1. C, D; 2. B

To Boo or Not to Boo

There comes a time in every Cub fan's life when his faith is tested. It's certainly understandable, given the many losing streaks he must endure just to get through each season. Hell, for some fans, this test comes after the very first time they root for the Cubs.[1] But somehow, the die-hard fan is able to rise above the 90 losses and come back Next Year, reenergized and ready for more.

It's a little something Cubs fans call "loyalty." You don't see much loyalty in sports today, with fans eager to jump ship at the first sign of a losing campaign. Take the New York Yankees, for instance. The team goes to the World Series every few years, but you wouldn't know it from the way the fans boo them when they lose two measly games in a row. And God forbid they lose three straight—that's cause for a mutiny. Now, some people will argue that Yankees fans just hold their team to a higher standard

---

1. This happened to my friend Tom, who moved to Chicago from Texas and decided to become a Cubs fan. Unfortunately, the Cubs were blown out 10–1 in the first game he ever attended. They had three errors, one rain delay, and Sammy Sosa struck out four times. And while none of this is actually true, I'm sure you can imagine the scenario, which is what's truly sad.

The Cubs Fan's Guide to Happiness

and the boos are their way of making it clear they've had enough of the mediocre play.

Those people are idiots.

Any fan who boos his own team isn't a real fan.

The majority of North Siders understand this. Admittedly, the last few seasons have brought a rash of boos from the home-field crowd, but they came mainly from the casual attendees, not the die-hards. An unfortunate side effect of a shrine like Wrigley Field is that it draws just as many people looking for a good time as it does people actually interested in watching the game.

The deeper issue is one of consistency. There's no honor in being a fair-weather fan. For those of you not familiar with the term, it refers to someone who is the biggest Chicago Cubs fan in the world when the team is playing

Notable Quote

Question: Do you ever wonder how Cubs fans have managed to stick with it all these years?

Kasper: The thing you learn right off the bat is that although Cubs fans may not always be thrilled with what they see on the field, and they may think, "Here we go again," when something bad happens, they always care. And they care 365 days a year. Every other pro team in Chicago could win a championship in the same year, and the radio airwaves would still be filled with, "I'm concerned about the Cubs' fifth starter." If you're asking me to explain it, I can't, but I do think it's incredibly heartening that in today's disposable society, where everything seems to come and go very quickly, that a fan's bond to a team can remain so strong through a little thick and a lot of thin.

—Cubs TV broadcaster Len Kasper

Fans in the right-field bleachers litter Wrigley Field with beer cups and assorted other debris during an aggravating loss to the lowly Colorado Rockies in 1999.

well, yet will have nothing to do with the Cubs when they play like, well, the Cubs.

Fair-weather fanning is an ugly thing to watch. Seemingly loyal fans suddenly go sour over a little 11-run outburst by the other team (as was the case on July 16, 2006, when the New York Mets scored 11 runs in the sixth inning, causing Wrigley Field to erupt in boos), or a routine five-game losing streak at the hands of lowly clubs like the Minnesota Twins and Colorado Rockies. Next thing you know, foreign objects are raining down from the bleachers, along with a steady stream of boos and obscenities. Do these people have any idea how ridiculous they look booing the very player whose jersey they're wearing?

"You suck, Rizzo!" a fair-weather fan might yell at Cubs first baseman Anthony Rizzo. "I can't believe I paid $75 for your jersey, you bum!"

Yeah, that'll show him.

Checking out
skybox attendant's
cleavage

Necktie loosened
for maximum
"casualness"

Complimentary
champagne,
included with
company's
skybox rental

Honduran cigar
that he claims
is a real Cuban

Remote starter
to brand-new BMW

Ignoring
phone call
from wife

Bottle of
Propecia
hair-growth
pills

Size 8
Ferragamo
dress shoes

Skybox Guest

But the main pitfall of being a fair-weather fan is simple: all of your previous suffering goes to waste. Any credibility you earned by agonizing through awful seasons like 1981 and 1995 is immediately erased from

Did You Know?

Some Cubs fans didn't even know how to boo their own players until relief pitcher LaTroy Hawkins joined the team in 2004. Those people learned fast.

the record once you denounce the team in 2014. You become more than a joke—you become a traitor who can never recapture the purity of being a true die-hard Cubs fan. This might not seem like a big deal, but it will be if the Cubs ever make it to the World Series. That's the single best thing about being a Cubs fan. There's no bandwagon. A team that hasn't won a title in nearly a century just can't have one. As a loyal fan of the Cubs, you can always claim you were there from the start. If by some stroke of luck the Cubs should happen to win it all during your lifetime, that phenomenon will end. The fan base will split in two: one half comprising true Cubs fans, the other a ragtag bunch of bandwagoners and opportunists.

Indeed, nothing in the history of civilization will have been more vindicating for any group of oppressed people than a victory in the World Series would be for Chicago Cubs fans.[2] Even Boston Red Sox faithful would have nothing on us. We would rule the sports world, and all other fans would envy our courage, our struggle, and most of all, our dedication. Who wouldn't want to be a part of

---

2. This may be an exaggeration.

Top Five Most Booed Cubs in Team History

5) Todd Hundley, 2001–02
   Reason: paid $6.5 million per year to hit like two homers
4) Malachi Kittridge, 1890–97
   Reason: couldn't hit his way out of a potato sack
3) Joe Carter (broadcaster), 2001–02
   Reason: he no talk very good
2) Carlos Marmol, 2006–13
   Reason: so much talent, so little control
1) LaTroy Hawkins, 2004–05
   Reason: single-handedly ruined the 2004 Cubs season

Carlos Marmol had a particularly ignitable effect on fans at Wrigley Field.

that? You'd have to be dumb, or a White Sox fan, not to want in on that sweet action.

Finally, how does this apply to life?

Oh.

It doesn't. I just wanted to get some things off my chest, and now that you've already read this chapter, there's nothing you can do about it. Now you feel like a real Cubs fan: a sucker.

Chapter 9
Quiz

1. The fan next to you is booing the Cubs manager. You should:
    A) Disregard this entire chapter, and join right on in
    B) Pretend you don't hear him
    C) Politely ask him to keep it down
    D) Tell security you saw him buy beer for those minors over there

2. Which of these statements is accurate?
    A) You should only root for the Cubs when they win
    B) You should only root for the Cubs and whoever is playing the White Sox or Cardinals

Answers

1. D; 2. B

CHAPTER 10

Sabermetrics?
No, Cubbiemetrics!

According to Wikipedia, Sabermetrics is "the term for the empirical analysis of baseball, especially baseball statistics that measure in-game activity. The term is derived from the acronym SABR, which stands for the Society for American Baseball Research. It was coined by Bill James."

In other words, superfan and statistician James decided to try and quantify the game in a new way, hoping to understand and perhaps even predict success based on numbers and probability.

When the Cubs hired Theo Epstein in 2011 to run the club, they were getting not only a proven front office man—they were also jumping on the Sabermetrics bandwagon.

This is excellent news for Cubs fans.

Because now, instead of focusing on numbers like 106 (years since the Cubs last won the World Series) or 74,021 (third base busts since Ron Santo retired, probably), Sabermetrics hones in on the meta-stats. Anyone looking at the big picture of Cubs baseball over the past century or so would obviously become disheartened. But when you only look at things like Defense-Independent Component ERA (DICE), suddenly turning a franchise around seems more manageable. It's a simple formula after all:

$$DICE = 3.00 + \frac{13HR + 3(BB + HBP) - 2K}{IP}$$

Now, instead of guessing which free-agent pitcher will have the best ERA next season, the Cubs can simply look to the equation. If the Cubs had been using DICE back in the 1980s, you can bet your throwback Greg Maddux jersey the team wouldn't have let the Hall of Famer leave for Atlanta. Unfortunately, personality clashes and money were valued over the stats, and the Cubs were deprived one of the greatest pitchers of all time in the prime of his career.

Let's look at some other ways math can distract from abysmal on-field shenanigans.

Here's a list of the most commonly used Sabermetric stats compared to the ones the Cubs employed before 2011.

Base Runs vs. Coulda Woulda Shouldas

Base Runs (BsR) estimates the number of runs a team "should" have scored given its component offensive statistics, as well as the number of runs a hitter/pitcher creates or allows. Prior to BsR, the Cubs depended on the less accurate stat Coulda Woulda Shoulda (CWD), as in "Boy, the Cubs really Coulda won that game if they didn't hit into a double play with the tying run at third and the winning run at second in the bottom of the ninth, and then they Woulda been less than 12 games back in the division…at least that's what Shoulda happened."

Wins Above Replacement vs. Salary Above Performance

Wins Above Replacement (WAR) determines the value of a player's total contributions to his team based on hitting, fielding, base running, and pitching. It's designed to demonstrate the number of additional wins a player would contribute to a team compared to a "replacement level player" at that position. For example, let's say the Cubs are

trying to decide between signing an over-the-hill catcher, or keeping their current backstop on the team. Thanks to WAR, the decision is simple. You look at the numbers and you select who best helps the team. Unfortunately, Cubs front office people in the pre-Epstein era used Salary Above Performance (SAP). Paradoxically, the team almost always hired the player with the highest salary-to-performance ratio. Typical SAP contracts include those of catcher Todd Hundley, outfielder Alfonso Soriano, and any contract ever given to Neifi Perez.

On-Base Plus Slugging vs. Off-Base Plus Strikeouts

On-Base Plus Slugging (OPS) is the sum of a player's on-base percentage and slugging average. It is used to evaluate a batter's ability to get on base and also hit for power. Elite players often have OPS numbers above .900. These people frequently wear St. Louis Cardinal, New York Yankee, and even Cincinnati Red uniforms. On the North Side of Chicago, however, from 1909 to 2011, the Cubs preferred to emphasize Off-Base Plus Strikeouts (also OPS). This statistic made it easier to see which players got on base the least, combined with their ability to strike out at alarmingly high rates. As those were the attributes valued most highly by the Cubs front office, it's no surprise Cubs players led the league in that statistical category 90 of the past 100 seasons.[1]

---

1. Most likely. It's too painful to actually research the stats and crunch the numbers.

Win Shares vs. Loss Shares

A Win Share represents one-third of a victory. So, if a team wins 90 games (someday, Cubs fans!), then there are 270 total win shares to distribute among the various players. Based on a complex formula, each player is assigned a win share number, making it easier to determine which players to sign, release, and so forth. The Cubs actually used a very similar model for most of the team's history: Loss Shares. On the one hand, this makes a bit of sense. There have certainly been more loss shares to go around than win shares. And maybe it started out as a deterrent. "You don't want more loss shares, do you Shawon? Now get out there and hit over .300 already. That dude in the bleachers has a Shawon-O-Meter and everything!" But at some point, the team seemed to reward loss shares, making the change in focus to win shares extremely welcome.

As you can plainly see, this organizational shift should give Cubs fans plenty of hope. Simply by focusing on different stats, the team is almost sure to be in contention during the Epstein era.

CHAPTER 11

The
Heckler

A Renovated Ballpark, A Renovated Future

Wrigley Field turned 100 years old in 2014, and while there's no denying it's a gem of a ballpark and a huge draw for the Cubs, it also might be the very thing that's holding back the franchise from winning another World Series. After all, the team has won exactly zero championships during the Wrigley Field era.

In an effort to break the Curse of Wrigley, Cubs chairman Tom Ricketts proposed a $300 million, five-year renovation plan in 2013. Some see it as a way to make the team more profitable than ever, but keen observers will notice what this renovation is truly about: winning the World Series.

Unconvinced?

Here are 10 stadium renovations that promise to turn the Cubs from Lovable Losers into State-of-the-Art Champions with a ballpark that is the envy of the entire league.

1. JumboTron
Nothing against the charming and historic scoreboard in center field, but a giant video screen was long overdue.

Firstly, it will block at least three or four rooftops from getting a free peek at the action on the field. By preventing neighboring scofflaws from pirating the game experience, and thus stopping them from stealing revenue from the club, the new video board will put money back in the pocket of Cubs ownership, 100 percent of which will obviously be used to increase payroll. Assuming the rooftop owners don't actually block the construction of the board, this video screen will be truly spectacular, and rumor has it select fans will be given fully functional remote controls on certain days.

Another benefit of the board is the embarrassment factor. A Cubs player will be a lot less likely to make a boneheaded blunder on the base paths when he knows the resulting gaffe will be shown on a two-story JumboTron for all to see. This public shaming will undoubtedly discourage all the lazy miscues that have gone on at Wrigley Field while players enjoyed relative anonymity on the field. No more hiding those errors, Cubs outfielders. Time to shape up or ship out, or at least be embarrassed in HD.

Plus, with a screen that's dozens of feet tall, can you imagine the Fan Cam beauties at that size? Wow! Everyone in the park will be in a better mood, including the umpires, who will be more likely to give the home team the benefit of the doubt as repayment for such great scenery.

Estimated Additional Wins Per Season: 3-5

2. Expanded Dugouts

Wrigley Field was originally built in 1914 over the course of seven weeks for a scant $250,000. That's like three hot dogs and a large soda in today's dollars, but that's irrelevant. The point is that at that price, it's no surprise the construction crew overlooked a few details. For example, a home dugout that could comfortably hold the entire team would have been nice. More than a century later, as rosters have expanded, the Cubs are still forced to squeeze into a dugout the size of a shoebox. Add 'roided up players to the mix and you've got a real space problem.

Is it any wonder Cubs players have trouble doing their jobs? You'd have a hard time staying loose too if you were packed on top of your teammates like sardines for half the game. Hell, it probably takes the average Cubs fielder two-thirds of an inning just to uncoil his muscles after leaving the dugout, and by then he's already committed two errors. It makes sense when you think about it. Imagine you had to hit a 95-mph fastball 30 seconds after being stuck in the back seat of a Honda Civic with two of your friends for 25 minutes.

By increasing the size of the dugout, the players will be able to rest (and stretch) properly before taking the field or heading to the plate.

"But wait," you might say. "Won't the opposing team's dugout also be bigger, meaning they'll enjoy the same benefits, thereby canceling out any significant advantage?"

The answer is no, for reasons that cannot be divulged. The gist is that, in this day and age, do you really think the Cubs are foolish enough to give their opponents the exact same dugout dimensions?

Oh, you do?

Well…here's hoping you're wrong.

Lastly, an expanded dugout might even add a new wrinkle: extra players. If there's one problem that's plagued the Cubs over the years, it's not having enough quality players in their dugout. Maybe with a larger dugout, they'll be able to hide an extra pinch-hitting option for the late innings in the corner, or they could sign five more catchers in hopes of solidifying the position.

Projected Annual Reduction in Errors: *27*

3. Batting Tunnels

If you've ever watched the Cubs fail to advance a runner in scoring position and thought to yourself "Man, it's like these guys don't even practice hitting!" you'd be right.

Because for the past 100 seasons, the Cubs have been forced to hit off a tee under the bleachers to get in their extra "batting practice" when they're at home. Never mind the fact that pitched baseballs routinely travel much faster than 0 miles per hour (aka Tee Speed), but all the other teams in the league have state-of-the-art cages in their own home parks. This means the Cubs get nowhere near the amount of batting practice as their opponents.

Which makes soooooooo much sense.

It really wouldn't be a problem if hitting wasn't such a crucial aspect of the game.

Unfortunately, it is, which explains why the Cubs routinely rank near the bottom of the league in batting average, runs, and the like.

Luckily, this is changing. With a fully functional batting cage nestled snugly below the lower deck, the Cubs are sure to improve their offensive output for years to come. Practice makes perfect, after all, and if the Cubs can get anywhere in the same universe as perfect, it'll certainly be an improvement.

Net Effect: 194 additional runs per season

4. Media Work Room and Dining Area

Is it possible that the Cubs aren't really as bad as history suggests?

Think about it: history is shaped by the people who write it. In the case of the Cubs, we're talking about sports journalists. Cranky, underfed sports journalists who are routinely crammed into old, subpar press boxes with spotty wi-fi and an even spottier bathroom. It stands to reason their daily reports of the Cubs exploits—or lack thereof—will be laced with anger and derision.

"Of course the team is one of the worst in baseball," Paul Sullivan might write. "They don't even have a proper dining area for the media. How could we expect them to execute a suicide squeeze?"

All that negativity adds up, game after game, season after season, until what the media presents to the public is a franchise so backward, we all simply assume the stories are true. Perception becomes reality.

Thanks to the newly renovated Media Work Room and Dining Area, those bad vibes will be a thing of the past. Now, instead of quickly hammering out a searing critique of the Cubs' latest loss, a journalist will be able to take a deep breath, enjoy a hot meal in the dining area, then retire to a desk in the designated work area. Suddenly, the game didn't seem so terrible for the Cubs. Silver linings begin to appear as a local or national scribe starts to type his or her game recap, all the while munching on a delectable ham on rye-pumpernickel topped with melty Swiss cheese, romaine lettuce, and organic Dijon mustard. Next thing you know, the Cubs almost won that 11–4 affair.

Get enough positive media mojo going and there's no telling what can happen. Imagine Starlin Castro reading in the *Tribune* about how those two errors weren't really his fault; it was just a sunny day and there were so many fans at the stadium to distract him. In that moment, the beleaguered shortstop might soar with confidence and find the inner resolve to be in the proper position and field that ball cleanly next time, dammit!

Press Coverage: *57 percent more positive*

5. Mini Triangle Building

Finally, after all these years, a building with three sides on the corner of Addison and Sheffield.

Cubs fans have been hearing about this structure for so long, it's taken on a legend all its own. Many believe that's where the team will put all the championship trophies it will win now that it has an asymmetrical building to properly house them in, while some fans insist the scalene structure will be home to the ghosts of Cubs legends, who will frighten opposing players until they agree to lose on purpose. Still others believe the triangle will not be a building at all, but a large pen that will hold more than two dozen goats, one of which will be sacrificed upon a stone altar every week of the season to appease the baseball gods.

Judging from the artist renderings, however, it's more likely the building will be home to a bar and grill, some merchandise shops, and maybe even a Cubs museum. While it's unclear what a franchise like the Cubs might actually include in a museum dedicated to its checkered past, the fact remains that by not adding a fourth wall, the Cubs are leaving open a portal to a new dimension in which championships grow on trees and can be plucked freely, possibly by the ghost of an inebriated Harry Caray.

Square Feet of Goat Roaming Space: 10,000+

6. Home Plate Club

Not to be confused with the Clean Plate Club—of which former Cub Aramis Ramirez was a charter member—the

Home Plate Club is a swanky tavern underneath the box seats directly behind home plate.

This will add some much-needed sophistication to the 100-year-old ballpark. And since the Home Plate Club is conveniently located underneath the lower seating deck, the new watering hole will displace the thousands of rats who used to roam free throughout the concession stockrooms that previously occupied the area. There's no word yet on where the rats will go, but the benefits of separating them from the actual food being served include fewer health violations for fans and players.

In addition to the obvious effect of healthier players on the field, fans who aren't experiencing food poisoning are sure to support the team with more enthusiasm. Ever tried to cheer while suffering from abdominal cramps and bloating? I didn't think so.

The club will also feature a diverse offering of libations, with some wine and spirits rumored to bring in hundreds of dollars per patron, the majority of which will, of course, be poured into building a perennial winner.

Decrease in Food Poisoning Incidents: *46 percent*

7. More Bathrooms

Did you know Wrigley Field only has one men's bathroom? Okay, that's not true. There are actually two men's bathrooms on the premises. At least that's what it seems like when you've had five overpriced Budweisers and your bladder is screaming in agony because the line is about 15 feet long for the john.

The point is: more bathrooms equals more of those awesome urinal troughs. And we all know winners pee in troughs. Look at the 1927 Yankees—they probably peed in troughs all the time.

Aside from the winner-to-trough connection, additional restrooms mean fewer fans relieving themselves in alleys and bushes after the game. This lack of a putrid urine smell in the air around the ballpark is sure to buoy the spirits of Cubs players and coaches, giving them more motivation to win for a city that actually doesn't smell like piss for a change.

8. New Locker Room

If you've ever taken a tour of Wrigley Field, you've likely marveled at many aspects of the stadium, such as the historic scoreboard, the ivy-covered outfield bricks, and, of course, the locker room smaller than the one at the junior high school you attended.

No other major league stadium features a clubhouse and locker room so small that players are forced to take turns getting dressed, as there isn't enough room for more than three grown men to put their pants on at the same time. Rumor has it the reason Kerry Wood famously smashed Sammy Sosa's boombox wasn't because of the music or any animosity between the star players, but instead because Wood was simply attempting to close his locker and his elbow knocked the CD player to the floor.

Making matters worse, the training "room" is actually a converted janitorial closet, where players are forced to soak their injured limbs in mop buckets filled with ice from the local 7-Eleven.

But now, no more! The Cubs will finally catch up with the rest of the league and enjoy luxurious amenities like a non-folding-chair in front of their lockers. The new, expanded clubhouse and locker room will also include multiple flat-screen TV's, which will make it easier to study game film than the old way (everyone heading to the coach's house after the game). Fancy technology like hydrotherapy machines will also be available, meaning Cubs players no longer have to use mop buckets or (when those are occupied) sit in beer tubs full of ice at Murphy's Bleachers to soothe their aching muscles.

There will even be a dedicated buffet area for the team before and after games, as opposed to the six TV trays that were used in the past.

Thanks to this spacious, state-of-the-art new setup, Cubs players will be loose, relaxed, and in much better mental health than when they had no choice but to shampoo each other's hair because the showers are so tiny, raising your arms above your own head was impossible.

Additional Wins Per Season: 3-4

9. Plaza, Hotel, and Office Building

It's not just Wrigley Field that's the problem—it's also the surrounding area. Sure, cookie-cutter Irish pubs are great, but where are the hotels? The office buildings? Can a franchise really call itself world-class if it can't even hire an intern because there's no office space left?

The answer is no, which is why the Cubs have included those amenities and more in their $300 million transformation.

Imagine a land full of farmer's markets during the summer, ice skating in the winter, and festivals of all kinds throughout the year. Sounds like paradise, doesn't it? Thanks to the renovation, those events will be a reality every year in Wrigleyville, right at the corner of Sheffield and Waveland.

Each contributes to a winning culture in its own unique way.

Farmer's Markets: Provide vital nutrients to fans and players while discriminating against rival players, who will be forced to eat GMO-laden produce from the non-organic aisle at Jewel.

Outdoor Ice Rink: Rumor has it the Stanley Cup champion Blackhawks will stop by to show the Cubs how to play hockey, as some of the North Siders may be better at it than baseball.

Office Building: Crunching all those Sabermetrics takes more than an iPhone app, okay? It takes a desk, fancy computers, and a cool whiteboard so Theo Epstein can excitedly scribble various equations in meetings while Jed Hoyer watches with puppy-dog eyes.

Hotel: Finally, the days of Cubs players having to bring barmaids and other recent college graduates all the way back to their Gold Coast or Lincoln Park apartments are over. A hotel just steps from the ballpark is much less taxing on the players over the long term.

Concerts and Festivals: The neighborhood that parties together wins championships together. That is a direct quote from some drunk dude outside Wrigley.

Estimated Additional Wins Per Season: 5-7

10. Marquee Restaurant

Want to intimidate opposing fans and players? Put a restaurant right underneath the historic Wrigley Field marquee. Obviously.

Here's the deal: imagine you're a fan visiting from St. Louis for the first time. You've heard all about Wrigley Field, but you've never seen it up close and in person. So there you are, wearing your wife beater and jorts (jean shorts), approaching the entrance to the ballpark.

"What's this? A restaurant before I even go inside? What kind of devilry is this?" you would probably be thinking. If a team has enough audacity to plant a restaurant at the corner of Clark and Addison...imagine what must be inside! Probably a championship-quality ballclub.

Again, it's Cubs logic and it just makes sense.

Intimidation Factor: High

Renovation Impact: The Final Analysis

After taking into consideration all the various upgrades and new amenities, you'd be hard-pressed to find any reason the Cubs won't win 15-20 additional games per season on average. Add those victories to even mediocre totals and it looks like Chicago finally has a perennial wild-card contender, if not a runaway NL championship club.

The Heckler

What Does All This Mean?

You're disappointed. I know. You purchased this guide to learn how to live your life like a Cubs fan, and all you got was a bunch of observations, clichés, and non sequiturs. You even got insulted once or twice. Maybe next time you should read chapter 8 first and work your way backward. That will give you just the perspective you need to fully enjoy this book.

Still, there's something else that's bothering you. You're wondering how all these ideas can coexist together. "How can you hold out hope for next year, yet not care if the team wins or loses?" you ask. "Then what the hell are you hoping for?"

That's an excellent, valid question. Admittedly, there isn't much rhyme or reason to any of it, almost as if the people living by these principles

Notable Quote

Question: What was it like playing for the Cubs?

Banks: It's a part of me, like my family. People who come out here are like my friends; people that play here are like my brothers. It's just a total picture of my whole life, being at Wrigley Field, and being around the players and the fans. In my life playing here, I just learned to forgive and forget and go on and enjoy each day and each person that I'm with.

—Mr. Cub, Ernie Banks

are crazy. News flash: they are. And that's exactly how I described them in the introduction of this book. They're Cubs fans, and they're willing to abide by whatever principles get them through the day. Today it could be TANY. Tomorrow might be "Beer Will Make It Better!™" The end result is the ability to cope with a difficult situation. That's the real lesson to be learned from these noble folks. In the face of adversity, they do whatever it takes to keep themselves happy. We should all be that single-minded in life.

So now that you're armed with this confusing set of rules to live by, what next? The practical applications in this book will only take you so far. A more comprehensive look at the Cubs fan is needed to fully understand what makes him tick. To achieve this, I considered a few different routes. One idea was to interview famous Cubs fans, but then I realized famous people add something unquantifiable to the mix. They aren't typical Cubs fans. No matter how much they love the Cubs, people like Bill Murray and Eddie Vedder have more important things to worry about than baseball. Most Cubs fans don't. So I only used a few insightful quotes from a select group of celeb fans. Hopefully they will inspire you to greatness, or happiness, or whatever else you're searching for in life.[1]

I also considered including a bunch of lists, like this one:

Top 10 Ways to Cook Dinner Like a Cubs Fan

10) While wearing your Corey Patterson jersey, because you sure as hell can't wear it in public.

9) Whatever you cook, make sure it's something that will leave a bad taste in your mouth.

8) Drink four beers before the water even starts to boil.

7) Refer to your kitchen as the Fridgy Confines.

6) Remind yourself it could be worse: You could be cooking like a White Sox fan, on one of those hot plates in the back of a house on wheels.

5) Predict greatness from your pasta, even though it's never been great before.

4) Buy all your ingredients from an overpriced Whole Foods, the Wrigley Field Premium Tickets of the food world.

3) Start everything off just right, then burn it. Burn it all.

2) Add a dash of Old Style, because Beer Will Make It Better!™

1) Prepare the worst meal ever, then promise yourself you'll cook something way better Next Year.

But then I thought it might be cheesy to do everything in

---

1. Unless you're searching for Scientology. I want no part of that.

Now that you've nearly finished this comprehensive guide, you are equipped with the tools to go out and enjoy life despite the heavy burden of being a Cubs fan.

list form, so I only used five or six of those. Another option was to include articles from *The Heckler*. Those are always good for a laugh, but I don't know how much life guidance can be gleaned from an article about the rebuilding Cubs trading their manager's desk to the Marlins for an ottoman to be named later, or White Sox fans celebrating a victory with a good old-fashioned tire fire. Plus, it would

This pair of smiling Cubs fans traveled all the way to New York's Shea Stadium in hopes of seeing the team's first win of the season after 14 straight losses to start the 1997 campaign. Their wish was granted, but not until after the Cubs dropped the first game of the doubleheader.

be a blatant plug for my website (TheHeckler.com), and I refuse to do that, even if it is the best satirical sports publication in the country.

That's www.theheckler.com.

At the end of the day, however, it seemed the best way to do justice to this lifestyle was to allow you, the reader, to take the principles at face value. Being a Chicago Cubs fan is a vague endeavor, after all. If you can somehow find a way to apply even one of these rules to your life, you've made progress on the road to happiness.

And if you think this is some sort of disappointing cop-out, welcome to the Cubs fan's experience.

If you have any questions about my controversial theories, life in general, or you just want to share one of your own Cubs-related anecdotes with someone who might actually give a damn, feel free to email me at george@theheckler.com. No White Sox fans, please.

15 Habits of Highly Happy Cubs Fans

Life is a series of habits and routines repeated over and over again. Some people's habits include smoking, drinking, and playing cards. Other people have a routine that revolves entirely around eating: breakfast, something, lunch, something, dinner, something—and so on.

While no two Chicago Cubs fans are exactly the same, a majority of them exhibit broadly similar habits. In many ways, this is borne out of their collective outlook on life, as described in the preceding chapters. In order to better understand how the brain of a Cubs fan operates, and to put yourself in a similar mindset, you need to program yourself with some of their habits. The more habits you pick up, the more you begin to experience life as a Cubs fan. And the more you do that, the closer you will be to unlocking the true happiness inside you.

The following list is certainly not exhaustive, but it does give you a glimpse into the soul of the Cubs fan. Or something profound like that.

Habit 1: High-five more often.

This is not a new concept. Since the dawn of time, mankind has celebrated accomplishment through the slapping of palms. When the first caveman invented shorts by hanging a bush around his midsection, his hunchbacked friends were there to give him a high-five (at that point in the evolutionary chain, it may have technically been a high-four, but that would be a total digression). While the specific manner in which the high-five is executed has changed over the years—it was even the low-five for a while—the premise remains the same. You get so excited about something you can't hold it in any longer, and you slap hands with the person closest to you.

If you happen to be celebrating a home run at Wrigley Field, you usually don't even know who the high-fivee is. But at that moment, during that ritual smack of flesh on flesh, you form a bond with your fellow man. This bond not only reinforces your humanity, it allows you to make a positive connection whenever you please, and that's the kind of experience Cubs fans seek out in life.

Habit 2: Laugh in the face of adversity.

Not in the figurative sense, either. Cubs fans literally laugh harder the worse things get for them. Why? Because when the Cubs blow a ninth-inning lead for the third time in a week, you just have to smile. Sometimes, if you're faced with an irrational situation, the only rational response is to act irrationally.

Doctors have long held the belief that laughter is "the best medicine." Did you hear that? "Best medicine." Not "good medicine" or "okay medicine" or even "medicine you should only use as a last resort." So why deny your body and mind a good, healthy guffaw when it needs it the most? You know it makes sense. On its face, it might seem inappropriate to laugh when your boss fires you, but that's really the best way to deal with the situation. Crying won't get you rehired. Laughing will make you feel much

better immediately, and considering the fact you're now unemployed, you'll need all the positivity you can get.

Habit 3: Buy someone a beer.

Nothing will endear you to your friends and coworkers more than a nice, frosty beverage. That's why Cubs fans are always buying beer for each other. Every time a fan over the age of 21 leaves the Wrigley Field seating area, he or she returns with two cups of beer. It doesn't matter if the intended destination of the trip was the bathroom or the hot dog stand, the beer station immediately becomes a stop on the way. It's a simple rule: come back with an extra beer, or don't come back at all.

Imagine if everything worked like that. It's Tuesday, let's pretend, and the end of the week is but a mirage, a mere blip on the radar. You're suffering through another snooze fest of a meeting led by your moronic boss, when one of your coworkers returns from the bathroom with two bottles of cold, refreshing Bud Light.

Nice.

Your coworker has just earned your eternal loyalty with 12 ounces of hops, barley, and water. And if you return the favor, you, too, will have a friend for life.

Habit 4: Leave work early.

Wrigley Field didn't get lights until 1988, meaning every home game played during the first 74 years of the stadium was played during the day. While Wrigley is no longer light-challenged, the schedule still leans heavily toward 1:20 starts, and Cubs players are constantly grousing about all the day games on the schedule.

"I don't have time to sleep off my hangover," they say. "How am I supposed to play well on such little rest?"

To the fans, however, the daytime starts are a godsend because they give Chicagoans yet another reason to leave work early. Of course, the Cubs aren't the reason anybody actually gives their boss. Common reasons include stomachaches, family obligations, phantom funerals, and the ever-popular dentist appointment. But the excuse is irrelevant. The bottom line is that being a Cubs fan gives you that much more incentive to get out of the cube and into life. So what if the Cubs aren't that great? Which would you rather do: watch the Cubs lose from the sun-splashed left-field bleachers or stare at a computer screen all afternoon while Big Brother breathes down your neck?

Habit 5: Throw it back.

When an opposing team's player hits a home run into the Wrigley Field bleachers, it doesn't stay there long. Tradition dictates that the ball immediately be tossed back onto the field. If it is not regurgitated in a timely manner, the surrounding fans join together in a relentless chant of "throw it back, throw it back" until the person holding the baseball is peer-pressured into sacrificing it to the bleacher gods.

As you might expect, this is a purely symbolic gesture.

The official scorer doesn't wipe the run(s) off the board when he sees the ball fly back onto the field of play. Nor is the opposing team discouraged from hitting more home runs into the stands.

So why, then, do Cubs fans get so excited about this peculiar practice of throwing it back? It just feels good. You dare to hit a home run off our pitcher? Screw you, pal! We don't need your pathetic baseball! In fact, you can have it back.

Juvenile?

Maybe.

Effective?

Big time.

The secret to ultimate happiness is denial. And denial can come in many forms, from throwing back a baseball to looking in the mirror and seeing 260 pounds of "thinness."

Habit 6: Heckle your rivals.

You should never let people get away with anything, even if they're just doing their job. As experts in the field of psychological warfare, Cubs fans understand how to get

inside an opposing player's head. This expertise comes from years of getting inside their own heads and reprogramming themselves to believe the Cubs have a chance to win the pennant. When this power is projected outward and focused on someone like Ryan Braun, the resulting heckles are truly inspired:

"Hey, Ryan, I still think you're innocent!"

"You've got some urine on you, and it's probably tainted!"

"What's that sticking out of your arm?"

"You're really good at hollow apologies."

"Your defense on the field is as bad as your defense during the Biogenesis scandal!"

"Hey, Braun! I'm wasted!"

At first blush, these heckles could be construed as goofy or frivolous, but I assure you I have seen the power of these putdowns in action. Barry Bonds himself has given me the cold stare of death. Rickey Henderson flipped off my friend. Adam Dunn was surprisingly annoyed by our pleas to "stick a fork in him." If millionaire athletes can be rattled by heckling, so too can your rivals.

People like your mother-in-law. Your teacher. Or even your neighbor, who thinks he's so cool with his new car and his fake-breasted second wife.

"Nice replacement!" you could yell. "I got my wife right the first time, loser!"

Heckling isn't just fun. It's also therapeutic. Telling your nerdy coworker he's more like a "codorker" will make you feel better about yourself.

Habit 7: Overcelebrate.

Life is fleeting. One minute you're enjoying a juicy steak at Gibsons Steakhouse, and the next thing you know you're dead. Unfortunately, there's nothing you can do about your mortality, but you can enjoy the hell out of the time you have here on earth.

Cubs fans do this by celebrating everything that even mildly resembles a positive outcome. They celebrate mediocrity, like a 4–4 home stand or a third-place season. Cubs fans will go so far as to praise a swinging third strike. Sure, the player failed in his attempt to make contact, but at least he made it to first. That's something we can all appreciate.

This propensity to overcelebrate really irks non-Cubs fans. For some reason, it upsets them to see us North Siders enjoying a season full of miscues, blown saves, and runners left in scoring position. Those non-Cubs fans will

not die happy. What they don't realize is that life is short, and being miserable is a gigantic waste of time. It's like calculus that way.

It's not too late for you to learn this lesson. Whenever you get upset about your dismal career, celebrate the fact you have a career at all. That way, if you die of a sudden heart attack, you can at least say you died as the happiest septic tank cleaner ever.

Habit 8: If you have to pee, pee.

Cubs fans know better than to hold it. In addition to the damage waiting too long to pee can do to your bladder, it's just not very comfortable. This is the reason Cubs fans leaving Wrigley Field have no problem urinating in nearby alleys—it's the healthy thing to do.

So what if the people living in the apartments surrounding the stadium can't stand this practice? They knew what they were getting into when they signed the lease.

Habit 9: Pay too much for stuff.

Bleacher tickets. Domestic beer. Starlin Castro jerseys. It doesn't matter how overpriced the particular item for sale may be, there's always a Cubs fan willing to buy it. Even the peanuts sold on Waveland and Sheffield, famously touted as "cheaper on the outside," can run you $5. Wrigleyville is like a mini-Manhattan, where saving money is not an option.

But it's not all bad.

It can't be, after all, if so many Chicago Cubs fans are able to stay happy amid the price gouging. So how do they do it? It's a matter of perspective. When you buy a six-pack of Old Style at the supermarket, you pay about $5.99. And that's exactly what it tastes like: $5.99 beer. When you spend roughly the same amount of money on just one Old Style at Wrigley Field, it tastes more expensive. Simply put, you appreciate a $6 beer more than you appreciate a $1 beer. The same can be said for a Junior Lake jersey. If you only paid $10 for it, you might be tempted to use it as a washrag around the house, but the extra $60 makes it that much more special. Bleacher tickets are the best example of the effect of overpricing. The higher price makes the ticket seem more exclusive. So even though you're in the only section of the stadium that doesn't feature assigned seats, seatbacks, or roving beer vendors, the $95 you paid the scalper makes it feel like the best section in the house.

Habit 10: Don't ask questions.

Life is hard enough when you don't question everything. Why am I here? Should I go back to college? What the hell is that lump under my arm?

Cubs fans try not to be too inquisitive, because the answers to most of life's questions are not "you're rich!" or "there's an easy solution to your problems!" Nobody ever asks himself how to spend his vast fortune, either. That would be too easy. People ponder hard things, like how to make $800 a month feed a family of four or whether they can get cancer from their cell phone.

Who needs all that information?

A bleacher bum doesn't ask how a team with no bullpen is going to win 90 games this season. Such concerns undermine the blind euphoria Cubs fans have come to know and love.

Habit 11: Wait in line.

If there's one thing that doesn't bother Cubs fans—aside from losing—it's waiting in line. And why should it? The things they stand in line for are usually worth the wait. Each February, for instance, the Cubs dispense thousands of bracelets with random numbers on them. A lottery is drawn, and the person with the winning bracelet gets the first opportunity to buy tickets for the upcoming season. Last year, scores of Cubs fans curled around the stadium in frigid temperatures just for the chance to buy Cubs tickets. To non-Cubs fans, this probably appears to be a gigantic waste of time, but those of us on the inside know it builds

character and is the only chance we have at beating the scalpers.

So we're okay with it.

Other things Cubs fans wait in line for are beer, the pisser, and entrance to the ballpark. All worthy causes. The lesson? If you have to wait in line, it's probably for something good. Think roller coasters, movie premieres, and dance clubs.

"But what about the DMV?" you say. "Why should I enjoy waiting in line there?"

That's a good question, and I could tell you there's a great answer for it, but I will instead refer you back to Habit 10.

Habit 12: Spend time in the sun.

Seriously. You need a tan.

Habit 13: Live life to the fullest.

Hot dogs. Nachos. Pretzels. Cotton candy. French fries. Peanuts. These are all things you should eat every chance you get. Even the slimmest of Cubs fans realizes the importance of inhaling as much food as possible over the course of nine innings. It may not be totally healthy for you,

but it sure is fun. And the best part is that it's guilt-free.

"Oh, I wouldn't normally eat six hot dogs and a lemon ice," you could say. "I'm only doing it just this once. I'm at the Cubs game, after all."

But you don't even have to be at the Cubs game. If you treat every day as a chance to enjoy the best life has to offer, then eat as many hot dogs as you want. If you're worried about being fat, don't be. Next to Green Bay Packers fans, Cubs fans are some of the fattest people on earth, and you don't see them worrying about it.

Habit 14: Sing drunk.

Much like the Wrigley Field bleacher section is the biggest singles party in America, the seventh-inning stretch is the biggest karaoke song since Neil Diamond's "Sweet Caroline." Every game, 40,000 people (attempt to) sing "Take Me Out to the Ballgame" in unison. Roughly half of these people are fall-down drunk, so the ensuing performance provides a pretty good show.

More important than the theatrics is the bonding experience. You've never really lived until you've sung arm-in-arm with your sloppy friends in the bleachers at Wrigley. Something about the stadium, the tradition, and the booze forms the perfect milieu of happiness.

Milieu.

Look it up.

If Harry Caray taught us anything, it's that we should all sing drunk more often. So the next time you're out at the bar, drape your arm over the shoulder of the person next to you and belt out a few verses of "American Pie," "Sweet Caroline," or "Welcome to the Jungle."

Habit 15: Go nuts!

Cubs fans are crazy. You'd have to be to keep rooting for a team with a tradition built entirely on losing. Through it all, however, the smiles never fade. It could be the last month of an absolutely dreadful season, and Joe Cub Fan will still find a reason to be glad he's at the game or watching it on TV.

Does this make Cubs fans insane?

Yes.

Is that a bad thing?

Hell, no.

It's better to be nuts and happy than sane and sad. Whatever it is in the makeup of a Cubs fan that allows him or her to rationalize losing—and turn it into something positive—it's certainly a quality to be admired.

We should all strive to be more irrational. In fact, you should make it a point to do something irrational on a daily basis. Today it could be asking out that woman at work, even though she's already married. Tomorrow you could buy three cars, just because you have good credit.

Whatever makes you happy, no matter how crazy it sounds—that's the Cubs fan's motto.

The **Heckler**

A Century of Losing: 100+ Years, 100+ Frustrations

When the Chicago Cubs beat the Detroit Tigers in the 1908 World Series, they were probably feeling pretty good about themselves. Not only had they won two championships in a row—the Cubs defeated the Tigers in 1907 as well—the franchise had compiled an amazing 322–136 record from 1906–08. That's an average of 107 wins per season.

Little did the North Siders know, the 1909 campaign would kick off the most infamous championship drought in American sports history: 106 years and counting. With the Boston Red Sox finally ending their own drought (86 years) in 2004 and the hated cross-town rival White Sox ending theirs (88 years) in 2005, the Cubs are now alone in their misery.

So how did it ever come to this? How did the proudest franchise in the National League become the laughingstock of professional sports? It hasn't just been the losing, although that surely would have been enough. It's also been the way the Cubs have lost and everything else surrounding the team. Cubs fans themselves don't even understand the extent of the damage; they just kind of sense its presence with them every summer. Outsiders have no clue. Oh, sure, most sports fans have heard of Steve Bartman and the 1969 Cubs, but that's just the tip of the iceberg with this franchise.

In order to fully understand how to live like a Cubs fan, you must first understand what it's like to be a Cubs fan. You must see what these people have been through over the last century and change. This section will touch on the major disappointments over the years, from the 1969 collapse to the Lou Brock trade to the renaming of the famous outfield bleachers.

1. Cubs' Monumental Collapse (1969)

The Cubs' strong 1969 season was the culmination of a five-year roster build-up by manager Leo Durocher. The team started off well, good enough to have an NL-leading 71–41 record on August 7. Yet the center did not hold for the Cubs when the team got into a race with the white-hot New York Mets in late August and early September. Stars Ron Santo and Glenn Beckert slumped, and "Mr. Cub" Ernie Banks had an appalling .186 batting average and hit only one home run throughout September. Chicago went 8–17 that month. While it's easy for statisticians to point the finger of blame at the Cubs offense, and superstitious fans to attribute it to the infamous "black cat" incident at Shea Stadium during a Cubs-Mets game, perhaps the one most responsible for the meltdown was the architect of the team. Durocher could be a very difficult manager to work with, as he confused berating his players with motivating them. In the face of the Cubs' difficulties in late 1969, all he could do was scold those around him. The season would eventually become known as "the one that got away."

2. The Bartman Play (2003)

Just five more outs. Wrigley Field was on the verge of erupting in celebration as the Cubs, leading 3–0 against the Florida Marlins in Game 6 of the National League Championship Series, looked to reach their first World Series in 58 years. In the eighth inning, Luis Castillo popped up a foul to left, and Moises Alou ran over to make the catch as the ball sailed toward the wall. But as Alou leapt to snag it, front-row fan Steve Bartman snatched the ball out of the air above Alou's glove. Cubs fans pelted Bartman with garbage as stadium personnel escorted him out of the park. It's uncertain whether Alou could have actually caught the ball, and Chicago still coulda—and shoulda—stopped the Marlins from subsequently scoring eight unanswered runs. The Cubs also could have stopped the Marlins from reeling off three straight victories to advance to the World Series. Yet Bartman is reviled among most of Cub Nation, which blames him for the team's failure.

3. Cubs Trade Lou Brock (1964)

If the 1969 season epitomizes the Chicago Cubs' penchant for failure, trading Lou Brock demonstrates the club's inability to recognize talent. The year was 1964, and the Cubs were in the midst of another losing campaign (76–86). On June 15, they decided to trade Brock, a promising young outfielder, to the Cardinals. The most notable player they got in return was right-handed pitcher Ernie Broglio. It's unclear whether the Cubs were just tired of waiting for Brock to blossom or if they thought he never would. Either way, the deal is considered one of the worst trades in baseball history. Brock's accomplishments as a Cardinal border on comical: two World Series titles (the first of which came in 1964, the year he was traded), six All-Star appearances, Babe Ruth Award, Roberto Clemente Award, Lou Gehrig Memorial Award, Hutch Award, league leader in stolen bases eight times, and holder of a .391 career postseason average. In his 19 seasons, Brock accrued 3,023 hits and 938 stolen bases. He was a first-ballot Hall of Famer. As for Ernie Broglio, he spent two and a half seasons with the Cubs, going 7–19 with a 6.00 ERA.

4. Sox Fans (Since the Dawn of Time)

Superman has Lex Luthor. The Smurfs have Gargamel. And Cubs fans have Sox fans. A teeming mass of tattooed, mulletted hooligans, Sox Nation is the bane of every North Sider's existence. Even before their team won the World Series in 2005, Sox fans delighted in celebrating every Cubs failure over the years. In 1969, they rioted in the streets, probably. After the Cubs blew the 2003 NLCS, the most deafening roar didn't come from South Florida— it came from the South Side. And every time the Sox beat one of their American League foes, the fans leaving U.S. Cellular Field inexplicably chant, "Cubs suck." In addition to the baseball-related issues Cubs fans have with their crosstown counterparts, there's also the matter of crime. When a car goes missing on the North Side, you can be sure a Sox fan is behind the wheel. When someone mugs a guy in a Cubs hat, it could be random, but the odds say it was some Sox fan unhappy with how much more money the Cubs fan makes at his cushy white-collar job. Now, with a recent championship under their belts, Sox fans won't rest until they've ruined the lives of every die-hard Cubs fan in Wrigleyville.

5. Cubs Lose to Padres in National League Championship Series (1984)

It was finally going to be the year...and this time for real. Buoyed by Rick Sutcliffe's 16–1 record and future Hall of Famer Ryne Sandberg's breakout season, the 1984 Cubs ripped off an impressive 96–65 record, claiming the NL East crown. After winning the first two games of a best-of-five against the San Diego Padres in the NLCS, the North Siders needed one measly win to make it to the fall classic for the first time since 1945. But thanks to the TV network's demand for night games, the Cubs, whose record earned them the right to home-field advantage, would instead be forced to play three consecutive games in San Diego. They ended up losing all three, including Game 5, due (in large part) to a routine ground ball that went through the legs of first baseman Leon Durham. The Cubs wouldn't have another winning season until 1989, when they again failed in the playoffs.

6. Tribune Company Buys the Cubs (1981)

People often criticized the Tribune Company for not caring whether the Cubs were a successful franchise. Nothing could be further from the truth—the Tribune wanted the ballclub to be as profitable as possible. Those coffers had to be filled somehow, and people like former team president Andy MacPhail made it happen by passing on the responsibility to the fans in the form of higher ticket prices, convenience charges, illegally scalped tickets, concessions, and merchandise. By any business standard, the Cubs were totally successful during the Tribune years. They were a cash cow.

7. Cubs Don't Re-Sign Greg Maddux (1992)

In 1984 the Cubs signed a promising pitching prospect named Greg Maddux, and the rest was Chicago baseball history. Until 1992, that is. He tallied 20 victories and won the Cy Young Award that season, but difficulties with the Tribune Company over contract negotiations led to a move to Atlanta the following year. Maddux won 195 games over the next 10 seasons for the Braves, who notched 10 straight division titles and a World Series victory over that time span. And how did the Cubs do over that same period, you ask? One wild-card berth and one NL Central title. Maddux returned to the Cubs in 2004, but he was already past his prime, so while the signing conjured nostalgia for the fans, it failed to produce a championship on the field, let alone a playoff appearance. In 2006, with the team once again hopelessly out of the playoff race, Mad Dog was traded to the Los Angeles Dodgers, where he returned to young Maddux form despite his extreme old age.

8. White Sox Win World Series (2005)

Seeing one cursed team—the Boston Red Sox—victorious in the World Series before the Cubs was uncomfortable enough for North Siders. Seeing their crosstown rivals win it all the very next season was excruciating. Like the Red Sox, the White Sox had a curse rooted heavily in baseball lore. The "Black Sox" scandal of 1919 involved a payoff of key Chicago players, who threw the World Series against the Cincinnati Reds. As a result of the scandal, eight members of the Sox roster, including star outfielder "Shoeless" Joe Jackson, were banned for life. And so the legend began and was seemingly borne out by the team's drought of series victories between 1920 and 2004. However, they made the playoffs in 2005 with a tremendously talented roster and had home-field advantage throughout. To make matters worse for Cubs fans, the White Sox did absurdly well, executing one of history's most dominant postseason runs. They lost only one game before popping the champagne and hoisting the Commissioner's Trophy.

9. Cubs Lose to Detroit Tigers in World Series (1945)

It started innocently enough. The Chicago Cubs had just won 98 games—out of just 154. In the World Series, they faced off against their longtime rivals, the Detroit Tigers. Despite going only 88–65, the Tigers proved a formidable opponent, and the Series was extended to seven games. Still, the Cubs were favored to win. They had a vastly superior team and were not yet the punching bags of the National League. All that would change after Game 7, however, when they were blown out 9–3. The loss marks the last time the Chicago Cubs have been to the World Series. It also marks the start of the cursed era, thanks to the famous billy goat incident. Couple that with the beginning of the pennant drought, and 1945 is the defining season in Cubs history.

10. Ernie Banks Retires without Championship (1971)

More specifically, Ernie Banks retires without ever reaching the postseason. The Hall of Famer played 19 seasons, and not once did he get the chance to hit a home run in the playoffs or celebrate a National League pennant. It was the Cubs curse taken to the extreme: Even a player of Banks's caliber couldn't turn around a franchise that had long since lost its luster. Affectionately dubbed "Mr. Cub" by fans and teammates alike, Banks spent his entire career on the North Side. Unlike Billy Williams, Fergie Jenkins, and Ron Santo, Banks would wear no other uniform, for he was a Cub through and through. Which is why despite 512 home runs, 11 All-Star appearances, two MVPs, the Lou Gehrig Memorial Award, and a Gold Glove he has no World Series rings to show for it.

11. Ron Santo Not Elected to Hall Until After His Passing

The biggest misconceptions about the outrage surrounding Ron Santo not being in the Hall of Fame were that it's purely Chicago-based or born entirely out of pity. Neither was true. While you could argue Santo deserved special consideration for battling type 1 diabetes throughout his career—doctors told him he wasn't going to live past 25 years old—he didn't need the advantage. When he retired in 1974, he was arguably the second-best third baseman in history, behind Eddie Matthews. He went to nine All-Star Games and hit 342 home runs during an era known primarily for pitching (as opposed to, say, steroids). But it is defense that set him apart from other third basemen. He won five Gold Gloves, led the league in chances nine times, assists seven times, and in double plays six times. So why didn't Santo get voted into the Hall until two years after his death? Was it because he was a Cub? Whatever the reason, Santo was perhaps the most beloved of all Cubs players, and he epitomized what it means to be an eternal optimist in the face of eternal adversity.

12. Derrek Lee Breaks Wrist (2006)

All of the Cubs' hopes and dreams for the 2006 season rested on the bat and glove of All-Star first baseman Derrek Lee. Lee was not only the reigning NL batting champion, he was just the kind of player Cubs fans could rally around: humble, supremely talented, and durable. In his first seven years in the league, Lee had never been on the disabled list, and the Cubs were positive this trend would continue. That confidence was reflected in a five-year, $65 million contract the team gave Lee at the beginning of the season. But after a promising 9–5 start, Lee went down with a fractured wrist on April 20 in a game against the Los Angeles

Dodgers. Rafael Furcal, who was barreling toward first base after a bunt, bulldozed him. The Cubs dropped 40 of the next 59 games they played while Lee watched from the dugout with a cast on his arm. Lee returned at the end of June. He played well, but went back on DL in late July. By the time he returned again in September, the team's fate had long since been decided.

13. Kerry Wood Undergoes Tommy John Surgery (1999)

More than three decades ago, pitcher Tommy John had a relatively new medical procedure called ulnar collateral ligament (UCL) reconstruction performed on his elbow. John gave his name to this kind of surgery, which would go on to become commonplace among major league pitchers who blow out their elbows. Enter Kerry Wood. Coming off a stellar Rookie of the Year performance in 1998, a season that saw the young phenom strike out 20 batters in a single game and lead the Cubs to the NL wild-card, North Side ace Kerry Wood was forced to undergo Tommy John surgery in the off-season. He missed all of 1999. Upon his return, the speed of his pitches was maintained, and he eventually made an All-Star run in 2003, but he was never the same, physically. The resulting string of injuries would turn Wood from a hero to a goat over the span of just a few seasons.

14. Cubs Lose World Series to White Sox (1906)

The inclusion of the Cubs' World Series loss to their crosstown rivals as one of the team's worst moments hardly needs further explanation. And yet, few people today understand how big a disappointment it really was. Perhaps it's the amount of time that's passed since it happened or maybe it's simply selective memory, but not many Cubs fans know this was a huge upset. Unlike today, the North Siders actually were the better team in the city in 1906—they led the league in team hitting, fielding, and pitching—and were therefore heavily favored to win against the White Sox. However, the Sox, dubbed "hitless wonders" because of their anemic offense, managed to hold their own against the Cubs. The two teams won alternately two apiece in the first four games of the Series, which surprised many fans for its competitiveness. But the Sox's "hitless" offense exploded at the end when they scored eight runs in each of their final two victories to win the Series, 4–2. Fortunately for the Cubs, they'd win the World Series two years later against the Detroit Tigers. Unfortunately, it would be the team's last title until, well, you know.

15. Gary Scott Is a Third Base Bust (1991–92)

When Ron Santo left the ballclub in 1973 (he retired in 1974 after one season with the Chicago White Sox), Cubs fans knew they were losing one of the best third basemen in the history of the game. What they didn't know was that the hot corner would turn into a virtual black hole for the next three decades, sucking up and spitting out Santo wannabes by the dozen. From 1974 to 2003, the North Siders went through 98 subpar players in an effort to find a serviceable replacement for the supremely talented Santo. From Steve Ontiveros to Manny Trillo to a guy nicknamed "the Penguin," the Cubs simply couldn't find a third bagger worthy of holding Santo's jock, let alone occupying his position. Then came Gary Scott. Hailed by baseball experts as a can't-miss prospect—Santo himself said Scott could ultimately restore order at third base for the Cubs—the young infielder played just 67 games in parts of 1991 and 1992. He notched a .160 batting average in 175 at-bats and was quickly demoted to the minors. Scott would never again set food on a big-league baseball field.

16. Line Drive Hits Mark Prior on Elbow (2005)

If the curse on the Chicago Cubs is real, then it's probably doubly true for the team's pitching staff. Take Mark Prior, for instance, a guy with worse luck than Ben Stiller's character in *There's Something about Mary*. In 2005 Prior began the season on the DL, as he would the following year. He did well when he eventually came back, though, building up a respectable 4–1 record in just a few weeks. Unfortunately for Prior, he started in a fateful game against the Colorado Rockies on May 27. In the fourth inning, Colorado outfielder Brad Hawpe sent one of Prior's pitches back to him in the form of a 117 mile-per-hour line drive that nailed him in the elbow—on his pitching arm, of course. The resulting fracture put him right back where he started the year, and he was never the same player again. Well, unless you're talking about him getting injured every other day, then he was the same player entirely.

17. Curse of the Billy Goat (1945)

Most Cubs followers have a passing familiarity with the curse that has afflicted their team for the past 70 years, and if they don't, shame on them. For all the Cubs fans who spend most of their time on cell phones or throwing up on someone else's shoes, here's how it went down.

William Sianis, who went by the nickname "Billy Goat," brought a real, live goat with him before the start of Game 4 of the 1945 World Series, in which the Cubs led the Detroit Tigers 2–1. Funny thing was, after Sianis paraded his goat on the field, the ushers escorted him off and didn't want to let him use the seats for which he had paid. Sianis and his goat eventually were allowed to use the box seats only to have Cubs owner Phillip K. Wrigley kick them out later in the game. When Sianis asked why, Wrigley replied, "Because the goat stinks." An incensed Sianis then gave up, but before he left, he declared that the Cubs wouldn't win another World Series until the goat was allowed in. Sure enough, Chicago lost that game and the World Series. After that year, they didn't make it back to the big one again, falling spectacularly short on a few occasions. Sianis even managed to get a zinger in a few weeks after the incident. Following the Cubs' collapse in the 1945 World Series, he sent a letter to Wrigley that asked, "Who stinks now?"

18. Cubs Sell Out with Ads Inside Park (2005)

An argument could be made that anywhere the words "Wrigley Field" appear within Wrigley Field, it's a kind of advertisement. After all, it's not only the name of the former owner, but also his chewing gum company. In fact, Wrigley Field was the first ballpark in baseball to take its name from a corporation. That claim aside, the park managed to stay remarkably ad-free over the years, especially around the diamond itself. As former Cubs president Andy MacPhail once said in an interview with *Sports Illustrated*, "I'm not really interested in putting up some jumbo sign in right field to get an extra $2 million to devote to the payroll. I don't think we have to do that to win, and I think if you do that, you lessen the uniqueness of Wrigley Field." Two years later the Cubs introduced Sears signage into the ballpark, and it's been a steady stream of advertising ever since: McDonald's, Culver's butterburgers, MasterCard, and United Airlines, just to name a few. The kicker came in 2005, when the Tribune Company added a rotating advertising billboard behind home plate, so everyone in the country would be aware that the team sold out. Thanks to the ads, Cub Nation is starting to lose the only thing it had going for it: the Wrigley Field mystique.

19. Harry Caray Dies (1998)

Surprisingly, the broadcaster who became a Cubs institution had lengthy tenures as an announcer with both the St. Louis Cardinals and Chicago White Sox prior to calling games at Wrigley Field. Yet in spite of these prior professional allegiances, Harry Caray was beloved by Cubs fans everywhere almost from the moment he arrived in 1982. He was popular for both his offbeat delivery in the booth and his ubiquity in Chicago's nightlife, particularly in the bars on and around Rush Street. Even as his skills in both areas declined with age (Caray frequently made Yogi Berra–level gaffes during broadcasts), Cubs fans continued to admire him. But it obviously couldn't last forever. Caray died in 1998 of a heart attack. Unlike most of the Cubs' mishaps, setbacks, and tragedies, this one was inevitable. After all, Caray was a mortal man, and he had to go at some point. But deep down, most Cubs fans thought he'd somehow live forever.

20. Lights Installed at Wrigley Field (1988)

For its first seven decades of existence, night games were unheard of at the Friendly Confines. Built for a different era, Wrigley Field was designed for playing baseball on sunny summer afternoons, the way God intended. However, after the Tribune Company bought the team in 1981, it was only a matter of time. The new owners started talking about putting in lights almost immediately, but their efforts were hampered by a couple of very different groups early on. Naturally, the fans were resistant to the idea mainly because it detracted from Wrigley Field's uniqueness. Also, politicians got involved because the park is located smack in the middle of a neighborhood, and huge bright lights might have proved a tad intrusive for the Wrigleyville residents. But the Tribune Company was determined to get those evening dollars. They cajoled, then threatened, and finally offered the decisive ultimatum: give us the lights or we move to the 'burbs. After that, what could Cubs fans say? They certainly couldn't have called the Trib's bluff—otherwise, those drunken preppies and Trixies would be hopping on the Metra to Schaumburg to see games. They just had to accept their team would have a dozen or two night games on the schedule. Still, the baseball gods offered something of a sign to the corporate paymasters who broke with one of the team's grand traditions. The Cubs first-ever night game on August 8, 1988, was rained out after four innings.

21. Cubs Open Season 0–14 (1997)

Every Cubs season since 1909 has brought eventual disappointment with it; the only difference is when the fans are forced to give up hope. Sometimes it's in June. Sometimes the Cubs aren't out of it until August or September. In 1997, however, the die-hards didn't have to wait long to go into "There's Always Next Year" mode. Just a few weeks into April, it was evident that the team wasn't going anywhere that season—in spite of the fact they had a pretty solid lineup that included Sammy Sosa, Ryne Sandberg, and Mark Grace. The team kicked off the year with a 0–14 losing run and finished the first month with a 6–19 record. The culprit? Poor pitching: No team can contend if its most consistent performer on the mound is Kevin Tapani.

22. Sports Illustrated *Picks* Cubs to Win World Series (2004)

You just knew it was a bad sign when *Sports Illustrated* picked the Chicago Cubs to win it all. It was a worse sign that the cover of the April 5 issue featured only Kerry

Wood—because Mark Prior was going to begin the season on the disabled list. If the 2004 Cubs needed anything, it wasn't added pressure. They certainly didn't need yet another curse, this time of the *Sports Illustrated* variety. Referred to as the "*SI* Jinx," this phenomenon involves people or teams featured on the cover of an issue. Basically, they end up getting hurt or losing big or [insert negative result here]. Cub Nation had enough to contend with thanks to black cats, goats, and overzealous fans, so when *SI* added its own hex to the mix, along with the headline "Hell Freezes Over," it became too much for the otherwise-talented Cubs squad to bear. Despite coming within five outs of the World Series in 2003, the ballclub didn't even make the playoffs in 2004, collapsing down the stretch in typical North Side fashion.

23. Mark Prior and Kerry Wood Begin Season on DL (2006)

Losing Derrek Lee to injury for much of the season was bad enough for the Cubbies. But the Cubs being the Cubs, that wasn't the only pain the fans would endure in 2006. Adding to their woes was the fact that Mark Prior and Kerry Wood—two key members of the team's five-man starting rotation—began the year on the DL for the second season in a row. It only got worse when they came back: In the month-long period after both pitchers were reactivated, Prior and Wood combined for a grand total of one win. Worst of all is that the two accounted for $15.65 million of the team's nearly $95 million total payroll in 2006.

24. Cubs Trade Dontrelle Willis (2002)

It wasn't quite Lou Brock revisited when the Cubs traded left-handed pitcher Dontrelle Willis to the Florida Marlins for Matt Clement and Antonio Alfonseca in March 2002, but the exchange had profound effects on both ball-clubs the very next season. Willis—who looked to be just another ready-to-disappoint Cubs pitching prospect at the time of the trade—went 14–6 with a 3.30 ERA in 2003 and was named the NL Rookie of the Year. That alone would have been enough to warrant regret, but "D-Train" and the Marlins also beat the Cubs in the 2003 NLCS. The Marlins would go on to defeat the New York Yankees in the World Series, while the Cubs went home. Meanwhile, Clement went 9–13 for the Cubs in 2004, then left for the Red Sox, while Antonio Alfonseca had a 5.83 ERA in 2003 and bounced around the majors for the rest of his career.

25. Sammy Sosa Corks Bat (2003)

He may have been corking his muscles with steroids for years, but there was never any proof, so Sammy Sosa's reputation remained relatively untarnished the first 14 seasons of his career. The same cannot be said for season 15, when the prodigious slugger was caught using a corked bat in a game against the Tampa Bay Devil Rays. Rather than admitting his mistake, however, Sosa amplified Cub Nation's embarrassment, claiming that he used the illegal bat only for batting practice and home-run contests. The defense rang hollow and helped contribute to a falling out between Cubs fans and their once-beloved slugger. In true Cubs fashion, Sosa spent the next season and a half chipping away at his legacy and becoming somewhat of a joke, giving Cubs faithful a whole new reason to feel humiliated. On the upside, the corking incident would eventually take a back seat to Sammy's bizarre injuries, his ballooned ego, and the rampant steroid rumors, which would dog him even after retirement.

SAMMY SOSA'S HALL OF FAME BATS

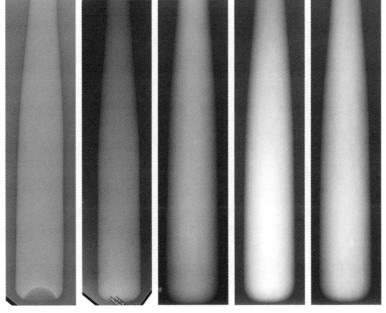

| 500th Career HR | 1998 HR's 64-66 | 1998 HR's 59-62 | 1998 HR 57 | 1998 HR 18 |

In the aftermath of Sammy Sosa's corking scandal, all of his bats were sent to the Hall of Fame to be x-rayed. Although no cork was found in any of them, the second one from the left showed traces of salsa on the handle.

26. Cubs Lose to Giants in National League Championship Series (1989)

If only Cubs manager Don Zimmer were taller, maybe things would have gone differently. Maybe San Francisco Giants slugger Will Clark wouldn't have been able to read Greg Maddux mouth the word "fastball" over Zimmer's head and hit that grand slam to seal Game 1. But Clark did hit that grand slam, and another impressive Chicago Cubs season (93–69) went by the board as they fell to the Giants 4–1 in the NLCS. Perhaps the saddest part about the series was Mark Grace's wasted performance: The first baseman hit .647, driving in eight runs. On the other hand, veteran slugger Andre Dawson had just two hits in the series, batting a paltry .105 and driving in three runs. Vaunted pitcher Greg Maddux was 0–1 with a 13.50 ERA. The Boys of Zimmer had been reduced to also-rans. They wouldn't win another division title for 14 years.

27. Jim Riggleman Hired as Cubs Skipper (1995)

After managing the San Diego Padres to a 112–179 record in just over two seasons, Jim Riggleman was hired to become the Chicago Cubs' sixth manager of the '90s. That's right: halfway through the decade, the North Siders were already on skipper number six, and this was the best guy they could find. It proved to be a perfect fit, as he would go on to helm the SS *Cubbie Blue* for five seasons, guiding the club to a record of 374–419. In 1999, Riggleman's last year as manager, he presided over a dismal 26–57 record after the All-Star break. He was summarily fired, and Cubs fans were excited about Riggleman's replacement, Don Baylor, right up until he led the Cubs to a 65–97 record in 2000, somehow besting Riggleman's worst record by two losses.

28. Cubs Collapse in Last Week of Wild-Card Race (2004)

It was the season after "the Season," and the Cubs were finally supposed to win it all. And with the end of the season just over a week away, the Cubs were in position to nab the 2004 NL wild-card. Then came the collapse, in every sense of the word. It wasn't just the losing, although dropping seven of their last nine games wasn't exactly fun. It was also the manner in which they lost: late. LaTroy Hawkins alone gave up more game-losing home runs in the final two weeks than most pitchers do in a lifetime. Sammy Sosa choked. Nomar Garciaparra choked. Just about the only guy who didn't was Prior. On September 30, he went nine innings and struck out 16, only to watch his teammates drop their second-straight 12-inning game. Management also self-destructed down the stretch, blaming WGN broadcaster Steve Stone for the team's troubles. According to some estimates, more than 10,000 fans cried themselves to death on the last day of the season.

29. Cubs Lose to Atlanta Braves in National League Division Series (1998)

North Side fans were given all sorts of false hope going into the 1998 playoffs, buoyed by Kerry Wood's Rookie of the Year performance, along with Sammy Sosa's heroic battle with Mark McGwire for the single-season home-run record. Cub Nation just figured Sosa and Wood would carry the club into the World Series, or at least the NLCS. What happened instead was a total deflation. The Atlanta Braves easily swept the wild-card Cubs, outscoring them 15–4 in three games. Sosa batted .182, going 2–11 with 0 RBIs, and an injured Kerry Wood pitched well in the final game, only to have the bullpen get jacked for five runs in four innings. Wood subsequently underwent Tommy John surgery in the off-season, and he was never the same again.

30. Cubs Go 11 Seasons without a Winning Record (1973–83)

Seven different men managed the Chicago Cubs from 1973 to 1983, and each proved equally capable of helming a loser. The only season during this stretch the Cubs didn't lose more games than they won was 1977, when the team somehow pulled off a none-mbarrassing 81–81 mark. But that minor achievement would be overshadowed by a 704–943 (.427) record in one of the worst dry spells in Cubs history. Combined with Ernie Banks's retirement in 1971 and the end of Leo Durocher's reign as manager in 1972, these years also marked the end of an era: Ron Santo left the Cubs in 1974; Billy Williams in 1975; Randy Hundley retired in 1977; and Fergie Jenkins retired in 1983. The other notable change was the purchasing of the Chicago Cubs by the Tribune Company in 1981 during a strike-shortened year, so the club wouldn't have a chance to celebrate the new ownership until 1982, when they went 79–83.

31. Cubs Produce "Believe" Bracelets (2005)

Always looking for a new expressway to Profit Town, the Chicago Cubs cashed in on a trend in 2005, hopping onto the fashion bandwagon started by Lance Armstrong's yellow "Livestrong" rubber bracelets, which were sold in packs of five and 10 in an effort to raise $5 million for cancer research. The Cubs' goal was equally noble. They wanted to bring in the dollars. The blue "Believe" bracelets were unveiled January 21, 2005, at the 20th annual Cubs Convention. Thousands of attendees gobbled them up for the attractive price of $2 apiece, then quickly turned around and sold them on eBay for between $10 and $20 each. By the start of the 2005 season, 94 percent of all Cubs fans were wearing the blue bracelets, but no amount of manufactured belief would save the ragtag Cubs squad, which finished the season in fourth place with a 79–83 record. While Believe bracelets still exist, they do so mostly in private, hidden in sock drawers.

32. Cubs Lose to Boston Red Sox in World Series (1918)

Despite featuring starting pitchers with names like Hippo, Lefty, and Claude, the Chicago Cubs fell to the Boston Red Sox 4–2 in what would be Boston's final World Series victory for 86 years. The Cubs, meanwhile, were just 10 years into what has bulged to a 106-year championship drought. While North Side fans had no way of knowing what struggles the next 10+ decades would bring, this Series should have provided some clues, as the Cubs' pitching staff had a combined 1.04 ERA but was only able to eke out two victories. On the bright side, the Cubs were able to hold Babe Ruth to just two RBIs in the Series, but that provided little solace as Ruth went 2–0 on the mound with a 1.06 ERA.

33. Beer Price Tops $4 (2004)
Enough said.

34. Cubs Open Wrigley Field Premium Ticket Services (2003)
What's the only thing worse than waiting in line for Cubs tickets? The Tribune Company answered that question when it established its very own ticket brokerage. Wrigley Field Premium Ticket Services, which billed itself as "the only licensed ticket broker endorsed by the Chicago Cubs," in fact had something of an incestuous relationship with the team. These two kissin' cousins were both owned by the Trib.

See, Wrigley Field Premium Ticket Services "purchases" tickets from the Cubs, inflates the prices (often many times over, depending on the game and seat), and then sells them to some sucker, maybe you. There are several problems with this arrangement. First of all, it borders on scalping. Second, buyers pay more in two ways: one on the mark-up from Wrigley Field Premium Ticket Services and another from the City of Chicago's 8 percent amusement tax, which is exacted on the difference between the face value and the ticket broker's resale price. Finally, as others have pointed out, the Tribune Company finally found a way to recoup at least some of the expense involved with paying their proportionate percentage of MLB dues from ticket sales via the brokerage. The corporation could sell off blocks of the tickets to another company it owned, which then resold them at a much higher price but only reported their income from face-value ticket revenues to the league each year. There's nothing wrong with this in and of itself, but if the Trib employed the same level of cunning to fielding a great team during its ownership tenure that it applied to financial matters, the Cubs would be going for their 10th straight World Series title in 2014.

35. Lee Elia Drops F-Bombs on Cubs Fans (1983)

Lee Elia, the Cubs' manager in 1983, was clearly frustrated by the team's slow start, but he was even more aggravated by the fans' very vocal disparagement of the players on the field. In an April 19 postgame press conference, he reached his breaking point. The following is an edited sample:

F——k those f——kin' fans who come out here and say they're Cub fans that are supposed to be behind you rippin' every f——kin' thing you do. I'll tell you one f——kin' thing, I hope we get f——kin' hotter than s——t, just to stuff it up them 3,000 f——kin' people that show up every f——kin' day, because if they're the real Chicago f——kin' fans, they can kiss my f——kin' ass right downtown and *print it*. They're really, really behind you around here...my f——kin' ass. What the f——k am I supposed to do, go out there and let my f——kin' players get destroyed every day and be quiet about it? For the f——kin' nickel-dime people who turn up? The motherf——kers don't even work. That's why they're out at the f——kin' game. They oughtta go out and get a f——kin' job and find out what it's like to go out and earn a f——kin' living. Eighty-five percent of the f——kin' world is working. The other 15 percent comes out here. A f——kin' playground for the c—suckers. Rip them motherf——kers. Rip them f——kin' c—suckers like the f——kin' players.

Now, all of us succumb to the temptation to drop an f-bomb or two every now and then. But Elia's tirade was the verbal equivalent of Hiroshima. Needless to say, it didn't go over well with the Cubs front office or fans, and he was gone by the end of August.

36. Mike Ditka Sings Seventh-Inning Stretch (1998)

For almost all Chicagoans, Mike "Da Coach" Ditka is a legend. He led the Bears to a Super Bowl that is still talked about in Chicago as though it happened last week, he was a key element of one of the most popular and long-running sketches on *Saturday Night Live*, and his restaurant serves the best pork chops in the Windy City, if not the United States. However, his star faded a little bit when he sang "Take Me Out to the Ballgame" during the seventh-inning stretch at Wrigley Field in 1998.

To be fair, this was Ditka, a gruff, cigar-smoking ex-coach with a nasally midwestern accent. No one expected a Pavarotti-esque performance from him. However, his rendition of the song fell even lower than the fans' very low expectations. According to Chip Caray, Ditka was running late because he had played a round of golf earlier that day. When he arrived at Wrigley Field, he flew up the steps and unceremoniously grabbed the microphone, then rushed through the song while out of breath. The result was that Ditka, who sounded like he just had his wisdom teeth taken out, was off key, off beat, off pitch, off everything.

Amazingly, he has been asked back nearly 10 more times.

37. Shawon Dunston's Mediocre Cubs Career (1985–97)

Shawon Dunston never quite lived up to his potential. Oh, sure, he went to two All-Star Games, but this guy was supposed to be special. He was supposed to go to 10 All-Star Games, win the MVP, and hit .300 every other year. He was also supposed to turn his absolute canon of an arm into a sniper rifle so he could win multiple Gold Gloves. Instead, Dunston's career was a maddening enigma for Cubs fans, who loved the shortstop to death but just couldn't understand why he never figured it out. First, there was his arm. The guy could throw an egg through a brick wall, whatever that means. The only problem was that Dunston often had no idea where his throws were going. If it weren't for Gold Glove first baseman Mark Grace, Dunston's already-high error totals would have been shockingly awful. At the plate, Dunston was as streaky as they get. He inspired the unforgettable "Shawon-O-Meter," poster-board signs that fans held up displaying his average that day in hopes that he would someday reach .300. The signs also featured the words, "And rising…!" but it usually wasn't the case. Despite all the potential, Dunston turned out to be a career .269 hitter.

38. Mitch Williams Busts as Cubs Closer (1990)

The Chicago Cubs caught lightning in a bottle in 1989, when newly acquired closer Mitch Williams had 36 thrilling, volatile saves for the playoff-bound North Siders. Never mind the fact that the Cubs gave up Rafael Palmeiro and Jamie Moyer in the eight-player deal…this seemed like a good trade at the time. But there was always something bad brewing beneath the surface, as his nickname, "Wild Thing," indicated. Despite his 36 saves in 1989, Williams gave up 52 walks in 81.7 innings pitched. The next season this wildness boiled over: Williams surrendered 50 walks in 66.3 innings, had a 1–8 record, and saved only 16 games. His blown saves were a major frustration as the Cubs went 77–85 just one year after they won 93 games. Williams was traded to the Phillies following his brutal 1990 season, and he eventually returned to form in 1993, saving 43 games. But his Cubness didn't leave him for long; in the 1993 World Series he had a 20.25 ERA, blowing two saves and serving up a bottom-of-the-ninth Series-losing home run to Joe Carter.

39. Mark Grace Wins World Series—with Diamondbacks (2001)

While hardly a slugger, Mark Grace was consistent, getting more than 2,500 hits over the course of his 16-year career. He was also a solid fielder, winning four Gold Gloves. However, Grace occasionally clashed with the team's management over his raucous participation in Chicago's nocturnal social scene. Also, there was something of a running feud between him and Sammy Sosa. These issues came to a head in 2000, when the Cubs opted not to renew his contract. After leaving Chicago, he was snatched up by the Arizona Diamondbacks, a team that had gobbled up many talented free agents in the previous few years thanks to big-spending owner Jerry Colangelo. Grace turned out to be one of the team's key contributors that season, with his seminal moment coming in Game 7 of the World Series. Down 2–1 in the ninth inning, he hit a leadoff single against feared Yankees closer Mariano Rivera that commenced his team's game- and Series-winning rally. This play gave the expansion Diamondbacks a World Series victory within their first five years of existence and one more than Grace's former team had managed to win in the previous nine decades.

40. Ryne Sandberg Walks Away (1994)

If it were up to Cubs fans, Ryne Sandberg would play second base at Wrigley Field forever. With the possible exceptions of Ernie Banks and Ron Santo, no Cubs player was more beloved by the fans during his career than the slick-fielding, smooth-swinging Sandberg. Or Ryno, as everybody called him. You never want to see a player like him leave the game prematurely, but that's exactly what Sandberg did on June 13, 1994, when the struggling second baseman retired in the middle of the season. According to Sandberg, in his book *Second to Home*, "The reason I retired is simple: I lost the desire that got me ready to play on an everyday basis for so many years. Without it, I didn't think I could perform at the same level I had in the past, and I didn't want to play at a level less than what was expected of me by my teammates, coaches, ownership, and most of all, myself." It was a crushing blow to Cubs fans, and coupled with the player's strike, which came two months later, 1994 became a season to forget on the North Side.

41. Cubs Lose to New York Yankees in World Series (1932)

You can't really blame the Cubs for losing to the juggernaut 107–47 Yankees squad. It was the way the Cubs lost. Their pitching staff had a combined ERA of 9.26, and the Yankees swept the Cubs 4–0 in a total rout of a Series, but this fall classic will forever be remembered for Babe Ruth's called shot. In the fifth inning of Game 3 at Wrigley Field, Charley Root was on the hill, and Ruth was at the plate with the score tied 4–4. Down two strikes, Ruth gestured toward the bleachers, then crushed the next pitch into the center-field seats. The Yankees won 7–5 and completed the sweep the next day with a 13–6 drubbing of the Cubs. Ruth's called shot would begin an ominous trend of Cubs games being remembered more for achievements by opposing players than for anything the Cubs themselves actually did on the field.

42. Cubs Unveil Precious Moments Giveaway (2002)

One might argue the Chicago Cubs could use as many precious moments as they can get their paws on. But one wouldn't argue that if one were a self-respecting baseball fan. So when the Cubs announced they were giving away miniature ceramic collectibles known as Precious Moments on Mother's Day 2002, it marked a new low in the franchise's promotional history. What ever happened to normal giveaways like baseball cards or beer mugs? The Cubs have enough trouble trying to prove they aren't wimps without distributing sappy figurines to eager fans once a year. But Cub Nation being Cub Nation, the 2002 promotion was a huge success, so every May since, the fans have lined up well before first pitch for the chance to take home a little piece of the Cubs' collective masculinity. Clearly a prelude to pink Cubs attire, the Precious Moments figurine is the bane of every Cubs fan who ever got called a "sissy," "wimp," or "Sally."

43. Todd Hundley Signs with Cubs (2001)

It sure seemed like Todd Hundley would be a great asset for the Cubs when the team signed him to a four-year, $23.5 million contract in 2001. A two-time All-Star catcher with the New York Mets who hit 41 homers in 1996, he was also the son of Cubs catcher Randy "the Rebel" Hundley and thus had some sense of the team's proud tradition.

Indeed, the younger Hundley showed that he was intimately familiar with that tradition by absolutely sucking during his two-year stint with the North Siders. When he wasn't on the DL or out drinking his sorrows away at various Wrigleyville pubs, he averaged .187 and .211 at the plate during 2001 and 2002. He had a grand total of 28 home runs and 66 RBIs in those two seasons…combined. By the end of his tenure in Chicago, he had even inspired a website called DumpToddHundley.com. Hundley continued to haunt Wrigleyville after he was traded away in 2003, as the Cubs were still on the hook for a part of his outlandish contract money.

44. Cubs Lose to Detroit Tigers in World Series (1935)

Ten years before the more notable postseason matchup between the Chicago Cubs and the Detroit Tigers, there was this one, which the Cubs lost in six games. Generally forgettable, the 1935 World Series did provide some fireworks in Game 3, when umpire George Moriarty ejected Cubs manager Charlie Grimm and shortstop Billy Jurges in the third inning. The Cubs ended up losing the game 6–5 in extra innings, thanks to an unearned Tiger run in the eleventh. While it's not exactly clear what prompted the ejections, MLB commissioner Judge Landis levied $200 fines to everyone involved after the season: Moriarty, Grimm, Jurges, Woody English, and Billy Herman. The Cubs followed their 100-win season in 1935 with two second-place finishes before winning the pennant in 1938, only to be crushed by the New York Yankees in the World Series.

45. Cubs Lose 100 Games for First Time (1962)

From 1947 to 1961, the Cubs enjoyed exactly zero winning seasons. And just when fans on the North Side thought it couldn't get any worse, the once-proud franchise endured the unthinkable: 103 losses. With a 59–103 record, the 1962 Chicago Cubs established a new low in Wrigleyville. It was a frustrating season for the offense (Ron Santo hit just .227, and a young Lou Brock just .263), but the pitching is what really crushed any chance of success. The staff featured a bloated ERA of 4.54, yielding 159 home runs and 601 bases on balls. Coming on the heels of the failed "College of Coaches" experiment, 1962 provided no relief as the Cubs went through three forgettable managers that aren't even worth mentioning, except one of them, Charlie Metro, because he had a cool name.

46. Cubs Lose 100 Games for Second Time (1966)

Of his 1966 ballclub, first-year manager Leo Durocher said, "Wow, these guys suck." Well, he probably said that, given how horribly the team played en route to its last-place finish and second 59–103 season in just five years. This time around, the pitchers were once again the problem, ranking dead last in the National League in a variety of key areas: ERA, hits, runs, home runs, shutouts, and angry fans shouting, "We need a pitcher, not a belly itcher." Durocher would eventually pull it together and prove to be a decent manager, but only until 1969, when the extremely talented Cubs self-destructed during a pennant race with the New York Mets.

47. Sammy Sosa Hit in Head by Pitch (2003)

Just one plate appearance after tying Eddie Murray for 17th place on Major League Baseball's all-time home-run list, Sammy Sosa stepped into the batter's box against Pittsburgh Pirates hurler and fellow Dominican Republic native Salomon Torres. Arguably, it would be the last time in Sosa's career he would feel comfortable at the plate, because the pitch Torres threw was a 90-mph fastball directly at Sosa's head. The ball connected with Sosa's left temple, smashing his helmet and leaving the Cubs slugger dazed and upset. While he escaped the incident without major injury, the mental toll from the horrific beaning would ultimately lead to the twilight of Sosa's career. A mere two months later, a struggling Sammy was caught using a corked bat in an effort to reignite his stagnant swing. The beaning also prompted him to stand much farther from the plate, making him susceptible to outside strikes and all but eliminating his opposite-field power.

48. Joe Carter Hired as Cubs Broadcaster (2001)

It would be tough for anyone to replace Steve Stone in the Cubs broadcast booth, but that doesn't mean anyone couldn't have done a better job than Joe Carter. When Stone left as WGN's color commentator (the first time), the geniuses in the Tribune Tower knew they had to pull in a heavy hitter. Unfortunately, they weren't able to do that, so Hall of Fame slugger Joe Carter would have to do. It's important to mention Carter's Hall of Fame standing, as he often used tales of his playing days as a crutch whenever he couldn't think of something to say about the actual game being played right in front of his eyes. While there's no way to verify the exact number, it's estimated that Carter casually mentioned his World Series–winning home run off Mitch Williams approximately 3,000 times during his two-year stint in the WGN booth. He also failed to build a rapport with play-by-play man Chip Caray, other than to step over his partner's words a few times a minute. Carter was not particularly gifted in grammar or math, often leading to gaffes combining his two weaknesses, such as the time he said, "Kerry Wood's fastball takes less time to get to the plate, so hitters has more time to react."

49. Jerome Walton's Sophomore Slump (1990)

Unlike many Cubs prospects, Jerome Walton actually lived up to the hype. At least for a few months. The year was 1989, and the Chicago Cubs were playing well. Walton, their young center fielder, looked to have a bright future in the big leagues. He had a decent bat, good speed, and was an above-average outfielder. But it was his remarkable 30-game hitting streak that catapulted him into the national spotlight, earning him the National League Rookie of the Year Award. Cubs fans couldn't help themselves when it came to expecting a long, All-Star-studded career from Walton. What should have concerned them was that Walton hit .338 during his streak, the lowest recorded batting average for any 30-game hitting streak in Major League history (20 of the 30 games were single-hit performances). Outside the streak, Walton hit a pedestrian .274. Which is better than the .263 average he put up in 1990 as he regressed into a pronounced sophomore slump. The bloom was off the rose as Walton had just 21 RBIs and was 14–21 in stolen base attempts. His glove slumped, too: he went from a .990 fielding percentage with three errors in 1989 to a .977 fielding percentage with six errors in 1990. Despite Walton's stellar rookie performance, he spent just a few years as a Cub, and his career petered out over the course of 10 seasons with five teams. His second-longest hit streak was like six or seven games, probably.

50. Cubs Give Up on Corey Patterson (2006)

When the Cubs used the third overall pick in the 1998 draft to select an 18-year-old Corey Patterson straight out of high school, the team was sure the decision would change the franchise forever. Hailed as a "five-tool" player, Patterson was supposed to blossom into the next Lou Brock (the one the Cubs wouldn't trade) and be a cornerstone of the organization. Just a few years later, Cubs brass couldn't wait any longer, so they rushed Patterson to the big leagues. The inexperienced center fielder struggled mightily, striking out with alarming frequency and drawing just 28 walks in his first 793 at-bats. Not exactly the type of numbers you want from a five-tool speedster. After a successful first half in 2003, Patterson suffered a season-ending knee injury. He regressed in 2004 and 2005, batting .245 in his final two seasons as a Cub. He was traded to the Baltimore Orioles in January 2006 for two minor leaguers and is generally considered the most overhyped player in Cubs history. But the Cubs being the Cubs, they learned

Corey Patterson, shown after striking out with the bases loaded for the second time in a 5–3 loss in 2004, is widely regarded as the most overhyped Cub ever.

nothing, drafting Eric Patterson, Corey's younger brother, a few years later. He also never panned out.

51. Bleacher Tickets Become Outrageously Priced (Ongoing)

There was a time when you could buy a bleacher ticket for $4. That time was not 1960, 1970, or even 1980. It was 1987. Since then, prices have steadily increased, easily outpacing the rate of inflation. In 2013, the total cost for a bleacher ticket (including taxes and "convenience charges") ranged from $39 to $69 per game. But that's not really the price, because odds are you can't get bleacher tickets at face value from the Cubs official ticket office. Odds are the scalpers got them first and will now sell them to you for $60 to $200 per ticket, depending on the game. So why the jump in prices? It's not like the club has become some sort of division-winning juggernaut. The answer, as is always the case, is much simpler: the fans will pay the price, no matter how high it goes. Thanks in large part to night games, the Wrigley Field bleachers have been transformed into a giant singles party.

52. Cubs Lose to Philadelphia Athletics in World Series (1910)

Just two years into what would become the longest championship drought in major sports history, player/manager Frank Chance led the Cubs to a stellar 104–50 record in the regular season and a date with the Philadelphia Athletics in the World Series. Alas, it was not meant to be, as the Cubs were nearly swept away in a 4–1 Series rout, with the

Cubs' only victory coming in Game 4 after 10 innings and three Athletics errors. Adding insult to injury, Philadelphia needed only two pitchers in the entire series—durable righties Jack Coombs and Chief Bender combined for a 2.76 ERA in a whopping 45.7 innings pitched—while the Cubs ran out seven hurlers of their own but were still outscored 35–15 in five games.

53. Ryne Sandberg Comes Back (1996)

To the delight of most Cubs fans, Ryne Sandberg's "retirement" barely lasted longer than a year, and he was on the field again at the start of the 1996 season. It started well enough: his first hit in a regular-season game was a home run off Pedro Astacio. And he had a decent year all around, with 25 home runs, 92 RBIs, and 82 double plays. Still, Sandberg would not be like Moses leading the Chicago Cubs to the promised land, as so many of the team's supporters had hoped. Really, Ryno's comeback did little more than pad his own stats (he finished with 277 homers, the most ever for a second baseman at the time) and promote his bid for the Hall of Fame. He retired again for good the following year, with Chicago finishing below .500 in both 1996 and 1997.

54. Leon Durham's Error in National League Championship Series (1984)

Leon Durham had a good seven-plus-season career with the Cubs and was a key member of the team that went to the NLCS in 1984. Alas, his most significant contribution that year was a huge negative for the team, and one that's earned him eternal ire in the hearts of Cubs fans. It was the sixth inning of the decisive Game 5, and things were looking good for the Cubs. The team led 3–0, but a pair of sacrifice flies in the bottom of the inning drove in a couple of runs for the Padres. The next inning, a visibly tired Rick Sutcliffe walked Carmelo Martinez, who advanced to second on a Garry Templeton sacrifice fly. Next up was Tim Flannery, who ripped a grounder toward first base. Durham attempted to field the hit, but it went through his legs like a croquet ball through a wicket, and Martinez plated. To be fair, the game was only tied 3–3 at that point, and the Cubs allowed three more runs in a 6–3 Padres victory. And Durham's overall numbers that year suggest he was a key factor in their playoff run. But Cubs fans will always remember him as, "That asshole who ruined '84."

55. Mike Harkey Injured Doing Cartwheel for Bleacher Chicks (1992)

Pitching prospect Mike Harkey was drafted in 1984 by San Diego, but he decided not to sign with the team, something that Padres management must have been happy about in hindsight. Of course, when he reentered the draft three years later, the Cubs were only too happy to pick him up. In a few ways, Harkey was the quintessential Cubs player. For example, he only won 26 games in the five seasons he played in Chicago, about five per year. Also, he was on the DL a lot. One of the most memorable injuries for Harkey came early in 1992 as a result of a little hot-dogging. In an effort to impress some babes in the stands, Harkey turned a cartwheel on the field in front of them during batting practice. While he can't be faulted for relying on this time-honored pick-up technique—if you ever want to impress a girl at a bar, simply turn a cartwheel in front of her—it backfired when it led to a season-ending injury. The Cubs let him go the following year, but for some reason, he wound up playing for two more teams at the major-league level after pulling this failed gymnastics stunt.

56. Dusty Baker Doesn't Get It Done, Man (2003–06)

When Dusty Baker was named Cubs manager in November 2002, Wrigleyville finally had reason to believe. Not only did Baker have a reputation as a cool customer, but he was also a three-time NL Manager of the Year coming off a season in which he led the San Francisco Giants to the World Series. They didn't win it, but so what? The 2002 Cubs could barely dream of getting to the fall classic, let alone actually winning it. And then, in 2003, it almost happened. Thanks in large part to aces Mark Prior and Kerry Wood, Baker and the Cubs shocked the world by going 88–74. They won the NL Central and nearly marched to the World Series—only to collapse in Game 6 of the NLCS against the Florida Marlins. Still, despite the disappointment of being only five outs away from the Promised Land (and then not making it), Baker had ushered in a new era of Cubs dominance. Only…he hadn't. Baker led the Cubs on a steady decline over the next three years, with the North Siders ultimately losing a whopping 96 games in 2006, good for last place in the National League.

Even the magical 2003 can't change the fact that Dusty Baker's reign will go down in the annals of Cubdom as yet another unmitigated disaster.

57. Will Clark Reads Greg Maddux's Lips Before Grand Slam (1989)

At the Republican National Convention in 1988, then-candidate George Bush made the famous proclamation: "Read my lips: no new taxes!" Of course, nearly everyone who read his lips was pretty peeved a few years later when President Bush broke his word and raised taxes. A year after the RNC, another lip-reading situation would garner headlines, this time in the world of sports. In Game 1 of the 1989 National League Championship Series, slugger Will "the Thrill" Clark faced Cubs ace Greg Maddux in the latter's first postgame outing. Maddux's inexperience showed: Clark bloodied his nose early when he drove in two runs with a double in the first inning, then hit a solo homer in the third. He wasn't done yet, though. Facing Maddux in the fourth, Clark stood and watched as manager Don Zimmer came out to the mound for a chat with his green pitcher. Clark later confessed he saw Maddux say "fastball in" during this discussion. Unlike Bush, Maddux delivered exactly what he said he would. Knowing what was coming, the Thrill nailed the pitch for a grand slam that gave the Giants a 7–3 lead on their way to an 11–3 rout of the Cubs that set the tone for the series. And Maddux? He now covers his mouth with his glove whenever he converses with anyone on the mound.

58. Steve Stone Gets Bitter, Then Steps Down (2004)

Following a solid, 11-season pitching career, Steve Stone stepped into the broadcast booth for Tribune-owned WGN television in 1983. He joined legendary announcer Harry Caray, and Stone's insightful commentary proved to be a great complement to the entertaining malapropisms of his senior partner. After Harry Caray's death in early 1998, his grandson Chip joined Stone in the booth. While no one could replace Caray (not even his descendant), Stone and Caray III meshed well. Health problems sidelined Stone between 2001 and 2002, but he came back in time for the Cubs' playoff run—and epic collapse—in 2003. Stone returned to the booth the following year a changed man. He was much more critical in his comments, particularly where Dusty Baker's management style was concerned. Moreover, Cubs pitcher Kent Mercker heckled Stone right back for what he perceived to be unfair disparagements of the team. (The idea of Stone, who won the Cy Young Award and achieved a 25-win season, being jeered by the middling Mercker, the Ford Taurus of pitchers, is nauseatingly amusing.) All of this got to be too much for Stone, who stepped down at the end of the 2004 season. In spite of his withering critiques of the team, he remained popular with fans until the very end—probably because they realized the Cubs deserved so much worse than what Stone dished out.

59. Tinker, Evers, and Chance Infield Broken Up (1911–13)

Not many teams in baseball history truly deserve to be called dominant in a given era. Cincinnati's Big Red Machine of the early to mid-1970s certainly qualifies, as does just about any Yankees squad from the late '20s through the late '50s. Believe it or not, the Chicago Cubs once had a dominant team as well. At the core of this collection of world-beaters was an incredible infield comprised of future Hall of Famers Joe Tinker at shortstop, Johnny Evers at second, and Frank Chance at first (as well as third baseman Harry Steinfeldt, to a lesser extent). These guys played together with few respites from 1903 to 1910.

How good were they? The Cubs won four pennants and two World Series during that span. In addition, the team got 116 wins in a 154-game season, a record that still stands today. (The Seattle Mariners tied this total in 2001, but they played 162 games that year.) Tinker, Evers, and Chance even inspired a poem that was famous in its day. It was penned by nationally known news columnist Franklin Pierce Adams, who titled it "Tinker to Evers to Chance."

However, there were problems off the field. Although they became friends many decades later, Tinker and Evers despised one another during their playing days, and the latter had a nervous breakdown in 1911 that shut him down that season. That same year, Chance got plunked with a pitch that nearly killed him. The dissolution was complete by 1913, when Chance went to New York to manage the Yankees and Tinker took over as manager for the Cincinnati Reds.

60. Red Sox Win World Series (2004)

One of the things that made the Cubs' cursed-by-fate status tolerable was the fact that there was another storied, prestigious organization out there that also couldn't win it all: the Boston Red Sox. In fact, the Red Sox's curse actually seemed worse. While the Cubs' hex involved a barnyard animal, Boston's torment was the result of having dealt away Babe Ruth, the best baseball player ever. In 1920 Red Sox owner Harry Frazee traded the Babe to the New York Yankees (back then an ally of Boston, along with the Chicago White Sox) for cash in order to purchase Fenway Park, which he didn't own at the time. He actually traded a few more stars to the Yanks that year, too, to put his proverbial thumb in the eye of American League president and antagonist Ban Johnson and the "Loyal Five" clubs aligned with him. Of course, the popular narrative goes that Frazee sold the Babe to finance an asinine Broadway theatrical production called *No, No, Nanette*, which is what the Curse of the Bambino was based on. That's right, it was all a lie.

Yet the "curse" enjoyed a good run and helped explain the Red Sox's 80+ years of failure to win the World Series in the minds of both the team's fans and followers of baseball. This was reinforced by incidents like Bill Buckner's infamous error in Game 6 of the 1986 World Series. However, the jig was up in 2004, when Kevin Millar, Johnny Damon, David Ortiz, Curt Shilling, and the other "cowboys" completely reversed the momentum in an amazing ALCS against the now-hated Yankees, then swept the St. Louis Cardinals in the World Series. The jig was up for the Cubs, too, who couldn't rely on their scapegoat the way they had before. Plus, now they were completely alone in their loserdom. (Unless they counted the White Sox, which, being Cubs fans, they didn't.)

61. LaTroy Hawkins (2004–05)

When the Cubs signed former Minnesota Twins reliever LaTroy Hawkins in December 2003, they were getting the best setup man in baseball. But when Cubs closer Joe Borowski went down with an injury in early 2004, Hawkins was forced to change roles and become the worst closer in the majors. It was a role in which Hawkins would thrive. Despite his respectable 2.63 ERA, the righty struggled all season long, converting just 25 of 34 save opportunities. He was particularly adept at blowing one-run-save chances. The fans at Wrigley Field commended Hawkins for his poor play by booing him periodically throughout the year. But it was the final two weeks of 2004 that cemented the fans' hatred for Hawkins. He blew every save opportunity down the stretch in excruciating fashion as the Cubs went 2–7 in their last nine games of the season. Hawkins was not solely responsible for the collapse, but he was certainly the biggest part of it. In 2005 the Cubs were forced to trade Hawkins to the San Francisco Giants after the combustible closer blew four of his first eight save opportunities. The deal ended one of the ugliest fan-player relationships in Chicago Cubs history.

62. Grant DePorter Blows Up Bartman Ball (2004)

How do you exorcise the demons of the Cubs' cursed 2003 National League Championship Series? Why, blow up the ball used during the play that may or may not have anything to do with the team's loss, of course. That's the conclusion that Grant DePorter came to, anyway. DePorter, the Chicago restaurateur who owns—among other establishments—Harry Caray's Restaurant, apparently decided that the ball had absorbed all the Cubs' bad juju when Bartman made his fateful grab in Game 6 of the NLCS against the Florida Marlins. Thus it had to be destroyed. First DePorter had to get it. To that end he spent $113,824.16. Then he hired a Hollywood special-effects professional to detonate the ball in a much-ballyhooed, nationally televised ceremony outside of Harry Caray's Restaurant. It was even given a "last meal" of steak and lobster. It turned out to be a terrible investment. Oh sure, the stunt generated lots of publicity for the restaurant. And it raised significant proceeds for diabetes sufferers. However, in terms of alleviating the Cubs' curse, it was probably the worst $113,824 plus change ever spent.

63. Cubs Acquire Pitcher Ernie Broglio (1964)

When the Cubs traded outfielder Lou Brock to the St. Louis Cardinals for pitcher Ernie Broglio in 1964, it seemed like a very good deal. The Cubs were getting rid of someone who hadn't performed well by anyone's standards, and they were getting an ace who had pitched a 21-win season with the Cards and gotten 18 victories the year before the trade. However, something clicked in Brock when he went to St. Louis. He helped lead the team to the World Series championship that same year and did the same in 1967 as an All-Star. And Broglio? He had a 4–7 record and 4.04 ERA with the Cubs during the remainder of the 1964 season. Sadly, that would actually be his best year with the team. Throughout 1965 and 1966, Broglio won a grand total of three games and dropped 12. The Cubs released him after that. "Brock for Broglio" is emblematic for Cubs followers today because it demonstrates the other aspect of the curse: not the part that causes the team to melt down late in the regular season or in the playoffs, but rather the part that makes the Cubs' seemingly sensible trades look ridiculous in retrospect. Also, it makes the Cubs' "loser" status glaringly obvious, as players who don't perform while on the team go on to have great careers—often including an elusive World Series victory—after they're traded.

64. Film Rookie of the Year *Released (1993)*

The Cubs' World Series hopes were put off for at least another century with the release of *Rookie of the Year*, a schmaltzy, contrived film about a boy who becomes a pitcher for the North Siders and leads them to...a division title. The plot goes something like this: 13-year-old Henry Rowengartner breaks his arm, but it heals exceptionally well. He finds out just how well while attending a Cubs game. When he catches a home run in the bleachers, he throws it back—to home plate. Needless to say, the team immediately signs this promising young prospect as a reliever. With Chet Steadman (played by a not-yet-psychotic Gary Busey) as a guide, young Henry manages to register save after save through that season, all while navigating the difficulties of fame, fortune, and scheming agents. Of course, there's the climactic showdown near the end of the movie where Henry must win the most important game of his life. Naturally, he does, but it's not Game 7 of the World Series, nor is it even a playoff game. It's actually the finale of the regular season, which simply gives the Cubs the NL Central title. (Hey, that's still a pretty good year.) But Henry decides he can't take all the pressure and attention anymore, plus he trips on a baseball in that last game and loses his 100-mph fastball when he falls on his arm. Thus, he goes back to his regular life of Little League baseball. The kicker, though, is the deus ex machina at the very end, which shows a Cubs World Series Championship ring on his finger. Accept it, Cubs fans: This is as close as you're going to get to a World Series win for a long time.

65. Cubs Sign Mel Rojas (1997)

For fans who remembered Ernie Broglio, the Cubs' acquisition of reliever Mel Rojas must have seemed like a really bad instance of déjà vu: A hot-shot, sure-thing pitcher comes onto the roster, then immediately collapses in epic fashion. In the case of Rojas, the Cubs were getting a pitcher who had notched 36 saves the previous season for the now-defunct Montreal Expos. He was going to be a surefire asset for the team. At least the Cubs paid him like he would be: Rojas received $4,583,333 in his first year with the team, a sum second only to the salary of Sammy Sosa. He earned more than Cubs stars like Mark Grace and Ryne Sandberg. The term "earned" is used loosely here, though. Rojas blew save after save for the team in his first month as the Cubs' closer. In fact, they dropped their first

14 contests; their first win came in the second game of a doubleheader against the New York Mets on April 20. They would go on to lose 19 that month. Suffice it to say, Rojas only stayed in Chicago for half a season. But the damage was done. Even though the team had a couple of strong runs later in the year, by that point they were a nonfactor in the playoff race: the Cubs finished fifth in their division at 68–94.

66. Cubs Replace Don Baylor with Bruce Kimm (2002)

It's hard to believe in hindsight, but Cubs fans were actually excited about the 2002 season. In the previous year, the team had finished third in the NL Central with a winning record, and baseball pundits and buffs alike were expecting big things from them in '02. Yet the Cubs stumbled out of spring training and into a very lackluster regular season. Most blamed the Cubs' stumbling start on manager Don Baylor, who many felt had affected the team's chemistry with some controversial personnel moves the year before. With a 5–1 loss to the Atlanta Braves on July 4, 2002—just before the All-Star break—the Cubs fell to 34–49. Baylor was canned the very next day. This move was understandable.

What was not understandable was management's choice to replace him: Bruce Kimm, then skipper of the Cubs' Triple-A affiliate in Iowa. Giving one of the most coveted and demanding manager positions in baseball to a largely unproven minor-leaguer defied logic, unless the Tribune Company had written the season off by that point (a definite possibility). In any case, it sucked for the fans: the only thing more depressing than having to fire a losing manager is hiring another losing manager, and Kimm was definitely a loser. The Cubs went 33–45 during Kimm's tenure and finished fifth in their division with a 67–95 record. He didn't even last the rest of the season. The announcement of his exit went out before the final game of the year, along with news of his replacement: Dusty Baker.

67. Team Uses Cell Phones to Call Bullpen (2006)

One of the things fans visiting Wrigley Field can expect to see are attendees—usually clad in the latest Abercrombie & Fitch clothing line—yapping away on cell phones. What they might not expect to witness is the Cubs managers talking on cellies. Yet this is exactly what happened last season. Apparently taking a cue from the fashion plates up in the bleachers, Cubs manager Dusty Baker began using a cell phone to send instructions out to the bullpen, which is little more than 100 feet away from the dugout in Wrigley Field. Exactly why the team decided to switch to cell phones when the regular landline or even hand signals would suffice isn't known for sure. What is clear is that this is completely unnecessary. The White Sox don't even use cell phones in the dugout, and they play at U.S. Cellular Field.

68. Wrigley Field Starts Falling Apart (2004)

One of the most venerable venues in all of sports, Wrigley Field is more of a draw than the team that plays there.

So when the Friendly Confines started to crumble in the summer of 2004, true baseball fans everywhere (except those on Chicago's South Side, perhaps) were upset. On a couple of different occasions within the span of a month, concrete debris fell on or near attendees. The first instance involved an elderly woman getting hit in the foot with a brick-sized chunk that collapsed from the upper deck. Following this incident, another piece fell inches away from a man and his five-year-old son. Understandably, people began to worry. Of course, no one was more worried than Chicago mayor Richard M. Daley. A lifelong White Sox fan from Bridgeport, Illinois, Daley threatened to shut down Wrigley Field if the Cubs owners didn't repair the stadium immediately. They fixed it shortly thereafter to the tune of $2 million, which should have been the end of it. But the city of Chicago fined the Cubs $6,725 for not having the proper permits, then charged the team $36,010 for retroactive permits for the renovations. This episode served as a lesson of sorts for the team's followers. Fans who insist that Chicago is a Cubs town were reminded that the 800-pound gorilla in city hall didn't see it that way.

69. Bleachers Renamed Bud Light Bleachers (2006)

The presence of blatant marketing at Wrigley Field is a relatively recent phenomenon, and perhaps no better example of this trend is the "Bud Light" prefix on the hallowed outfield bleachers. Game attendees who come in the famous entrance at the intersection of Sheffield and Waveland

Avenues are now greeted by a sign that reads "Bud Light Bleachers." This is an affront to Cubs fans for a couple of reasons, the most important of which is the fact that Bud Light is a product of Anheuser-Busch, the same corporation that has its name plastered on the stadium where the rival St. Louis Cardinals play. Given these circumstances, Cubs fans might expect that Anheuser-Busch had to plead with and throw boatloads of money at the Tribune Company for these naming rights. They'd be right on the second count, but wrong on the first. "The Cubs approached us with this opportunity, and it seemed to us a unique way to improve our presence in Chicago," Anheuser-Busch's vice president of global media and sports marketing Tony Ponturo said of the deal. According to Ponturo, the "Bud Light Bleachers" cost just under $1 million a year.

70. Village People Release "YMCA" (1978)

Back in the late 1970s, a group called the Village People, whose shtick was dressing up as masculine American stereotypes, put out a disco song that covertly explained how homosexual males could meet up at the YMCA to "hang out with all the boys." Not that there's anything wrong with that. For some reason, though, the Cubs decided this would be a great song to play during the seventh-inning stretch. Perhaps it's because it's a catchy pop tune, or maybe it's an homage to the rainbow-bedecked Boys Town area in the nearby neighborhood of Lakeview (which actually has a YMCA). Whatever the reason, the song caught on at Wrigley Field, where fans do the famous dance that accompanies it. Even the beer guys get into it. Yet it's just fuel for the fire for South Siders, who don "Wrigley Field: Home of the World's Largest Gay Bar" T-shirts at every White Sox game.

71. Van Halen Releases "Jump" (1984)

The distinctive synthesizer sounds and sonic screams of lead singer David Lee Roth made "Jump" a radio hit for Van Halen in 1984. That was also the year the Chicago Cubs started playing the song on the ballpark organ during pregame introductions. For the next two decades, Cubs players would run out onto Wrigley Field with this ditty as a musical backdrop. In 2006 "Jump" was played significantly less, as the team decided to go with a handful of songs in a rotation format, but fans at Cubs games can still catch it fairly frequently. The decision to hold on to this song for as long as they did is somewhat strange. It definitely lacks the hard, kick-ass edge of, say, "Thunderstruck" by AC/DC (the pregame anthem for the White Sox). Plus, while it's an undeniably appealing power pop-rock anthem, "Jump" isn't a particularly great motivational device. In fact, the lyrics were inspired by a suicide attempt from a building ledge.

72. Jeff Gordon Sings Seventh-Inning Stretch (2005)

"Rainbow Warrior" Jeff Gordon is one of the most hated men in NASCAR. He made himself extremely disliked in yet another sport when he came to Chicago's North Side in 2005 to sing "Take Me Out to the Ballgame" during the seventh-inning stretch. Before he started singing,

Ozzy Osbourne's rendition of "Take Me Out to the Ballgame" was the weirdest to date, but he still got a group hug.

Gordon greeted the fans by stating how happy he was to be at "Wrigley Stadium." From then on, it was boos aplenty. As Gordon progressed through the song, he began to slip up on the lyrics, which made the fans jeer and heckle him even more. In all likelihood, he'd never encountered such a negative reaction to a performance, even among his most bitter antagonists at Daytona Arena...err, Daytona International Speedway.

73. Ozzy Osbourne Mumbles Seventh-Inning Stretch (2003)

Back in the 1960s and 1970s, Black Sabbath front man Ozzy Osbourne could really belt out some monster tracks. Few rock stars before or since could wail like he did in songs like "Iron Man," "Sweet Leaf," and "Crazy Train." The man who showed up at Wrigley Field in 2003 was a far cry from that heavy metal icon. Ozzy came into the booth with Chip Caray and Steve Stone to sing but proceeded to mutter his way through what might have been lyrics. Only about half of the tune seemed to have been sung in any language at all, much less English. Ozzy certainly provided Cubs fans with the most peculiar version of the song they've ever received, if not the absolute worst (*see*: Jeff Gordon). However, Caray said it was one of the best experiences he had with a guest singer: "As everyone just stands back in shock, he says to every member of our crew that was in the booth—the cameraman, the lighting people, Steve, me, our production assistant—'Thank you very much. My wife and I had a lovely time. Give me a hug.'"

74. Cubs Suffer First Sub-.500 Season Since 1908 (1915)

The 1915 Chicago Cubs went 73–80, which put them in fourth place (out of eight teams) in the National League. It marked the first time since the 1908 World Series that the club had failed to win more games than it lost. In many ways, it was the birth of a new, more inconsistent Cubs franchise. Suddenly losing seasons started to outnumber winning ones, and the postseason failures began to add up. This instability spread to the dugout, where managers were changed like underwear. Nineteen fifteen was Roger Bresnahan's first and only year as Cubs skipper, but this would prove to be perfectly normal in this era. From 1912 to 1917, the Cubs went through six different managers: Frank Chance, Johnny Evers, Hank O'Day, Bresnahan, Joe Tinker, and Fred Mitchell. The low point of the season came when the Brooklyn Dodgers beat the Cubs 13–0 and George Cutshaw went 66 at the plate, tying a record not achieved in 14 years. This was also the last season the Cubs would play at West Side Grounds. In 1916 the club's home games were played in what would eventually become

Wrigley Field, a stadium that has never seen a World Series victory—by the home team, anyway.

75. Kevin Orie: Yet Another Third-Base Bust (2002)

With 98 different Cubs third basemen between the Ron Santo and Aramis Ramirez eras, we could focus on any number of busts, but Kevin Orie stands out as a guy who should have succeeded. His numbers were respectable in 1997, his rookie season: a .275 batting average, five triples, and 44 RBIs in just 114 games. But things fell apart the very next year. Orie was dreadful at the plate in 1998, hitting just .181 in 64 games. The Cubs traded him to the Florida Marlins in the middle of the season, and he struggled there, too. In 2002 Orie tried to return to the Cubs after a few years out of the big leagues, but it was not to be. He retired with a .249 average in only 316 career games.

76. Neifi Perez Given Two-Year Contract (2006)

Baseball contracts have become somewhat of a joke ever since Alex Rodriguez was handed a quarter of a billion dollars by the Texas Rangers in 2001. Suddenly everyone was making the big bucks, even ineffective middle relievers. But over the last 15 years, there has been no bigger show of GM idiocy than when Jim Hendry signed utility man Neifi Perez to a two-year, $5 million contract for 2006–07. The first problem was the money: $5 million for an aging backup infielder with no power and a penchant for popping the ball up every other at-bat? The second—and more fundamental—slap in the face to Cubs fans is the fact the Cubs signed Perez for two years. The whole point of a multiyear contract is to lock up a player so you don't have to compete with other teams to re-sign him. Other than a local softball team or two, who the hell is going to be interested in a subpar, 34-year-old pine rider with a weak bat and fading defensive skills? The only saving grace here is that Perez was traded to the Detroit Tigers halfway through his contract for a minor league catcher.

77. Dennis Eckersley Becomes a Great Closer (1987)

With Oakland, of course. Following a three-year stint as a Cubs starting pitcher, during which he compiled a pedestrian 27–26 record with a 4.31 ERA, Dennis Eckersley was traded to the Oakland Athletics for three minor leaguers. Those guys never quite panned out. Eckersley, on the other hand, became one of baseball's premier closers, helping his team get to the World Series in 1988 and win it in 1989. He hadn't won a single award as a Cub, but after he was traded, Eckersley's accomplishments were many: an MVP, a Cy Young Award, two Rolaids Relief Man Awards, ALCS MVP, and *The Sporting News* Pitcher of the Year. The handling of Eckersley is just another example of the Cubs' inability to utilize talent. By the time he became a Cub, the bloom was off Eckersley's rose as a starter, yet the Cubs kept running him out there, not even considering a move to the bullpen, where he would eventually flourish and play his way into the Hall of Fame.

78. Cubs Fan Steals Chad Kreuter's Hat (2000)

If Cubs fans have one thing going for them, it's their reputation as a happy lot. They're fans of baseball's "Lovable
Losers," after all, so they are supposed to be lovable, too.
This started to change in the late 1990s as ticket prices
went up, beer sales skyrocketed, and fans became much
more interested in winning (even though the team
wasn't). The new wave of drunkenness and anger boiled
over on May 16, 2000, in a game against the Los Angeles
Dodgers, when a fan sitting near the visitor's bullpen stole
reliever Chad Kreuter's hat. Kreuter and several teammates
went into the stands to retrieve the hat, and a nine-minute
mêlée ensued—as the rest of Wrigley Field cheered it on.
It was a sad turning point for Cub Nation. This was the
kind of violence that occurred across town at U.S. Cellular
Field, not the Friendly Confines. Coupled with a disturb-
ing new trend of throwing objects onto the field to show
disapproval, the hat incident helped chip away at the positive image of the Wrigley Field faithful. Instead of happy-
go-lucky, some people started seeing Cubs fans as angry
and disenchanted.

79. Cubs Block Rooftops with Wind Screens (2002)

During its ownership tenture, the Tribune Company
might have had a reputation for being greedy, but it sure
didn't act like it. No matter what dollar-grabbing stunt
they pulled, the good folks at the Trib always came up
with a sensible explanation. Such was the case in 2002,
when they installed "wind screens" on the fence lining

Wrigley Field's bleachers. According to the Tribune Tower, the fans needed protection from the elements. Never mind the fact that bleacher bums have been surviving the wind for decades without incident. Also never mind the fact the Cubs were in the middle of a dispute with local rooftop owners when they decided to put up the "wind screens," which conveniently blocked the view of Wrigley Field from the buildings across the street. According to the Tribune Company, the rooftop owners were getting a free product they weren't entitled to—Chicago Cubs baseball—and that was hurting everybody. Turns out everybody is the same group of people who knew what the Cubs were really up to: squeezing more cash out of a subpar baseball team. In the end, the rooftop owners ponied up about $2 million per season, and the wind problem at Wrigley suddenly went away, along with the screens.

80. The Virtual Waiting Room (2004)

As if purchasing Cubs tickets wasn't painful enough in the pre-technology era, the Cubs took things a step further with the "Virtual Waiting Room" in February 2004. A white rectangle that occupies your computer screen and repeatedly counts backward from 30 to 0, the Virtual Waiting Room is supposed to be where you wait for your chance to buy individual game tickets for the upcoming Cubs season. A more appropriate name would be the Virtual Torture Room because nothing on this earth is more excruciating than waiting *to be allowed* to buy a Cubs bleacher ticket for nearly $50. Especially when it takes three to four hours per purchase, if you're lucky enough to get into the actual system at all. And the odds are you won't get past the Virtual Waiting Room until late afternoon, which means the only tickets left will be for the nosebleed section on a frigid April day game against the Miami Marlins.

But it's not all bad. There is, surprisingly, hope. When the gods created the awesome frustration force that is the Chicago Cubs, they didn't account for computer geeks, who quickly figured out that you can press Control N (Option N on a Mac) to open as many windows as your screen allows. Instead of waiting like a chump in one Virtual Waiting Room, you could be waiting like a chump in 80 or 90 of them.

81. Nomar Garciaparra Fails as a Cub (2005)

The 2004 trade deadline seemingly had passed without the Cubs making a significant move to upgrade the club that had come within five outs of the World Series in 2003, but then news came of "the Trade." It was a four-team deal between the Cubs, Red Sox, Twins, and Expos. The result was Nomar Garciaparra in a Cubs uniform for at least two years. Everyone figured Cubs GM Jim Hendry had struck gold—just like he did with Aramis Ramirez in 2003. After all, Garciaparra was a two-time American League batting champion and a five-time All-Star shortstop. Unfortunately, in becoming a Cub, the former Red Sox standout was forced to trade in his talent for a string of injuries. He played just 43 games over two months for the 2004 Cubs, hitting a respectable .297 but knocking in just 20 runs. The Cubs missed the playoffs. Still, everyone was pretty sure Garciaparra would be his usual, stellar self in 2005. Instead, he collapsed with a torn groin three weeks into the season. He was only hitting .157 at the time. He played a grand total of 62 games in 2005, finishing with a flurry to bring his batting average up to a modest .283. The ultimate kicker would come in 2006, when he returned to form and had an outstanding season...for the Los Angeles Dodgers.

82. Cubs Unveil '80s Night (2005)

It was bad enough the Cubs' marketing department decided to foist '70s Night on Chicago fans in 1996. Adding an '80s version a few years later was just plain offensive. It would be different if the franchise actually had any decent memories from the decade. But as it stands, all '80s Night did was remind every Cubs fan that not only did the team compile a 735–821 record during that time period (plus two October choke jobs), but we were all wearing the dumbest fashions ever concocted while we watched them do it. From the tight-rolled, stonewashed jeans to the ripped, off-the-shoulder shirts, it was a fashion nightmare. And that doesn't even take into account the hair: bangs for the ladies and mullets for the men. But in yet another case of the Cubs not caring about their increasing cheese factor, they went ahead with the promo anyway. So instead of a washed-up actor singing the seventh-inning stretch, this particular night was commemorated by a washed-up '80s personality like Debbie "now call me Deborah" Gibson doing the honors, while everybody reminisced about how great the 1985 Chicago Bears were.

83. Cubs Unveil '70s Night (1996)

As if Cubs fans needed another reason to feel embarrassed about supporting a team that hasn't won a championship since 1908. Now they're supposed to do it wearing bellbottoms and a fake Afro. One can just imagine what's going on in the minds of the random WGN viewer when he sees 40,000 people dressed like Disco Stu doing the cellphone wave as the hapless Cubs drop another one, 10–2. The front office says it's all about fun at the ballpark, but you almost get the feeling they're just trying to come up with ways to distract fans from what's happening on the field. Don't watch another Cubs pitching phenom blow out his elbow! Instead, check out the chick next to you in the halter top and hot pants! Hot pants! And no '70s Night would be complete without 20 or 25 renditions of "YMCA" blasting over the loudspeakers while fans try to remember if the Cubs made the playoffs in the 1970s. Upon realizing the team didn't, however, the fans will simply shrug and order another $7 beer.

84. Andre Dawson Hit in Head by Eric Show (1987)

Andre Dawson went through many hot streaks in 1987 en route to winning the National League MVP Award, but "the Hawk" was never hotter than he was moments before San Diego Padres pitcher Eric Show hit him in the face with a fastball on July 7, 1987. The plunking came after Dawson had homered in three of his last five plate appearances, and it was pretty obvious to everyone involved that Show had beaned him on purpose. While Dawson lay on the ground, dazed and bleeding from a cut that would eventually require 24 stitches, his teammates picked fights all over the field. Eric Show had to be removed from the stadium for his own safety. The fans were angry and scared, and many were positive that this was another "Cubs moment" unfolding: surely Dawson's season would be over. Surprisingly, and uniquely, a moment of frustration and fear turned into a good thing for the North Siders as a young Greg Maddux proved his mettle by nailing Benito Santiago in the ribs in the next inning. Dawson returned to the lineup in short order, finishing the season with a career-high 49 home runs and his first and only Most Valuable Player Award.

85. Sammy Sosa Leaves Game Early (2004)

There was a time when Sammy Sosa was treated like a king in Chicago. That time was not 2004, when an aging, broken-down Sosa was on the outs with Cubs brass as well as Cub Nation. The decline had been steady and punctuated by events like the corked bat incident in 2003, the sneeze incident in 2004 (he allegedly had to go on the disabled list because of a "violent sneeze"), and the growing steroid rumors. Coupled with the fact that Sosa's numbers had fallen dramatically—he would finish the season with his lowest home run and RBI totals in over a decade—and everything finally came to a head on the last day of the season, when Sosa walked out on the team before the game was over. The Sammy Sosa era was officially over in Chicago, as the once-proud Cub would end his career with a pathetic 2005 season in Baltimore (14 HR, .221 average).

The man who looked to replace Ernie Banks as Mr. Cub had become the goat of Chicago, an impressive feat considering the outlandish, record-breaking stats he compiled in 13 seasons at Wrigley Field. To this day, he remains the only major league player to hit more than 60 home runs three separate times. He's also the only Cub with more than 500 career home runs who nobody likes.

86. Sammy Sosa "No Speak English" at Steroid Hearings (2005)

Technically, he was a Baltimore Oriole at the time, but that didn't make things any better when Sammy Sosa was subpoenaed to appear before a senate judiciary committee in March 2005 to discuss the problem of steroids in sports. Everyone knew Sammy as a Cub. And thanks to all the focus on steroids over the previous two years, everyone assumed Sammy was on the juice when he broke all those records. Just like Mark McGwire. Just like Barry Bonds. But nobody expected Sosa to claim "he no speak English" as his defense. The guy spent his entire major league career extolling his own virtues as a "gladiator" during press interviews. No English? That's all the slugger had to say for himself? It was embarrassing enough for baseball, let alone the people of Chicago. The only saving grace came when he was out-embarrassed by McGwire, who repeatedly "refused to talk about the past," and Rafael Palmeiro, who denied ever using steroids...then failed a drug test a few months later. For Sosa, the hearings would prove to be the final nail in the coffin of his legacy as a Cub.

87. Steve Goodman Releases "A Dying Cub Fan's Last Request" (1983)

How do you know your team might be doomed? Probably when people write entire songs about its futility, as was the case with folk singer and longtime Cubs fan Steve Goodman. Here's how WGN radio man Roy Leonard described Goodman's unveiling of the song on his program: "The most memorable of all the visits, however, occurred on March 16, 1983, when Steve [Goodman] and Jethro Burns walked into our WGN studios around 11:00 AM. They had just finished a weekend at Park West, and Steve said he had introduced a song the night before that he would like to sing on the radio for the first time. With Jethro on mandolin and Steve's guitar for accompaniment, 'A Dying Cub Fan's Last Request' was heard on the radio the first time. Little did we know." Nearly six minutes in length, the song tells the tale of a dying Cubs fan and his feelings about the team in general. The most famous stanza goes like this:

Do they still play the blues in Chicago
When baseball season rolls around?
When the snow melts away
Do the Cubbies still play
In their ivy-covered burial ground?
When I was a boy they were my pride and joy
But now they only bring fatigue
To the home of the brave
The land of the free
And the doormat of the National League.

88. Cubs Lose to New York Yankees in World Series (1938)

Losers of five straight World Series appearances, the Chicago Cubs successfully made it a six-pack in 1938 against the formidable New York Yankees. Swept 4–0 and outscored 22–9 in the Series, the Cubs were no match for the likes of Lou Gehrig, Joe DiMaggio, and the rest of the Bronx Bombers. Even Dizzy Dean and Bill "Spaceman" Lee couldn't help the Cubs scratch out a lone face-saving victory, as the two hurlers went a combined 0–3. On the bright side, the 1938 Chicago Cubs did make plenty of history, helping the Yankees set multiple postseason records: New York catcher Bill Dickey tied a World Series record with four hits in one game; pitcher Lefty Gomez won his sixth straight World Series start; and the Yankees became the first team ever to win three consecutive World Series titles.

89. Hawk Harrelson's Vocabulary

How can another team's broadcaster frustrate Cubs fans so much? For starters, Ken "Hawk" Harrelson works in the same city. As the White Sox's color commentator, Harrelson and his many catchphrases reflect poorly on all Chicagoans. He also appears on local television 162 times per season, which means Cubs fans are subjected to terms like *ducksnort* and *can of corn* much too often. Other regrettable Harrelson sayings include: Texas-leaguer; grab some bench; Hiney Bird; I tell you what; mercy; he gone; chopper two hopper; rack 'em up; stretch; hang wiff'em; zone 'em in, reel 'em in, and light her up; sacks packed;

time to cinch it up and hunker down; that one had eyes on it; that'll get the job done; down to the last bullet; ball-four base hit; and you can put it on the boards, yes.

Harrelson is also as much of a homer as you can get. His favorite pastime is criticizing umpires about their strike zones, claiming, "There have been two different zones today, one for them and one for us."

90. Cubs Ballgirl Marla Collins Fired for Posing in *Playboy* (1986)

Thanks to Marla Collins, the attractive Cubs ballgirl, the franchise actually had something decent to look at on the field in 1986. God knows it wasn't the baseball, as the Cubs would finish the season 20 games under .500 at 70–90. Instead, it was Collins's short shorts. But in July, perhaps on a whim, Collins decided to lose the familiar striped uniform and pose nude in *Playboy*. The photos didn't actually appear in the men's magazine until the September issue, but Cubs brass decided to fire Collins immediately upon learning of the pictures in late July. The real losers were the fans, who were forced to watch game action for the duration of the season. The pictures, meanwhile, turned out just fine, especially the one that featured Harry Caray pointing to a tattoo on Collins's exposed thigh. Caray was not fired.

91. Home Opener Snowed Out (2003)

Opening Day is supposed to be about hope, new beginnings, and the promise of a successful season. Such was the case in 2003, when three-time National League Manager of the Year Dusty Baker was set to manage his first home game with the Chicago Cubs. That's when Baker and Cub Nation were reminded who was really in charge in Chicago: the weather. Amazingly, the April 7 opener against the Montreal Expos was postponed because of snow. Not rain or sleet, but the white stuff. It was also plenty cold. Fans who had taken the day off to see their Cubs start a new era were instead treated to nothing but hassle. While the home portion of the season began on Tuesday, April 8, most ticket holders were unable to skip two days of work in a row. On the upside, the Cubs defeated the Expos 6–1 to bring their record to 4–3. On the downside, we all know how 2003 turned out.

92. Ronnie Woo-Woo's Voice

It's somewhat novel the first time you hear it, but after 10 consecutive minutes this shriekish cheer makes you want to tear your own ears off: "Cubs woo! Cubs woo!" Or "Rizzo woo! Rizzo woo!" Or the ever-popular "Beer woo! Beer woo!" You get the idea. For decades, Ronnie "Woo-Woo" Wickers has roamed Wrigley Field, supporting the Chicago Cubs with his trademark shriek. If you attend only one game a year, it probably won't bother you much. But for regular fans, especially those who frequent the bleachers, where Wickers spends most of his time, the act tires quickly. Despite his claim of being the biggest Cubs fan in the world—his stated goal is to be the team's unofficial mascot—Wickers is more of a nuisance than anything. Dressed in his dingy Cubs uniform, he loves being the center of attention, whether it's at Wrigley, in Arizona during spring training, at the Cubs Convention, or dancing with some drunken chick at a Wrigleyville bar. That's what's so frustrating about Wickers: he claims to be doing it all for the glory of the Cubs, but he spends most of his time drawing attention to himself. And then after the game he goes from bar to bar asking for "donations," in the form of money, food, or help with his electric bill.

93. Bruce Sutter Wins World Series—with Cardinals (1982)

It's always a bittersweet moment when an ex-Cub wins the World Series with another team. Bruce Sutter's championship in 1982 was especially tough on the North Side, as it came just two years after the Cubs traded Sutter to division rival St. Louis. The future Hall of Famer began his career with the Cubs in 1976. Over the next five seasons, he compiled a stellar 2.39 ERA, saving 133 games. He went to four All-Star Games as a Cub and even won the Cy Young Award in 1979. Apparently, all this success wasn't what the Cubs looked for in a reliever, so they decided to trade Sutter to the Cardinals after the 1980 season. To nobody's surprise, Sutter flourished in St. Louis, winning the World Series his second year with the Cards and saving a career-high 45 games in 1984. Because he was in the same division as the Cubs, he also spent a great deal of his time stymieing Chicago hitters. Sutter was inducted into the Hall of Fame in 2006—as a Cardinal.

94. Cubs Acquire Jeromy Burnitz (2005)

Sammy Sosa was finally gone. After an amazing Cubs career, Sosa had worn out his welcome over the previous few summers, so Wrigleyville was more than happy to see the aging slugger leave for Baltimore. But...Jeromy Burnitz? That's who the Cubs chose to carry on the legacy of Andre Dawson and Sammy Sosa in right field? In the pantheon of disappointing Cubs signings, it wasn't quite Todd Hundley bad, but it was not much better. Burnitz was coming off a decent offensive season in Colorado. Which means the 30+ homers and 100+ RBIs totals were essentially meaningless. Justin Bieber could hit 30 home runs in the thin air of Colorado. Burnitz also had a track record of striking out at an alarming pace, to the tune of a strikeout every other at-bat...or at least that's what it felt like. Overall, he wasn't nearly the offensive threat Cubs fans were looking for, especially considering that the team had also let Moises Alou go after the 2004 season. With such a big hole in the lineup, Burnitz had no chance to fill it. When he hit just .253 with 24 home runs and 87 RBIs in 2005, nobody was surprised.

95. Cubs Lose to Philadelphia Athletics in World Series (1929)

Joe McCarthy managed the North Siders to a 98–54 record, but the franchise would lose for the third time in its last three World Series appearances. By now fans were starting to get restless. It didn't help that 1929 also kicked off the Great Depression, so Cubs fans were unhappy in more ways than one. But while the Depression would fizzle out by the end of the 1930s, the Cubs' woes would only worsen.

In this particular Series, the problem was a lack of clutch hitting. Hack Wilson, who drove in 159 runs during the regular season—and just one year later would set a single-season record of 191 RBIs—had a grand total of 0 RBIs in five games. Rogers Hornsby batted .381 during the season, but just .238 in the World Series. At least he drove in more runs than Wilson, although it would be more accurate to say "run," as he only knocked in one. The lowest point came in Game 4, when the Cubs led 8–0 going into the bottom of the seventh inning. The Athletics scored 10 runs in the frame and eventually won the game 10–8, marking the biggest rally in World Series history. The Cubs had a chance to get out of the inning, but it was kept alive when star outfielder Hack Wilson misplayed a fly ball into a three-run, inside-the-park home run. Reportedly, this was the first time a fan said, "Only the Cubs" after a comically bad play. It would not be the last.

96. A.J. Pierzynski Hits Game-Winning Home Run (2006)

Any other team and it would have just been a tough loss. Any other hitter and it would have just been a game-winning homer. But it wasn't just any other team or any other hitter on Saturday, July 1, 2006. It was A.J. Pierzynski of the Chicago White Sox. Less than two months after brawling with Cubs catcher Michael Barrett after running him over at home plate, Pierzynski hit a 1–1 Ryan Dempster pitch into Wrigley's right-field bleachers for a three-run homer to erase a one-run deficit. The blast gave the White Sox an 8–6 victory over the poor Cubs, but that's not all it gave the South Siders. It gave them bragging rights all over again: The very player who incited the brawl was

Jimmy Buffett's party at Wrigley Field hasn't done anything in the way of improving the Cubs' bullpen woes.

needling the Cubs once more, only this time with his bat. It was bad enough that Sox fans were saying Pierzynski took Barrett's sucker punch with ease, but now their guy was taunting North Siders with his bat, too.

97. Jimmy Buffett Plays Wrigley Field (2005)

According to Amazon.com, sellers of the *Jimmy Buffet Live at Wrigley Field* DVD, "Wrigleyville was transformed into Margaritaville as Jimmy Buffett, his band, and many thousands of his dancing, beer-guzzling, Hawaiian shirt–wearing, lei-draped fans invaded the venerable Chicago baseball stadium over Labor Day weekend, 2005." We couldn't have said it better ourselves, but just for kicks, we'll try: lame. So very lame. When the Cubs first announced they would start holding concerts at Wrigley Field, it was a rather exciting new revenue source. Sure, the money wouldn't go to fielding a better team, but at least the Tribune would benefit.

Adding insult to injury, the Cubs gave first concert rights to Jimmy Buffett and his merry band of cheeseballs. So while the Cubs were off playing their way to a fourth-place finish, 40-year-old drunk dudes in coconut bras and grass skirts were soiling hallowed Wrigley Field. Once again, the Cubs had given die-hard fans a cornucopia of reasons to be ashamed of their favorite franchise.

98. Alex Gonzalez Fumbles Easy Grounder After Bartman Play (2003)

Everybody wants to blame poor Steve Bartman for the 2003 Cubs playoff collapse. Or, if they actually decide to point fingers at someone on the field, they choose Mark Prior, who quickly disintegrated in the eighth inning of Game 6 of the NLCS against the Florida Marlins. The guy nobody seems to remember is Cubs shortstop Alex Gonzalez. While the Bartman Incident set the scene, the rally didn't officially get out of hand until a few batters later. With the Cubs up 3–0, Marlins catcher Ivan Rodriguez singled to make the score 3–1. There was still no inkling of what was to come, especially when the batter after Rodriguez, Miguel Cabrera, hit a tailor-made double-play ball to Gonzalez at short. Unfortunately for Cub Nation, the normally sure-handed Gonzalez muffed the grounder. So instead of ending the half-inning by turning two, the Cubs let the door swing wide open— and the Marlins scored seven more runs. By the time the final out of the frame was recorded, the Marlins led 8–3 and were on their way to one of the most improbable turnarounds in NLCS history. Gonzalez was shipped to the Montreal Expos in 2004 as part of the four-team trade that brought his replacement, Nomar Garciaparra, to the Cubs.

99. Richard Marx Appears in Cubs Uniform in "Take This Heart" Music Video (1991)

There are so many things wrong with this particular Richard Marx music video; it's difficult to know where to begin. The hair? The lyrics? The horrible cinematography? In what might be one of the most confusing entertainment creations of all time, the video can best be described like this: Hall of Fame broadcaster Bob Uecker narrates the action as second-rate pop star Richard Marx hits a World Series–winning home run for the Chicago Cubs off Oakland Athletics closer Dennis Eckersley while a variety of major league players and coaches look on, including Greg Maddux, Tony La Russa, Jose Canseco, and Rickey Henderson, the last of whom fails to catch the ball despite a high-flying leap above the outfield wall. Between pitches, Marx and his longhaired bandmates do a rockin' version of "Take This Heart" all over an empty baseball stadium. Sometimes they're on the field, sometimes they're in the stands, sometimes we see the crew filming them, and sometimes we even flash back to see Marx training with the Cubs throughout the season. After the girlish pop star finally delivers the historic home run for the Cubs, despite an 0–2 count and a hopelessly awkward swing, he wakes up to discover it was all a dream! In a word: abomination.

100. Lou Piniella Can't Get It Done (2007–10)

Over the course of four years, Cubs skipper Lou Piniella did lead the team to a combined record of 316–293, so that's definitely an accomplishment. Not many Cubs managers can boast a +.500 tenure. Unfortunately, Piniella's teams also had no success in the playoffs, including being swept out of the first round of consecutive division series. Compounding matters was Piniella's penchant for appearing to fall asleep during games as he neared the end of his run in the Cubs dugout. On the bright side, "Sweet Lou" was always good for a few temper tantrums a season, which made for fun dustups with the umpires.

101. Mike Quade Era (2010–11)

Well, "era" might be an overstatement. After Lou Piniella left the team due to personal matters in the middle of the 2010 season, the Cubs promoted third-base coach Mike Quade to manage the club. The team went 24–13 down the stretch, prompting the Cubs to keep Quade on for the 2011 season. The result? A record of 71–91 and a fifth-place finish. He was promptly fired before the next season.

102. Alfonso Soriano's Megadeal Doesn't Pan Out (2007–13)

When you sign someone for eight years and $136 million, the fifth-largest contract in major league history at the time, you expect more than what Soriano provided. To be fair to the slugger, he had his moments with the Cubs, producing a number of multi-homer games and hot streaks that seemed to last for weeks. Those streaks were balanced by less impressive performances that occurred much more often. In seven seasons as a Cub, Soriano only drove in more than 100 runs a single time, and he was plagued by leg injuries that took away his speed. His transition from second base to left field wasn't exactly smooth either, meaning the Cubs were contractually tethered to a streaky power hitter with no speed and a bad glove. By the time the team actually traded Soriano to the Yankees, the bloom was many years off the rose. In typical ex-Cub fashion, Soriano immediately went into one of his streaks after joining the New York ballclub.

103. Cubs Swept Out of Playoffs Twice in a Row (2007–08)

Still stinging from the epic 2003 collapse, Cubs fans were nonetheless optimistic about the team's chances against the Arizona Diamondbacks in the 2007 National League Division Series. After all, the first-place Cubs were being helmed by new skipper Lou Piniella, and it seemed things were on the uptick. That was not the case, however, as the North Siders were summarily swept in the three-game series. The following year, the Cubs produced one of their best regular seasons in team history, amassing 97 victories and averaging an eye-popping 5.2 runs per game. Unfortunately, the Cubs were once again swept out of the postseason, this time by the Dodgers. The team has been in steady decline ever since.

104. Another 100-Loss Season (2012)

Tom Ricketts and family purchased the Cubs in 2009, ending nearly three decades of Tribune Company ownership. The change was a welcome one, with Ricketts being a lifelong fan who promised to bring quality baseball to the North Side. A year after taking over, Ricketts hired Theo Epstein, the architect of the Red Sox revival, to lead the charge toward a new era in Cubs baseball as team president. All things take time, however, as the team went into complete rebuilding mode yet again. And yet again, Cubs fans saw their team drop more than 100 games, this time under brand-new manager Dale Sveum, who would eventually be fired after the 2013 season.

105. Cardinals Win Another Title (2011)

Albert Pujols and the hated St. Louis Cardinals weren't supposed to be a factor in the 2011 postseason. They finished in second place, and many thought they'd be ushered out of the playoffs by the Philadelphia Phillies in the first round. Instead, the Redbirds defeated the Phils and Brewers en route to the World Series, where they rallied past the Rangers in epic fashion to win the chmpionship in seven games. It marked their 11th World Series title since 1926 and was yet another reminder that the Cubs' major rival was simply superior to them in every way (aside from their hometown and their fans, of course).

106. Cubs Tagged as "Lovable Losers" (Post-1945)

When a franchise becomes so synonymous with losing that people feel the need to put a positive spin on it, that's frustrating. It also doesn't strike much fear in the hearts of other teams. "Hey Yadier," St. Louis Cardinals manager Mike Matheny might say. "You think we'll be able to take two of three from, let's see here, the Lovable Losers? Oh, my mistake. I didn't realize we were playing the Cubs. This should be a walk in the park." The worst part about the nickname is that it suggests losing is okay as long as you're affable. Throughout the years, Cubs brass often latched on to this idea, worrying more about the "brand image" of the ballclub than the quality of the team on the field.

107. Cubs Unveil Their New Mascot...and Wrigleyville Implodes (2014)

On the face of it, fielding a mascot to make the game experience more kid-friendly shouldn't be that big of a deal. Almost every other team in Major League Baseball has some kind of giant stuffed animal to provide a little levity. But when the Cubs announced Clark, a cuddly cartoon bear, would be the newest member of the Cub family, fans went berserk. Maybe it was because the supposedly youth-targeted mascot wasn't wearing pants. Or maybe it was that his eyes looked like he was crying after yet another blown save. Or perhaps it was because his very existence was yet another nail in the coffin of baseball purity on the

North Side. Whatever the case, having the addition of a mascot be the most notable off-season move after a 96-loss campaign probably wasn't what Cubs fans had in mind going into 2014.

Frequently Asked Questions

Q: Am I supposed to take this guide seriously?
A: Yes. Too many self-help books are filled with small-minded theories about how to enhance your self-esteem or maximize your potential. Those books are difficult to follow and almost never result in an improved you. This guide is all about making yourself feel better no matter what life throws your way. It provides simple ways to deal with adversity and features easy-to-apply tactics such as "drink more beer" and "just don't worry about it."

Q: A lot of people make fun of Cubs fans. Will my friends mock me for reading this book?
A: They might, yes.

Q: I'm a New York Yankees fan. Will this book work for me?
A: It will probably work even better for you. Imagine you've taken chapter 1 to heart. Just when you're about to wait for Next Year, you realize your club is going to the playoffs this year. That makes this season that much sweeter. The same can be said for the other principles,

from the Power of Low Expectations to Beer Will Make It Better!™ Because in case you were wondering, yes, beer will also make winning better.

Q: Wouldn't it be easier for Cubs fans to just root for another team? In other words, aren't these people asking for trouble?

A: So you want them to give up? What are you, some sort of communist? America was founded on the ideals of perseverance and struggle. What if Ben Franklin or George Clooney had simply given up? Not only would you be reading this sentence by candlelight, we'd all be without one of Hollywood's most likeable leading men. Asking Cubs fans to switch their allegiance is like asking an American to root for France in the Olympics just because France has a better soccer team. It's not going to happen. And it shouldn't.

Q: Most of your practical applications seem to be geared toward men. Is that because this guide is more useful for males than for females?

A: Not at all. I'm just too lazy to think of unisexual examples. Hell, I'm too lazy to check if *unisexual* is even a word.

Q: What's the best postgame bar in Wrigleyville?

A: Man, that's tough, because every one of them sells beer. But I would have to go with Gingerman Tavern on Clark and Grace. The Full Shilling is pretty good, too. Steer clear of John Barleycorn's unless you're a meathead.

The 2003 Ford Taurus is the ideal vehicle for any Cubs fan.

Q: I'm thinking of getting a new car. What kind of car would a Cubs fan buy?

A: That's a great question. By patterning your purchasing habits after Cubs fans, you can really get inside their heads. As for the specific make and model, it's obvious: a 2003 Ford Taurus. It's all-American, not flashy, and you don't have to worry about it getting your hopes up. Okay, this car might be kinda ugly. It might even break down every once in a while, but most of the time it'll run just fine. And Cubs fans have always been comfortable with "just fine," so you should be, too.

Q: Since we're on the subject, what brand of clothing should I wear?

A: Well, you're gonna want something that will make you happy. Cubs fans usually wear Ernie Banks or Ron

Santo jerseys. That might not be appropriate in every situation, however, so you'll need a steady supply of Old Navy items.

Q: Who are some famous Cubs fans? Do they agree with the assertions in this book?

A: Noteworthy Cubs fans include Bill Murray, John Cusack, William Petersen, Bonnie Hunt, Jim Belushi, George Will, Joe Mantegna, George Wendt, Vince Vaughn, and Gary Sinise. As of August 25, 2013, all of these people subscribe to this book's theories, maybe, if you were to ask them.

Q: Wrigley Field has been around 100 years. Where are all the championship banners?

A: Ouch. That one hurts.

Q: What do Cubs fans do in the off-season?

A: That's the beauty of being a Cubs fan. There really isn't an off-season in the traditional sense. Cubs faithful find all kinds of ways to make rooting for their team a year-long process. If you're referring to the months between October and March, Cubs fans are typically busy during this time of year. From decompressing after the season in November and December to the Cubs Convention in January, to the start of spring training in February, these people are always thinking Cubs. It's also a great time to earn extra money so you can afford tickets for next season.

Q: I've never been to Wrigley Field. Where are the best seats in the stadium?
A: The left-field bleachers. On the flip side, the worst place to sit is right behind one of those steel girders holding up the upper deck. You can't see anything, and the friend you brought to the game will hate you all day.

Q: Is it ever appropriate to do "the wave" at Wrigley Field?
A: Sure. If you're a loser. Or if it's suddenly 1988.

Q: What would happen if I lived my life like a White Sox fan?
A: Initially, it might feel good to not worry about showering, shaving, or abiding by the laws of our country, but eventually, you'd probably end up lonely and incarcerated.

Beer Will Make It Better!™, but you have to know when you've had too much.

Q: You say that "Beer Will Make It Better!™" But how do I know how much beer it will take?

A: It's a long process of trial and error, but it's a fun one. A good rule of thumb is if you can stand on one foot, you haven't had enough. If you don't remember your name, you've had too much.

Q: Is it true you founded *The Heckler*?

A: Yes, I cofounded the satirical Chicago sports newspaper and website known as *The Heckler* (and TheHeckler.com) with my friend Brad Zibung. Brad is a lot more responsible than I am, so his title is editor in chief, while I am relegated to being second in command with a pathetic title of managing editor. I'm funnier, though, as anyone who knows both of us will tell you. I'm also more of an idea man, while he just talks on the phone and pushes papers around. Before we started *The Heckler*, Brad and I worked together on RightFieldSucks.com.

Q: I think I'm funny. Can I write for TheHeckler.com?

A: Maybe. Check out the site for details on how to submit content. If you're an embattled Cubs fans, odds are you might have just the kind of sarcastic mindset we could use.

The Heckler

Cubs Fan's Glossary

Alleys: The areas in the outfield between the fielders, or a place to pee behind that apartment building over there

Bad luck: The reason Cubs fans believe their team hasn't won a World Series in more than a century

Bartman, Steve: Unlucky Cubs fan who did the exact same thing you would have done if you were sitting in that seat (and you know it)

Beer goggles: Those things that make every girl in the bleachers totally sexy, even the one who actually turns out to be your uncle

Bison Dog: A fancy concession made of buffalo meat that was brought in to improve the fan's experience at Wrigley without actually improving the team's performance

Blanco'd: Term used in the late 2000s when backup catcher Henry Blanco drove in a run (i.e., You've been Blanco'd!)

Bleacher bum: A bleacher season-ticket holder and frequent beer consumer

Bud Light Bleachers: Formerly known simply as the bleachers, this section of Wrigley Field is now the largest singles bar in the country

Bullpen: Part of Wrigley Field that houses Cubs players who should still be in the minor leagues

Bush-league: Style of play often associated with Chicago's North Side franchise

Catcher's interference: When a Cubs catcher's inability to call a good game interferes with the Cubs winning

Cash cow: The Tribune Company's pet name for the Cubs when they owned the team

Caught Looking: When your girlfriend or wife catches you ogling the 22-year-old in the tube top three rows over

Cheese: A great fastball, or some yellow, goopy stuff that may or may not be edible but is usually poured on top of nachos anyway

Clubhouse: Where the Cubs go to lick their wounds after being shut out, again

Coffers: Where the Cubs keep the overwhelming profits made from the team

Crazy: Mental state of people willing to spend $60 on bleacher tickets for a Tuesday-night game against the San Diego Padres

Cubbies: Affectionate nickname for the team often said by people who are either five years old or attending their first game

Cubs Convention: Annual celebration of the team and its ability to milk fans for revenue, even during the off-season

Day-to-day: Catchall phrase used to describe how often the prognosis can change for a Cubs pitcher's most recent injury

Disabled list: Where 50 percent of Cubs players will spend any given season

Double play: What the Cubs hit into with one man out and the tying run at third in the bottom of the ninth

Doubleheader: A rare chance for the Cubs to lose two games in one day

Eamus catuli: A rooftop phrase used to confuse Cubs fans

Elbow: Ironically, a Cubs pitcher's Achilles Heel

ERA: How long it has been since the North Siders won a World Series...an entire era

Error: A mistake (i.e., former Cubs GM Jim Hendry made an error when he traded away pitching prospect Dontrelle Willis)

Fielder's choice: A Cubs hitter's version of an infield hit

Fork: What can usually be stuck in the Cubs around mid-July, as they are most likely done for the season

Friendly Confines: Wrigley Field's nickname, which arose shortly after the stadium's completion, when opposing teams realized how easy it was to win there

Front office: Part of the Cubs organization responsible for explaining away latest price increases

Fundamental: A basic skill or tenet of the game possessed by roughly 8 percent of all Cubs players

Grand slam: A Cardinal fan's favorite breakfast order

Happiness: An elusive state of well-being, if you're a Cubs fan

Heckler, The: A satirical Chicago sports publication known for being totally awesome and really funny

Hey, Hey!: Exclamation uttered by drunken bleacher fans when a tight-shirted female is spotted nearby

Holy cow!: Harry Caray's famous catchphrase—or one of those big fat nuns who attends the day games

Home run: What most Cubs players try to achieve with women after the game

Hope: A belief that things will get better, not worse, which is way more possible

Hustle: A characteristic former Cub Aramis Ramirez has not displayed once in his entire career

Hype: Misguided excitement that often surrounds the Cubs' mediocre minor league prospects

If: A pivotal word in the vocabulary of Cubs fans. Through *if* all things are possible, including overcoming a five-game deficit in the standings with only six games left to play.

Ivy: One of those "intangibles" that brings people to the park despite all the losses

Jail: Common hangout for many Chicago White Sox fans

JumboTron: A fancy video board designed to improve the fan experience, not run 300 ads per game, if that's what you were thinking

Kangaroo court: Ad hoc committee that fines Cubs players for doing things right

Lose: What the Cubs usually do when they play other teams

Mai tai: Overpriced alcoholic beverage used to "make self feel better about hooking up again this weekend"

Next Year: When the Cubs are rumored to win the World Series

Optimism: Thinking the Cubs won't get swept this weekend

Pop out: What a Cubs hitter is good for with two outs and the bases loaded

Proud partner: What the Cubs call a company that gives them overwhelming amounts of cash to splash its logo somewhere inside the stadium

Rally: Scoring a flurry of runs in a short span of time to erase a deficit. The Cubs are great at almost doing this.

Reliever: For the Cubs, this is typically a pitcher with a 5.00+ ERA

RISP: Runners in Standing Position (because they won't be going anywhere, that's for sure)

Sabermetrics: The analysis of baseball using complex statistics in a way that many Cubs fans actually believe will lead to a World Series victory for the team before 2070

Sacrifice: When a Cubs player takes one for the team after the game at John Barleycorn's

Save: An obscure pitching stat that doesn't come into play very often for the home team at Wrigley

Scalp: The part of a male Cubs fan's head that hair falls out of as a result of yet another one-run Cubs loss

Scapegoat: Cause of every problem to ever encounter any Cubs fan

Screwball: Former Cubs ace Carlos Zambrano

Shame: The emotion that should be (but probably isn't) felt by any member of the Hall of Fame who voted against Ron Santo being inducted

Shark: Nickname for Cubs pitcher Jeff Samardzija, probably because he looks like one

Single: The kind of women former Cub Kyle Farnsworth loved to get his hands on—though he'd take "Married" or "Any" as well

Skybox: Gathering place for "friends of the Cubs" and other rich people

Slump: What a Cubs hitter goes through from April to June, when the games actually matter

Streak: Two Cubs wins in a row

Strikeout: The outcome of a typical Cubs player's at-bat

Strike zone: An area above the plate Cubs pitchers usually have trouble finding

Talent: A trait rarely found in the Cubs' minor league prospects

Triple: The kind of cheeseburger Brewers fans prefer at Wendy's

Umpire: Who Hawk Harrelson tends to blame when things don't go his team's way

Urinal: Alley

Walk: The outcome of one out of every 1,000 Corey Patterson at-bats when he was a Cub

Walk of shame: Refers to how Cubs players exit the field after the end of a typical game

Wander: What Cubs shortstop Starlin Castro's mind tends to do when he's on the field

Wave, the: Ballpark activity that should have ended in 1994

WGN: We Got Nothing

Win: What the other team usually does when they play the Cubs at Wrigley

Woo-Woo, Ronnie: Self-anointed superfan and the guy in the Cubs uniform dancing with your girlfriend

Wrigleyville: Beer drinker's paradise

Wrigleyville Premium Ticket Services: "Legal" scalping operation owned and run by the Chicago Cubs

Yakker: A nasty curveball, or a fan that's had seven too many Budweisers

The **Heckler**

About
the Author

George Ellis is a lifelong Cubs fan. Despite that fact, he does smile every so often, perhaps because he's also a Blackhawks fan. When George isn't running TheHeckler.com with Brad Zibung, he works as an advertising creative director. He also dabbles in screenwriting and coined the phrase "Peanut Punch." His mortal enemy is the sun. For Chicago sports humor all year-round, visit TheHeckler.com.